A "Manly Study"?

A "Manly Study"?

Irish Women Historians, 1868–1949

Nadia Clare Smith

palgrave
macmillan

Cover Painting: *Girl Reading* by Edmund Charles Tarbell, 1909.
Photograph copyright 2006, Museum of Fine Arts, Boston.

First published in 2006 by
PALGRAVE MACMILLAN
Houndmills, Basingstoke, Hampshire RG21 6XS and
175 Fifth Avenue, New York, N.Y. 10010
Companies and representatives throughout the world.

PALGRAVE MACMILLAN is the global academic imprint of the Palgrave Macmillan division of St. Martin's Press, LLC and of Palgrave Macmillan Ltd. Macmillan® is a registered trademark in the United States, United Kingdom and other countries. Palgrave is a registered trademark in the European Union and other countries.

ISBN-13: 978–0–230–00904–2 hardback
ISBN-10: 0–230–00904–2 hardback

This book is printed on paper suitable for recycling and made from fully managed and sustained forest sources.

A catalogue record for this book is available from the British Library.

Library of Congress Cataloging-in-Publication Data

Smith, Nadia Clare
A "manly study"? : Irish women historians, 1868–1949 / Nadia Clare Smith.
p. cm.
Includes bibliographical references and index.
ISBN 0–230–00904–2 (cloth)
1. Women historians – Ireland – History. 2. Women historians – Ireland – Historiography. 3. Historiography – Ireland – History – 19th century. 4. Historiography – Ireland – History – 20th century. 5. Women historians – History. 6. Women historians – Historiography. I. Title.

DA908.S65 2006
941.5072′02—dc22 2006045753

10 9 8 7 6 5 4 3 2 1
15 14 13 12 11 10 09 08 07 06

Printed and bound in Great Britain by
Antony Rowe Ltd, Chippenham and Eastbourne

Contents

Acknowledgements

A book about Irish women historians should begin by thanking several Irish women historians for their help and support for this project. I am indebted to Margaret O hOgartaigh for her friendship and insightful critiques of my work, and Mary O'Dowd and Maria Luddy for their support and their many insights about Irish women's history. At Boston College I would like to thank Kevin O'Neill, Rob Savage, and Peter Weiler for their invaluable help and support over the years, as well as Alan Rogers, Lynn Johnson, Colleen O'Reilly and other faculty members and friends in the History Department and Irish Studies Program. I am grateful to John Atteberry and David Horn at the Burns Library at Boston College, and the staff at the O'Neill Library, for their help as well.

Many thanks to Michael Strang, Ruth Ireland, and the production team at Palgrave for all their help with this book.

I am immensely grateful to others working in history and Irish Studies on both sides of the Atlantic who generously shared their knowledge and discussed aspects of my work with me, as well as those who shared memories of the women historians who appear in this book. Thanks to Maria Walsh, Angus Mitchell, Eunan O'Halpin, Angela Bourke, Ilaria Porciani, James Donnelly, Timothy Meagher, Tom Desmond, and Kevin Whelan.

My own undergraduate students at Boston College have indirectly contributed to this book, more than they realize, and I thank them as well.

I would like to thank the staffs of the National Library of Ireland, the National Archives of Ireland, the UCD Archives, and the Trinity College Library for all their help. Every reasonable attempt has been made to contact the copyright holders of material reproduced in this book. I gratefully acknowledge permission from the Board of the National Library of Ireland to quote from material from their collections. I am also grateful to the Board of Trinity College for permission to quote from material from their manuscript collection. The image on the cover has been reproduced by the kind permission of the Museum of Fine Arts, Boston.

Introduction

The standard narrative of the emergence of the modern historical profession appears very different when women are placed at the center of the narrative. This book contributes to the reconsideration of the story by exploring the lives, works, and social and political activism of female historians in Ireland between 1868 and 1949. A social history of historiography, this study considers the role of women in the development of the Irish historical profession, and the place of Irish female historians in the wider context of women historians in the nineteenth and twentieth centuries. It discusses the careers of these women in light of major developments such as feminism and new educational and professional opportunities for women, Irish nationalism, and the emergence of the new Irish state in 1922.

This book is located within recent work on women historians in the modern Western world, gender and historiography, and Irish historiography and women's history. It also participates in histories of the social constructions of intellectual disciplines and in the recovery of women in the humanities and social sciences during a period when academic disciplines were becoming professionalized.[1] Bonnie Smith's *The Gender of History*, which proved instrumental in shaping debates in the field, presented an interpretive paradigm of Western women historians. Smith argued that between 1800 and 1940, female historians tended to write popular women's, social, and cultural history, while men wrote "high" political history that legitimized the state, simultaneously gaining greater access to political power and raising the profile of the historian-citizen.[2] Mary O'Dowd's article on Irish women historians discussed the contributions of nineteenth and early twentieth-century amateur historians, as well as university-based women historians in twentieth-century Ireland. In addition, O'Dowd analyzed the Irish historiographical revolution in the 1930s, the position of women academics in Irish universities, and the relationship of Irish women historians to "scientific" history. The position of Irish academic women historians, she argued, declined during the modernization of the university-based historical profession in the late 1930s and 1940s, and some of the women expressed ambivalence about the intellectual and philosophical underpinnings of the new academic history. Anne Colman addressed the range of genres chosen by Irish women writers in the nineteenth century; a novelist such as Emily Lawless, for instance, also wrote history.[3] Other historians have highlighted the importance of factors such as family support, education, relative affluence, and intellectual circles of friends in the formation of successful female historians,[4] as well as the central role played by women historians in the development of social and economic history.[5] Works by Maxine Berg and Julie des Jardins highlighted the political and social engagement of women historians in Britain and the United States respectively, which resonates with the focus of this study. The scholarly recovery of women historians in Scandinavia and Central and Eastern Europe[6] also resonates with this study, as Irish women historians, in many cases, had much in common with their counterparts in small, peripheral European countries with active nationalist movements.

A new interest in Irish historiography and in the origins of the university-based historical profession emerged in the 1980s. The narrative held that pioneering male historians R. Dudley Edwards and T.W. Moody, armed with doctorates from the University of London's Institute of Historical Research, had initiated a historiographical revolution in Irish universities in the late 1930s. Their promotion of objective, scientific historical practices professionalized the study of Irish history, undermining sentimental historical myths and partisan histories based on incomplete evidence and analysis. A critique of this narrative, and of the legacy of the founding fathers of the new "revisionist" school of Irish academic history, was offered by historian Brendan Bradshaw.[7] His intervention helped stimulate new debates about Irish nationalist and revisionist historiography, the history of the Irish historical profession, and the role of the historian. Women historians and the role played by gender, however, have often been excluded from the reconsideration of the development of the Irish historical profession.

This book argues that political affiliation and social and political engagement have been central to the identity and formation of Irish women historians over several generations between 1868, when two women wrote histories of Ireland and the country had not yet achieved independence, and 1949, when Ireland officially became a republic and Irish history seemed to have become a male preserve. Irish women historians were often public figures who intervened in political and historiographical debates, and challenged political and intellectual establishments through both their writing and their political and social activism. They were instrumental in reinforcing Irish nationalist and unionist identities and communal historical memories before and after independence, and in the writing of histories during the Free State era that sometimes bolstered and sometimes critiqued aspects of the new state and Irish nationalism. This study demonstrates that Irish female historians could gain access to political power in a new state through both their own political activism and the writing of histories with a political dimension. For example, Alice Stopford Green and Helena Concannon became senators, and Dorothy Macardle and Rosamond Jacob helped establish the Fianna Fail party.

This book also argues that, while the official contours of the discipline of Irish history were largely shaped by university-educated male scholars in the late nineteenth century, and by male academics in the twentieth century, women played a more significant role in the shaping of modern Irish historiography than has previously been considered. While some female historians identified unexplored topics and made original contributions, other women played a less direct role in the historical imagination of the profession, because they raised a discordant voice with which the male professional historians were compelled to engage. While this point need not be belabored, the contemporary discourse on popular nationalist historiography has at times been strikingly gendered. According to this discourse, a (masculine) scientific, objective, impartial history emerged to do battle with a (feminized) emotive, sentimental, partisan popular tradition produced by amateurs, including women, whose emotional excesses rendered them incapable of unbiased and objective scholarship. A distinctive modern Irish historical profession may not have emerged the way that it did without a popular, nationalist historiography, produced by amateur female and male writers, against which it could define itself and construct a new collective identity.[8]

This study has engaged with the work of Rosemary Ann Mitchell on women historians, considering how the factors Mitchell outlines, such as family, education, socio-economic background, mentors, access to libraries and manuscripts, and supportive circles of friends informed the development of the historians under consideration. As was the case with women historians throughout Europe in this period, almost all of the Irish women historians came from wealthy or middle-class backgrounds. They were the daughters of doctors, solicitors, Church of Ireland clergymen, and businessmen. Their families valued education, though some of the historians were educated by governesses, rather than at school. The historians born before the mid-nineteenth century were unable to attend universities, as opportunities for higher education were not yet available to women. The majority of the women were single, several were married and childless, and only one married and had children.[9] They found mentors, often male, who encouraged them and through whom they gained access to books and libraries. W.E.H. Lecky and F.J. Bigger were particularly noteworthy for the help they gave women historians.[10] Access to libraries was harder to obtain for non-academic women historians than for university- based ones. Most of the women had close friends connected with antiquarian, cultural, nationalist, feminist, and literary circles, who encouraged and supported them in their endeavors.

Religion also played a role in the formation of Irish women historians. The majority of the women in this study were Protestant;[11] during the period under consideration Protestants were often wealthier and had greater educational opportunities than Catholics. Most were nationalists, or combined political unionism with Irish cultural nationalism. Political and cultural nationalists had more of an impetus to write history, as they wished to refute negative representations of Ireland, to promote new Irish scholarship and national pride, and, later, to bolster the new state or critique it when it failed to live up to their expectations.

The careers of these women took place during a period in which the feminist movement brought about major changes in European politics and society. European feminists in the nineteenth and early twentieth centuries fought for the right to vote, as well as access to the universities and the professions. The feminist movement counted women historians among its supporters throughout Europe, including Irish historians such as Mary Hayden, Dorothy Macardle, and

Rosamond Jacob. While some feminists turned to the study of women's history, women historians in Ireland, with the exception of the non-feminist Helena Concannon, engaged less with women's history. The Irish feminist movement's early successes in obtaining the right of women to enter universities and vote (by 1918) helped structure the educational, professional, and political opportunities for women in the new Irish state after 1922.

Breakdown of chapters

This book is divided into three main sections. The first two chapters focus on women historians in pre-Independence Ireland, and cover the years between 1868 and 1922. Chapter 1 considers the careers of Mary Ferguson, Mary Agnes Hickson, Emily Lawless, and Eleanor Hull, most of whom combined political unionism with cultural nationalism. Chapter 2 addresses the careers of two popular nationalist historians of the period, Margaret Cusack and Alice Stopford Green, who constructed the persona of the Irish nationalist female historian as a politically and socially engaged public figure.

The next section focuses on academic women in Free State Ireland in the 1920s and 1930s. Chapter 3 examines the careers of the academic Irish women historians of the 1920s and 1930s in relation to the changing context of academic history in Ireland, and discusses the careers of the women who taught in the National University of Ireland's constituent colleges. Chapter 4 considers the careers of Constantia Maxwell, Olive Armstrong, and Jocelyn Otway-Ruthven of Trinity College.

Chapter 5 discusses "amateur" or nonprofessional female historians in Free State Ireland. Helena Concannon (the only one who produced significant works on women's history), Dorothy Macardle, and Rosamond Jacob were all nationalists and political activists, in the tradition of Alice Stopford Green. They were involved in national politics to an unusual degree in the early decades of the Irish state's consolidation. This chapter also discusses the less well-known Isabel Grubb, Grace Lawless Lee, and Ada Longfield, all of whom made innovative contributions to Irish religious, early modern, and social and economic history in the 1920s and 1930s. This study concludes with a comparative discussion of the women historians under consideration.

This book, then, contributes to the comparative study of women historians in the nineteenth and twentieth centuries, to Irish women's history, and to the study of Irish historiography. It writes Irish women into the international study of women historians, and women into the study of Irish historiography and the development of the Irish historical profession. Engaging the themes of gender and historiography, the social and political context in which history is written and received, and the relationship between politics and the writing of history, it reconstructs the lives of Irish women historians, and recovers and assesses their contributions to the historical discipline.

1
Unionist Women Historians, 1868–1922

"I am convinced that the thorough study of history is a noble, invigorating, manly study," William Gladstone announced in an 1875 letter to historian E.A. Freeman.[1] In the Liberal leader's time, however, a period marked by feminist and Irish Home Rule agitation, not all historians in the British Isles were men. Several prominent Irish historians writing during the last half-century of British rule in Ireland were women.

The following sections explore the work of Mary Ferguson, Mary Agnes Hickson, Emily Lawless, and Eleanor Hull. These four women were linked by their unionist political affiliation, status as nonprofessional historians, and shared interest in Irish history. It considers how factors such as family, education, socioeconomic status, access to libraries and archives, mentors, and intellectual circles shaped the careers of these women. While all four women were Irish Protestants and unionists, it is argued that their scholarship often expanded the possibilities for writing Irish history within a more nationalist framework, and that they helped pave the way for other Irish women who sought careers in history and related fields.

These women wrote at a time when far-reaching changes were taking place in the historical discipline. The professionalization of history and the establishment of university history departments in British, American, and Continental universities took place in the late nineteenth century. Academic journals such as the *Revue Historique*, the *English Historical Review*, and the *American Historical Review* were founded between the 1870s and 1890s. The new professional historians struggled to distinguish themselves from antiquarians and amateur writers of history, including women writers. However, "men of letters" and amateur female historians who wrote popular social and cultural histories were by no means displaced. Academic history could be problematic for women in the 1880s and 1890s, as they faced discrimination in higher education, and did not have access to the same academic training as men. Moreover, some women may have been alienated by academic historians' focus on political history and the nation-state, as they lacked full citizenship rights in the nation-state at this time. The late-nineteenth century feminist movement took place simultaneously with the professionalization of history, and as a result of feminist campaigns women gained entry to some universities by the 1870s. While amateur women historians continued to write, other women earned doctorates in history from the 1880s onwards in Scandinavia, Germany, Britain, and the United States. They published books and contributed to the new historical journals. A small number became history professors, especially in women's colleges in Britain and the United States, while the majority worked outside universities.[2]

The four historians under consideration wrote a range of works, from books on early Irish civilization to general histories of Ireland down to the modern period, and their books were influenced by their political stances. Unionist historians sometimes embraced Irish cultural nationalism, which coexisted with their political support for the Union between Ireland and Britain. Ferguson, who wrote on early Ireland, and Lawless and Hull, who produced general histories of Ireland, all revealed their cultural nationalism in their narratives of the nation. These three historians favored a moderate and conciliatory unionism, which allowed for critiques of British policy and reforms to conciliate nationalists. Hickson, perhaps the least sympathetic to Irish nationalism, wrote on seventeenth-century Ireland, and was significant in demonstrating the importance of using primary sources and for her prominence in a major historiographical debate in the 1880s. She would not be the last Irish woman to debate male historians whose work she opposed. While the historical works of these women reveal some similarities with other Western women historians writing in this period, they are best understood in light of the political and historiographical developments in late-nineteenth and early twentieth-century Ireland.

The political context of late nineteenth-century Ireland helped set the parameters in which Irish historians wrote their works. Irish nationalists contested British rule in Ireland throughout the nineteenth century, using both political and violent methods to overturn the Act of Union between Britain and Ireland. The militant, clandestine Irish Republican Brotherhood carried out a rebellion in 1867 that was easily put down. Charles Stewart Parnell, an Irish MP, championed land reform and constitutional nationalism in the 1880s with much popular support from an increasingly enfranchised Catholic electorate.[3] His Irish Parliamentary Party worked with Prime Minister William Gladstone and Liberal MPs to introduce a Home Rule Bill (intended to give Ireland a measure of autonomy) in Parliament, which was defeated in the House of Commons in 1886 against a backdrop of intense unionist opposition.[4] In 1893, after Parnell's death, a second Home Rule bill was passed in the Commons, but was defeated in the House of Lords.[5] Political polarization and militancy continued in Ireland for the next twenty years, as nationalists pushed for constitutional change, and pro-British unionists consistently opposed such change. In 1905, Arthur Griffith founded Sinn Fein, a nationalist movement more radical than the constitutional nationalism of the Irish Parliamentary Party. By 1914, the Home Rule Bill had passed the House of Commons, but was postponed for the duration of the First World War.[6]

Irish historiography between the 1860s and early 1920s was shaped by politicized debates between unionist and nationalist historians. William Lecky,[7] J.A. Froude,[8] Thomas Dunbar Ingram,[9] Richard Bagwell,[10] and Goddard Orpen[11] were among the leading unionist historians of Ireland during this period. With the exception of Froude, all were Irish Protestants.[12] Lecky and Froude took part in historical debates on Ireland between the 1870s and 1890s. Lecky, who was commended by nationalists for defending Ireland against hostile claims made by Froude, was widely considered to be the most objective and impartial Irish historian of his era. Froude, who was English, was a prolific writer whose works included *The English in Ireland in the Eighteenth Century* (1872–74). He was blatantly hostile to Irish Catholics, whom he believed were unfit for Home Rule.[13] Lecky was initially sympathetic to moderate Irish nationalism, but embraced unionism as Land League and Home Rule agitation gathered pace in the 1880s. He was elected to Parliament as a unionist MP for Trinity College in 1895.[14] In his *History of Ireland in the Eighteenth Century*, Lecky praised the autonomous eighteenth-century Dublin Parliament, dominated by landed Irish Protestants, which was dissolved after the 1798 Rebellion. His volumes were widely misinterpreted as nationalist documents and were used politically by Home Rulers in the 1880s and 1890s, since they praised an instance of limited Irish self-government and criticized the passing of the Act of Union.[15]

Thomas Dunbar Ingram, Richard Bagwell, and Goddard Orpen were also important unionist historians at the time. Ingram, a lawyer and a strong opponent of Home Rule, wrote openly partisan historical works on the Act of Union in the 1880s.[16] Richard Bagwell, a landlord from Tipperary, wrote significant multi-volume works on Tudor and Stuart Ireland based on the State Papers. He played an active role in unionist politics in the 1880s and 1890s.[17] Goddard Orpen, a Trinity College graduate, made a major contribution to the historiography of medieval Ireland by writing a groundbreaking four-volume work on the Normans in Ireland. He favored Norman feudalism over the decentralized medieval Gaelic polity.[18] Many of the reviews of Irish books that appeared in the *English Historical Review* between the 1890s and the 1920s were written by Orpen, who frequently censured works on Irish history written from a nationalist perspective. He appeared particularly concerned when less than admirable intentions were ascribed to England and its policymakers by historians of Ireland.[19]

Nationalist male historians of Ireland, who ranged from Home Rulers to republicans, also contributed to historiographical debates between the late 1860s and the early 1920s. Nationalist historians often wrote popular histories that reached a wide audience, and were therefore significant both in shaping a shared understanding of the national past and in the construction of Irish identity in the era preceding independence. Irish nationalist historians who produced significant works during this time included A.M. Sullivan, John Mitchel, Patrick Kavanagh, Justin Huntly McCarthy, J.G. Swift MacNeill, P.W. Joyce, and Eoin MacNeill.[20]

A.M. Sullivan, the editor of the *Nation* and later an Irish Parliamentary Party MP, wrote *The Story of Ireland*, an extraordinarily popular book which advanced the "seven hundred years thesis."[21] This interpretation of Irish history held that the native Irish had continually fought for independence from England since the Norman invasion of 1169. Sullivan was later criticized for his "Anglophobic and sectarian" tone,[22] which alienated unionists and Protestants. Luke Gibbons, however, highlighted Sullivan's political and social conservatism and his "sustained opposition to Fenianism and popular insurgency," adding that a tightly structured historical narrative like *The Story of Ireland* "can be seen as an attempt to co-opt and control the more unruly and refractory narratives of vernacular history."[23]

John Mitchel, one of the few Protestant nationalist historians, was a republican who had joined the Young Ireland movement in the 1840s. He wrote a *History of Ireland* in 1868, which covered the period since 1691.[24] One of Mitchel's historical contentions concerned the Famine. He believed that the British government's failure to prevent the massive death toll during the Famine was indicative of its genocidal intent to clear the land of its Irish inhabitants. James Donnelly writes that while no genocide took place in Ireland during the 1840s, "the idea of genocide had taken firm root in Irish political consciousness" because of mass evictions during the Famine. Mitchel's history, as well as his earlier political tract, *The Last Conquest of Ireland (Perhaps)*, simply reinforced a widely held view.[25]

Other nationalists who wrote histories at this time included a priest, two Irish Party MPs, a well-known educator, and an Irish language scholar. Patrick Kavanagh, a Franciscan from Wexford, was noteworthy for constructing a popular Catholic nationalist narrative of the 1798 Rebellion.[26] In his *Popular History of the Insurrection of 1798* (1870), he wrote out the secular republicanism of the United Irishmen, and presented the insurrection as a defensive action taken by persecuted Irish Catholics led by a selfless priest. Justin McCarthy, an Irish Party MP, wrote *An Outline of Irish History* (1883) and *Ireland Since the Union* (1887).[27] J.G. Swift MacNeill, also an Irish Party MP, wrote openly partisan works on the Irish Parliament and on the Act of Union, like Ingram, but from a Home Rule perspective.[28] Patrick Weston Joyce, the head of a teacher training college, was an influential history textbook writer as well as a scholar of early Ireland. A constitutional nationalist, he highlighted the achievements of both the Anglo-Irish and Gaelic Irish, and downplayed the theme of conflict.[29] Eoin MacNeill, the co-founder of the Gaelic League, was a leading scholar of Celtic Ireland in the early twentieth century, and became prominent both as a historian and as a public figure. In addition, he openly challenged unionist historians, such as Goddard Orpen.[30]

Four unionist women historians

Mary Ferguson (1823–1905)

Mary Catherine Guinness Ferguson was one of the first women historians in "the heroic age of Irish historiography," which lasted from the 1860s to the early 1920s.[31] She was important as an Irish female antiquarian and historian who commented on bias in historical scholarship and who helped promote a more sympathetic understanding of early Ireland and its cultural achievements, which came to be embraced by Irish nationalists. Ferguson's works were also noteworthy for revealing the outlook and historical understanding of a conciliatory, patriotic unionist in late nineteenth-century Ireland.

Mary Catherine Guinness was born into a wealthy, socially prominent family in 1823. Her father, Robert Guinness, was a Justice of the Peace, and her uncle was the chairman of the Guinness Brewery in Dublin.[32] Guinness met her future husband, the lawyer and antiquarian Samuel Ferguson, at a dinner party, where they discussed Irish missionaries in the early Christian period. They were married in 1848 and lived in Dublin.[33] Samuel Ferguson's life was later celebrated in *Sir Samuel Ferguson in the Ireland of His Day* (1896), a two-volume biography by his wife. It was not uncommon for women historians to engage in "the cultivation and enhancement of the posthumous reputation of male relatives" by writing biographies which included material from their correspondence.[34]

Samuel Ferguson (1810–86) was a central figure in Irish archaeology and cultural revivalism in the nineteenth century. He became the Deputy Keeper of the Records of Ireland in 1867, and the president of the Royal Irish Academy in 1881. He opposed Home Rule in the 1880s, although he had sympathized with both the romantic nationalist movement, Young Ireland, and the movement to repeal the Union in the 1840s.[35] Ferguson and other patriotic Protestant unionist antiquaries sought to undermine sectarian division and assert the cultural leadership of Irish Protestants by uniting the public in awareness and appreciation of archaeology and the ancient Irish past. This cultural initiative took place against a backdrop of threats to the social and political position of Irish Protestants during the nineteenth century, such as Catholic Emancipation, the Disestablishment of the Church of Ireland, and greater democratization. Despite their unionism, however, the work of Royal Irish Academy members influenced the development of Irish nationalism. By popularizing "the idea of 'an Irish nation,' rooted in antiquity," they inadvertently legitimized aspirations for Irish independence.[36]

Mary Guinness's marriage to Samuel Ferguson played a decisive role in her becoming a historian. She was encouraged by her husband, and joined him on archaeological expeditions to sites in Ireland, Brittany, and England. Mary's participation in archaeology was not unique in nineteenth-century Europe, as women in Britain, France, and Germany joined local antiquarian societies and sometimes worked alone or with their husbands on prehistoric sites in Europe, Africa, and Asia; later in the century, some women gained professional training as archaeologists.[37] Through Samuel, Mary gained access to manuscripts and translations of Irish texts in the Library of the Royal Irish Academy and in private collections. Mary Ferguson also became part of an intellectual circle of friends, a further source of encouragement and support. The Fergusons socialized with Irish historians such as R.R. Madden, A.G. Richey, and J.P. Prendergast, as well as literary figures and Celtic scholars. Mary shared Samuel's views on history as well as on politics. The Fergusons preferred Lecky to Froude as a historian of eighteenth-century Ireland, commending Lecky's integrity and impartiality, which they contrasted with Froude's condemnations of the Irish.[38] While both Fergusons were unionists who feared greater democratization and the end of elite rule,[39] they went further than some unionist contemporaries by their opposition to sectarianism and in their appreciation of early Irish history, culture, and antiquities.

Mary Ferguson wrote *The Story of the Irish Before the Conquest*,[40] a survey of Irish history from antiquity to the twelfth-century Norman invasion, in 1868. R.F. Foster notes that Ferguson's "accessible, effective treatment made popular both the stories of mythic heroes and heroines like Cuchullain and Deirdre, and the division of early Irish history into " 'The Mythic[al] Period' and 'The Heroic Period' and other categories … constructed a powerful sense of national destiny and nationalist amour propre."[41] Her popularization of antiquarian research in 1868 helped lay the groundwork for the Irish literary revival in the 1890s, though her contribution was not always remembered.[42]

Ferguson began her book by reflecting on bias and defending her sympathy for Ireland to an imagined English and Anglo-Irish readership. "If it be objected that a somewhat too favorable view is taken of a rude age and savage manners," she wrote, "it may with truth be said that any errors of sympathy are more than counterbalanced by the undue contempts [sic] of which, for many ages, all native Irish historic and legendary material has been the object."[43] Thus, she believed that in the context of nineteenth-century historiography, a positive presentation of Irish history satisfied the requirements of balance. A desire to counter anti-Irish prejudice in historical scholarship was not incompatible with the patriotic unionist political stance she shared with many of the leading antiquarians, such as George Petrie.[44] Mary Ferguson hoped that her book would promote tolerance, sympathy, and respect for the Irish.[45]

Ferguson emphasized such key figures and episodes as St. Patrick and early Irish Christian missionaries in Europe, the role of the Vikings, Brian Boru and the Battle of Clontarf, and the Norman invasion. St. Patrick was acclaimed for his role in Christianizing Ireland, and Irish monks were lauded for their scholarship and artistry, as shown by their illuminated manuscripts. She underscored the instrumental role played by Irish missionaries in spreading Christianity throughout Western Europe.[46] Ferguson criticized the Viking invaders for their violence, adding that the decentralized Gaelic polity could not organize a national resistance effort. However, she also highlighted cultural interchange and intermarriage between the Vikings and the Irish, as well as the contributions made by the Vikings to urbanization and commercial life.[47] She praised Brian Boru, the victor in the 1014 Battle of Clontarf against the Vikings and their Irish allies, as an outstanding Irish leader who promoted centralization, learning, and the building of churches.[48] Ferguson briefly described the events leading up to the Norman invasion of 1169, which inaugurated English rule in Ireland. She concluded her book on a unionist note, writing that the Norman Conquest resulted in Ireland's "admission to a larger sphere of civilization" and a share in numerous intellectual, cultural, and military accomplishments.[49]

Overall, Mary Ferguson was significant in legitimizing positive assessments of Celtic Ireland, and in popularizing nineteenth-century research on Ireland by antiquarians and Gaelic scholars. As an Irish Protestant and unionist who reached educated audiences in England and Ireland, her contention that Ireland had a culture and history worthy of respect carried weight. She used manuscript evidence to support her arguments. Ferguson also reinforced the view that

Ireland had an ancient civilization, a view embraced by Irish nationalists who appealed to tradition when staking out their claim to nationhood. Although Ferguson was not openly controversial and polemical, she felt the need to defend her positive presentation of early Irish history at the outset of her book. She believed that many English readers held certain preconceptions of the Irish, which would make them less likely to accept claims of an advanced early Irish culture. Early Irish history, however, was a less controversial period to write on than post-Reformation Irish history, when sectarian conflicts over history came to the fore. Ferguson, by expanding unionist historiography to include positive assessments of early Ireland, helped pave the way for advanced nationalist historians, including Alice Stopford Green, who ventured into the study of later and more contentious periods of Irish history.

Mary Agnes Hickson (1825–99)

Mary Agnes Hickson, who specialized in local history and in the history of seventeenth-century Ireland, differed from her contemporary, Mary Ferguson, in terms of socioeconomic circumstances, priorities, and motivations for writing history. While Ferguson was an affluent, socially prominent, patriotic unionist from Dublin who defended the Irish against charges of inferiority, Hickson was a socially and financially insecure Protestant unionist from Kerry who sought to defend unionist historical narratives at a time when they were being contested by nationalists and professional historians in a highly charged political and historiographical context. Hickson is significant both for her research in primary source documents and for her identity as a polemical female unionist historian engaged in scholarly and political controversies, standing in contrast to conciliatory patriotic unionist historians as well as nationalists. This section traces Hickson's formative influences and early efforts at historical scholarship, and demonstrates how her involvement in a major historiographical controversy in the 1880s both highlighted issues faced by female researchers, and led to Hickson's self-fashioning as a very public, confrontational unionist woman historian.

Mary Agnes Hickson was born in Tralee, County Kerry, in 1825. Her parents, John James Hickson, a successful attorney, and Sarah Day Hickson, a Church of Ireland clergyman's daughter, had thirteen other children, ten of whom would ultimately die of tuberculosis. While Mary's parents were committed Protestants, her paternal grandfather, originally a Catholic, had conformed to the Church of Ireland, and the Hicksons had Catholic relatives living in Kerry. Mary attended a girls' school in Tralee, followed by boarding school, where she excelled as a student. In addition to formally studying history at school, she learned about local history in a family setting, as her father discussed the history of Kerry and showed her the region's antiquities. This informal study ended with John James Hickson's death in 1839.[50]

The financial insecurity that Hickson experienced throughout her adult life, and which hindered her opportunities for research, began during the Famine. The Hicksons, who owned land in Kerry, suffered financial losses and eviction in 1847 when their tenants were unable to pay their rents, and several of the family's properties had to be sold. Mary lived with her widowed mother in rented rooms in Tralee until Sarah Hickson's death in 1852. Mary spent most of the 1850s and 1860s living with relatives in both Ireland and England, where, interestingly in light of her later attitudes, she converted to Catholicism. She returned to the Church of Ireland, and to Kerry, in the late 1860s, and began her career as a historian.[51]

Hickson's earliest forays into historical research centered on family history and local history, revealing similarities with the work of other non-academic women historians in the nineteenth century. As a prolific writer on Kerry history and antiquities for newspapers, such as the *Kerry Evening Post*, and for scholarly journals, she reached a wide audience, and can thus be viewed as a popularizer of historical scholarship. Like Mary Ferguson, she was also active in antiquarian circles, and joined the Royal Society of Antiquaries of Ireland.[52] Hickson edited *Selections From Old Kerry Records* in the early 1870s, combining her interest in county history with archival scholarship.[53] Writing on local history linked Hickson to Margaret Cusack, who also wrote on Kerry history, and to women historians in Britain and the United States, who produced local histories of their counties and states respectively.[54] Other women historians also edited records, and Hickson's English contemporary, Mary Anne Everett Green, was instrumental in the professionalization of the Public Record Office.[55] While Hickson was hindered by financial insecurity as an adult,[56] she had the advantages of a circle of friends connected with antiquarianism, as well as access to libraries, which she gained through her acquaintance with historian W.E.H. Lecky. Lecky also gave her books and critiqued her work.[57]

Hickson's major work, *Ireland in the Seventeenth Century; or, the Irish Massacres of 1641–2* (1884), propelled her into the midst of a historiographical controversy.[58] The main historical source on the 1641 Rebellion in Ulster, in which several thousand Protestant settlers had been killed by the Irish Catholic insurgents, was the evidence taken from surviving settlers, which included hearsay about various atrocities as well as testimony from eyewitnesses. Sectarian debate had raged about the authenticity of the depositions, with Catholic partisans viewing them as exaggerated or made up to justify the further confiscation of Catholic land, and Protestant partisans believing the deposition evidence testified to the slaughter of tens of thousands of Protestants.[59] Some Protestant unionists in the 1880s justified their opposition to Home Rule by citing the violence of 1641 "as an example of the way that Irish Catholics had behaved under home rule in the past."[60] J.A. Froude, who believed the depositions were valid, had reopened the controversy in the 1870s in *The English in Ireland in the Eighteenth Century,* in which he denounced the Irish Catholics for perpetrating the massacres. Irish historians J.P. Prendergast and W.E.H. Lecky, who were skeptical about the value of the depositions, responded to Froude in the 1870s.[61]

Mary Agnes Hickson, unlike Lecky and Froude, thoroughly studied and analyzed the depositions.[62] However, she consulted Lecky for advice about historical investigation. According to Lecky, "in dealing with evidence such as the depositions afforded, one should follow Voltaire's maxim and believe only the evil a party writer tells of his own side, and the good that he recognizes in his enemy."[63] Hickson tried Lecky's methods of historical analysis with mixed results. She wrote that one piece of evidence helped confirm the overall validity of the testimonies: "One of the many internal signs of truthfulness in the depositions is that they admit Sir Phelim [O'Neill, an insurgent leader] expressed regret for [the murder of] Lord Caulfield and his child's foster mother ... now if these witnesses were the prejudicial perjurers the (so called) nationalist writers want to make them out ... they would have" described O'Neill as utterly depraved.[64] However, her belief in the validity of the depositions led her to overestimate the numbers killed. She maintained that "about 27,000 Protestants were murdered by the sword, gun, ropes, drowning, etc."[65] Historians of early modern Ireland now believe that between 3000 and 4000 Protestant settlers were killed;[66] some of Hickson's contemporaries, including Lecky, also believed the Rebellion claimed approximately four thousand Ulster Protestant victims.[67]

Hickson presented her views and findings in the introduction to the depositions she selected and edited, which were published as *Ireland in the Seventeenth Century* in two volumes in 1884. She was concerned that the consensus of some recent (Protestant and unionist) historians came closer to the Catholic interpretation of 1641 than to the Protestant and unionist interpretation. Hickson lamented that many Irish Catholics had never accepted the 1641 narrative of the near-extermination of Ulster Protestants, and perceived their historic co-religionists as innocent victims of Cromwellian atrocities and land confiscation. This perception, she felt, was ominously reinforced by popular Catholic nationalist histories "unhappily ... in the hands of every Irish child and youth." She wanted to inform them of "the records of the crimes which led to those severities."[68] Hickson seemed to display a need to engage in moral one-upmanship, and to prove that Catholic insurgents killing Protestant settlers were more depraved than the Cromwellian forces killing Catholic civilians in retribution. For Hickson, the 1641 massacres were utterly without justification, while the deaths of Catholics in the 1650s, though regrettable, were mitigated by the need to avenge the 1641 atrocities and pacify Ireland. Hickson wanted to privilege and enshrine the Protestant narrative of victimization, at a time when it was being interrogated by scholarly historians, while simultaneously puncturing Catholic narratives of historic victimization. Thus, her work may be seen as an inversion of partisan Catholic histories featuring exercises in moral one-upmanship, in which Protestants were the depraved aggressors and Catholics the innocent victims.

The book was not calculated to appeal to the popular audience in Ireland that Hickson wished to enlighten. Having J.A. Froude write the preface to her book hardly added to its credibility and worth in the eyes of Irish Catholic nationalists and of many professional historians. Froude believed that the depositions should be published as an "eternal witness of Irish barbarity."[69] The 1641 massacres had historically been invoked to justify the treatment of Catholics, which factored into Catholic distrust of the depositions, and rendered them less likely to empathize with the Protestant victims. Hickson was unable to engage with a popular Catholic readership while doing full justice to the experience of the victims of atrocities in 1641, whereas Lecky, who was also a Protestant and a unionist, was more successful in this project. His tone was calmer, and he contextualized 1641 while condemning the atrocities.

Hickson's book received mixed reviews. It was praised by a unionist writer in the *Edinburgh Review*, but S.R. Gardiner, a British early modernist, wrote a less favorable review. While Lecky had praised her research efforts, he did not think she had proved her case regarding the depositions.[70] In 1886, Robert Dunlop, a seventeenth-century specialist at the University of Manchester, wrote about the depositions in the *English Historical Review*. Like Lecky, he downplayed the validity of the depositions as a historical source.[71] Hickson disputed Dunlop in the pages of the *EHR*, defending her work and the validity of the deposition evidence.[72] Although she was a non-professional woman historian who had not received a university education, she was not afraid to confront a credentialed male historian based in a university history department. Her sparring with Dunlop foreshadowed Alice Stopford Green's confrontation with him over criticism of her work more than two decades later.

Hickson's defensiveness about the credibility of the depositions raises interesting questions about historical writers and the "politics of empathy". Unsurprisingly, she was emotionally involved with her material, which contained graphic accounts of extreme violence. The victims were not an undifferentiated mass for Hickson, but individuals with names and occupations, whom she had come to know and humanize through her study of the depositions. She questioned the propriety of historians raising doubts about the testimony of victimized people. However, the fact that the victims were Protestants made her empathize and identify with them more.

Her status as an insecure Protestant in predominantly Catholic and nationalist southwestern Ireland in the 1880s lent a polemical edge to Hickson's writing, and sometimes led her to conflate past and present.[73] She was unable to empathize with Irish Catholics, whom she perceived as a dangerous political threat, believing that they had always been manipulated and controlled by priests interested in fomenting unrest and sectarian hatred.[74] Hickson condemned the historic involvement of the Catholic Church in politics, as well as local agrarian and political activism in the 1880s. Local incidents reinforced her perceptions and value judgments about the people of Ireland. In an 1887 letter to Lecky, she expressed her anger about recent events in Mitchelstown, Co. Cork. Police had charged into a crowd at a political meeting, whereupon the crowd had stoned them. Three men were shot and killed by the police in the disturbance, but Hickson was most anguished about the stoning of a Protestant policeman named Leahy, who had given evidence against nationalist MP William O'Brien. "The mob acted like cowardly assassins to poor Leahy," she wrote. She blamed the nationalist journalist and politician Timothy Harrington for fomenting crime and unrest through his provocative speeches and writings, insisting that he had "deliberately trad[ed] in agitation to enter Parliament."[75] This underscores her tendency to view the Irish Catholics, past and present, as easily manipulated by priests and politicians, and to value Protestant victims of violence over Catholic ones.

Ireland in the Seventeenth Century, then, may be understood as a late nineteenth-century document as well as a seventeenth-century one. Hickson wrote as a defensive, marginal member of an old elite group whose former political dominance was being undermined by the advance of Irish nationalism, though unionists were hardly powerless in the 1880s.

Hickson was aware of the challenges facing women historians of her era as they embarked on original research and the editing of documents. Unlike many of her male contemporaries, she lacked a steady income as a landowner or a university-based historian or other professional. As a woman, she was less likely to obtain employment with the Historical Manuscripts Commission. This contrasted with Sir John Gilbert, whom Hickson greatly resented for his access to resources, mistrust of the 1641 depositions, and nationalist sympathies.[76] Her public clashes with Gilbert, like her debate with Robert Dunlop, highlighted the power struggles between amateur women historians and professional male historians in positions of institutional and academic power.

In conclusion, then, Hickson is significant not only for using primary sources on early modern history in the 1880s, but also for being more public and polemical than other women historians at the time. She was involved in a high-stakes, public historical controversy, and was unafraid to defend her work to men such as Robert Dunlop who were better educated than she. Hickson was a defender of an imperiled status quo, as a unionist and as a historian. Her assessment of the numbers of Protestants killed in 1641 was not considered credible by some of her contemporaries, whose lower figures are accepted by professional historians today. She wanted to protect Protestant narratives of victimization in 1641 by placing them on an irrefutable documentary basis after factoring in obvious exaggerations, but her numbers and analysis did not stand the test of time. In addition, scholarship on 1641 has broadened to include studies of other aspects of the depositions that Hickson could not have anticipated, such as the information they provide on "attitudes, social structures, wealth and indebtedness, literacy and possessions."[77] Hickson's importance also lies in defining an identity as a public female historian unafraid to enter into disputes, a persona redefined by the historian Alice Stopford Green.

Emily Lawless (1845–1913)

Emily Lawless wrote *The Story of Ireland*, a general history in the "Story of the Nations" series, in 1887. She was not, however, primarily a historian, and was best known as a novelist and poet whose works of fiction sometimes dealt with historical themes.[78] Such versatility was not uncommon for nineteenth-century women writers in Europe and the United States, many of whom wrote fiction and poetry as well as history. It is argued here that Lawless was significant for producing a survey of Irish history from a moderate unionist perspective, and for reaching the political establishment through her historical and political fiction.

Emily Lawless was born into an aristocratic Irish Protestant and unionist family in Celbridge, Co. Kildare, in 1845. The Lawlesses were relative newcomers to the Protestant Ascendancy, as Emily's Irish Catholic great-grandfather had converted to Protestantism in the eighteenth century. Her grandfather had favored the United Irishmen in 1798, and had denounced the Act of Union.[79] Emily's father was the third Lord Cloncurry of Lyons Castle, and her mother, Elizabeth Kirwan, came from a landed family in Galway. Several members of the family struggled with depression. Her father committed suicide when she was fourteen, and two of her sisters took their own lives as well. Emily became a heroin addict later in life.[80]

Lawless's distinguished literary career began in the 1880s. James Cahalan contends that Lawless, "raised by her mother, prompted to write by [Scottish novelist] Mrs. Oliphant, and inspired throughout her career by the example of [Irish writer Maria] Edgeworth ... clearly experienced female tradition and mentorship as central shaping influences."[81] Her first novel, *Hurrish* (1886), dealt with peasants and the Land League in rural Ireland, and brought Lawless to the attention of Prime Minister William Gladstone. He thought the novel dramatically depicted Irish alienation from the law, and *Hurrish* helped him shape his arguments promoting Home Rule legislation.[82] Lawless eventually met and corresponded with Gladstone, who sought her out for her knowledge of Ireland. He was later taken in by Lawless's *With Essex in Ireland* (1890), set in the Elizabethan period, "a work of fiction so well grounded [in history] as to deceive Mr. Gladstone into believing it reprinted from a genuine journal kept by Essex in 1599."[83] In 1892, Lawless wrote *Grania*, centered on a woman living in the Aran Islands, "the most clearly feminist nineteenth-century Irish novel since those of Sydney Owenson at the beginning of the century."[84] She wrote *Maelcho*, a work of historical fiction set in early modern Ireland, in 1894, and a biography of Maria Edgeworth a decade later, linking her with other women historians who wrote female biographies.[85]

Lawless found another mentor in historian W.E.H. Lecky, with whom she discussed history and politics. She had relied on his treatment of eighteenth-century Ireland for her own historical survey,[86] and found his chapters on Ireland in his last two volumes of *A History of England in the Eighteenth Century* both edifying and highly engaging, adding that she favored dramatic, character-driven history.[87] Lawless shared Lecky's opposition to Home Rule and his concern about greater democratization. Discussing the fall of Parnell in 1890, she wrote that "one cannot help hoping that *that* bogy [Home Rule] is dead and done with for ever. There is no knowing however how soon even the most discredited scarecrow and impostor may not be galvanized into an appearance of new life." She hoped that the discredited Parnell would retain his leadership of the Irish Party, believing that would prevent Home Rule.[88]

Lawless's political and ideological stances are reflected in *The Story of Ireland*, a survey of the country from prehistory to the nineteenth century. As a cultural nationalist and feminist, she praised early Celtic Ireland for its literature, laws, and the active role it appeared to allow to women. In regard to "the treatment of his women – the Irish

Celt seems to have always stood in favorable contrast to most of the other rude races [in northern] Europe."[89] She commended the intellectual life, art, and spirituality of early Christian Ireland, like Mary Ferguson, and denounced the Viking invaders for their brutality.[90] She was critical of both the medieval Norman invaders and of the excesses of the Cromwellian forces in the seventeenth century.[91] In her discussion of the eighteenth century, Lawless, like Lecky, valorized notable Anglo-Irish Protestant elites, such as Jonathan Swift, Edmund Burke, and especially Henry Grattan, a leading member of the autonomous Dublin Parliament in the 1780s and 1790s. She lauded Grattan for "being consistently loyal [to England] and consistently patriotic."[92] Lawless condemned republican rebels such as the United Irishmen and the Fenians who rebelled in 1867. She concluded her book with a discussion of two related contemporary issues, Land League agitation and Home Rule. She empathized with the landed class she belonged to, since its position was being undermined by the increasing strength of the Catholic tenant farmer class. Lawless expressed her anxiety about Home Rule, and hoped for the continuance of the Union.[93] The book underscored her cultural nationalism, exemplified by her positive assessment of early Ireland and Gaelic culture, and her relatively liberal unionism and commitment to elite rule, which allowed her to critique past English policies and praise Grattan's Parliament, while still upholding the Union.

Emily Lawless died in England on 19 October 1913. While her most important achievements were in Irish literature, she was also significant in the 1880s as a woman writing a popular history of Ireland through the nineteenth century from a moderate unionist perspective. By positively assessing early Ireland and the eighteenth-century Dublin Parliament, and by occasionally criticizing past English policies, she helped expand the boundaries of what was acceptable in unionist histories of the modern period, in contrast to Mary Ferguson, whose book concluded with the arrival of the Normans. Lawless helped popularize Lecky's presentation of eighteenth-century Irish history, particularly his promotion of Henry Grattan, the autonomous Dublin Parliament of 1782–1800, and the eighteenth-century Anglo-Irish landed aristocracy. In doing so, she helped reinforce an alternative historical memory for the southern Irish Protestant minority before and after the establishment of the Free State, centered on the perception of an eighteenth-century golden age for the Anglo-Irish aristocracy. Lawless was significant as an Irish female historian who influenced the political establishment through her writing, as Gladstone sought her out for her knowledge of Ireland as he formulated policy. Lawless's public role and engagement with the political establishment also has implications for the careers of Alice Stopford Green and politically influential women historians of the Free State period, such as Helena Concannon and Dorothy Macardle.

Eleanor Hull (1860–1935)

Eleanor Hull was one of the leading female Irish-language scholars of her era, as well as a historian and folklorist. An independent scholar, Hull was important in bridging the gulf between non-professional antiquarianism and academic Celtic Studies, an interdisciplinary field incorporating early history, literature, language scholarship, and archaeology. Hull's work also reveals that she reflected on conceptual issues pertaining to the writing of history, and that she believed an understanding of history could illuminate contemporary politics. The shifts in Hull's political thought, registered in her historical writing, reveal the trajectory taken by some moderate, conciliatory southern unionists after 1916.

Eleanor Hull was born in England in 1860 to Irish Protestant parents, but spent her formative years in Dublin. Her father, Edward Hull, who had roots in County Down, was a professor who taught at the Royal College of Science. Eleanor attended Alexandra College, a Protestant girls' secondary school in Dublin, and then studied at the Royal College of Science. Her major intellectual interest was the Irish language, which she studied with noted scholars Kuno Meyer and Robin Flower. Flower was a lifelong mentor and associate who later headed the Council of the Irish Texts Society.

Hull, who spent most of her adult life in London, was the honorary secretary of the Irish Texts Society, which she co-founded in 1899. The members of the Society edited, translated, and published Irish manuscripts.[94] The Society provided her with an intellectual network and a circle of friends with shared interests. Hull, who shared the Gaelic League's goal of promoting the study of the Irish language and early Irish history, organized Gaelic League classes and lecture series in London focusing on early Irish history. Like Emily Lawless, Hull was aware of the dramatic potential of history, and recommended interspersing Irish historical narratives with myths and legends to appeal to a wide audience.[95] She was especially interested in reaching children and adolescents, like many other women historians, and published two histories pitched towards a younger audience, *Pagan Ireland* (1904) and *Early Christian Ireland* (1905).[96] Like Mary Ferguson and Emily Lawless, she expanded the boundaries of the acceptable within unionist historiography by presenting early Irish culture in a positive light.

The emerging field of Celtic Studies was where Hull became most influential. Mary O'Dowd contends that Hull, as honorary secretary of the Irish Texts Society, played a key role in raising the scholarly status of Irish language scholarship and textual editing, moving these endeavors away from the realm of antiquarianism. In doing so, she helped pave the way for the institutionalization of interdisciplinary Celtic Studies in Irish universities. Hull also mentored female Celtic scholars in the Irish Texts Society, opening up the emerging field to women. For example, Agnes O'Farrelly and Kathleen Mulchrone, both of whom had edited texts for the Society, ultimately attained academic jobs, O'Farrelly as a lecturer in Irish at University College, Dublin (UCD), and Mulchrone as a Professor of Celtic Studies at University College, Galway (UCG).[97]

Unlike the other unionist women historians, Hull lived to witness the Easter Rising. On April 24, 1916, republicans, disillusioned with constitutional nationalism and the postponement of Home Rule, occupied key points in Dublin, such as the General Post Office, and exchanged fire with British troops before surrendering on April 30. The executions of fifteen male insurgents helped to radicalize Irish public opinion.[98] Initially a relatively liberal political unionist and a cultural nationalist[99] like Mary Ferguson and Emily Lawless, Hull was taken aback by the 1916 Rising. Unlike other unionists, however, she did not wholeheartedly denounce the insurrectionists, one of whom, Patrick Pearse, had been an acquaintance. She wrote that she would have sympathized more with the insurgents if their goal had been to implement Home Rule right away, but the insurrection "was as much against Redmond [the leader of the Irish Parliamentary Party] and Home Rule as it was against England." She appeared to have been moving towards a moderate Home Rule stance, and was now concerned that Sinn Fein, which she believed was dominated by "syndicalists," had displaced moderate nationalists such as Redmond who opposed complete independence. While Hull thought the work of cultural nationalists had been undermined by the Rising, she concluded that "it is impossible not to grieve for the young men who have gone down in this struggle – many of them pure-spirited and talented though I think misguided ... the whole thing is heartbreaking."[100]

An article Hull wrote during the Treaty negotiations in 1921, entitled "Ireland's Allegiance to the Crown," demonstrated her view that history could be used to understand the present. Surveying centuries of Irish history, she argued that the Irish had traditionally been loyal to the Crown, but had never been rewarded for their loyalty. "The chief rebellions of the Irish people were directed not against the Crown as such," Hull maintained, "from it they rather looked for relief." Irish insurrections resulted from such causes as religious persecution and land confiscation. Local officials who enforced such policies "rooted in the minds of the Irish an ingrained distrust of English rule."[101] Irish support for the Stuart cause, Hull maintained, was a striking example of Ireland's traditional loyalty to the monarchy.[102] She concluded by asserting that Irish leaders such as Grattan, O'Connell, Parnell, and Redmond had all favored an Irish Parliament and the retention of the link with the Crown, rather than full independence. Ireland, she wrote, "united to the Empire by the imperial link, will take a higher and more dignified position than as a small and isolated independent State."[103] By 1921, then, she was supportive of a mild Home Rule settlement that was no longer revolutionary, a stance that linked her with conciliatory southern unionists and moderate nationalists opposed to republicanism and complete independence. Her article is unusual in arguing for the historic loyalty of the Irish Catholics in the early modern period, and stands in sharp contrast to the work of early modernist Mary Agnes Hickson, who believed Irish Catholics were generally disloyal and rebellious.

Hull's major historical work was a history of Ireland in two volumes. She began working on *A History of Ireland and Her People* as early as 1913, but publication was delayed and the volumes appeared in 1926 and 1931 respectively.[104] Her book was used as a textbook by Trinity College history students beginning in 1929, and was recommended to NUI students into the 1950s.[105] The first volume, which covered the pre-Christian period through the sixteenth century, is examined here, as it made more of an impact and because Hull's expertise was in early and medieval Irish history. Hull sought to achieve balance by maintaining that troubled Anglo-Irish relations in the medieval and early modern periods were not so much the fault of the English or the Irish, but were largely attributable to "the officials who intervened between the English Crown and the Irish people."[106] She emphasized the importance of primary sources and the reports of witnesses to past events. Hull was skeptical of linear teleologies of historical development, arguing that "Irish history is a series of contradictions ... it refuses to march along the simple lines marked out for it by the modern political writer."[107]

While Hull believed there had been no golden age in early Ireland prior to English rule, her treatment of early Ireland was generally positive, in keeping with her cultural nationalism. She concurred with Emily Lawless that women in early Ireland had legal rights and property rights within marriage.[108] Hull emphasized the scholarly achievements of Irish monks and the role of Irish missionaries in Europe during the early Christian period.[109] She praised Brian Boru as a noble leader. Hull was ambivalent about the Normans, who were frequently celebrated by unionist historians, believing that many of Ireland's later problems originated in the manner in which they governed the country during the medieval period. The Norman nobles, she wrote, ruled Ireland in their own interest, while the monarch's power receded. The Irish became alienated from the English Crown; to the Irish, "the English remained a foreign nation, whose right was disputed, and whose rule was accepted only through necessity."[110] She believed that some Normans had assimilated into Irish culture, and she criticized the Statutes of Kilkenny, which tried to check Norman assimilation to ensure continued loyalty to the Crown.[111]

Hull was more critical of the English in Ireland during the Elizabethan period, although she highlighted the shortcomings of the Irish leaders as well. She described Essex as one of the many cultured sixteenth-century noblemen who "in their dealings with 'native' races lost all sense of honour or feelings of natural compassion. In his relations with some of the Irish and Scots alike Essex acted with callous and hideous cruelty."[112] Hull ended her book with the Flight of the Earls in the early seventeenth century, following the loss of the Nine Years' War and the end of the clan system. In her conclusion, she underscored the problems inherent in the clan system and the violence and instability of medieval Gaelic society. However, she added that "there was little to choose between the methods of the Irish chief and the English officer so far as terrorism and bloodshed were concerned."[113] Hull further maintained that "there is a real difference in the humanity shown by [Irish] leaders toward the vanquished [and towards captives] ... the behaviour of the Irish chiefs showed a sense of honour and courtesy of which we have lamentably few examples on the part of the English officers in their dealings with them."[114] Overall, she tried to maintain balance by discussing the limitations of both sides, rather than uncritically celebrating either the Irish or the English.

Two historians who reviewed *A History of Ireland and Her People to the Close of the Tudor Period* were Goddard Orpen, a unionist, and Alice Stopford Green, a nationalist. Orpen praised Hull's competence and vivid writing, but felt that she was overly sympathetic to the native Irish and that she failed to praise the Normans highly enough for their achievements.[115] Green wrote that Hull's work was weak in its treatment of the law in Gaelic Ireland and in contextualizing early modern writers who shaped opinion on Ireland.[116]

Eleanor Hull died in 1935. She left a varied intellectual legacy as a historian, folklorist, and Irish-language scholar. Hull shared an interest in early Ireland with the other historians, especially Mary Ferguson, and her contribution to the editing of texts linked her with Mary Agnes Hickson. Like women historians elsewhere in the West, she disseminated historical knowledge through textbooks. Her writing reveals that she reflected on philosophical and ideological issues linked with historical scholarship. While her cultural nationalism and liberal unionism related to the stances of Ferguson and Lawless, she lived to witness the revolutionary period and the creation of the Irish Free State, and her acceptance of greater political autonomy for Ireland signified the political possibilities of conciliatory unionism in a changed political context.

Conclusion

This chapter has examined the careers of Mary Ferguson, Mary Agnes Hickson, Emily Lawless, and Eleanor Hull in the context of Irish political history and Irish historiography in the years between 1868 and 1922. All four women were Irish Protestants and unionists. The unionism of Ferguson, Lawless, and Hull encompassed cultural nationalism and a favorable outlook on early Irish history and culture.

The four historians differed in terms of relative advantages concerning family, education, wealth, mentors, and access to sources and to intellectual networks and circles of friends. Ferguson, the only married woman of the four, was mentored in her historical endeavors by her husband, through whom she also gained access to sources and a circle of scholarly friends. Emily Lawless's mother was a source of support, while Hickson and Hull came from families that valued formal schooling for girls. None had attended university, as higher education was denied to women born before the mid-nineteenth century, and opportunities were still limited for women of Hull's generation. Hull had the greatest educational advantages of the four, as she attended the rigorous Alexandra College, and studied at the Royal College of Science. With the exception of Mary Hickson, who as an adult lived in reduced circumstances, all were middle-class or wealthy. W.E.H. Lecky served as a mentor to Emily Lawless, and to a lesser extent Mary Hickson, while Hull's mentors included Celtic scholars Kuno Meyer and especially Robin Flower. All had circles of friends involved in antiquarianism, history, language studies, and literature. These factors all helped shape and reinforce their commitment to historical research and writing.

The historians under consideration made different impacts on the course of Irish historiography. Mary Ferguson, Emily Lawless, and Eleanor Hull all reinforced positive perceptions of early Irish culture, expanding the boundaries of the acceptable in unionist historiography on Ireland. This was more controversial when Ferguson wrote in the 1860s, but her assessment carried weight because of her position as a Protestant and unionist, and because she used textual evidence to support her assertions. She was significant in popularizing the new scholarship on early Ireland carried out by Royal Irish Academy members, and indirectly gave support to Irish nationalists, who appealed to the notion of Ireland as an ancient civilization to bolster their political claims to nationhood. Lawless and Hull took the historical narrative into later and more contentious periods. They again expanded the boundaries of the acceptable in unionist-oriented Irish historiography by sometimes criticizing English policy, and by celebrating aspects of the Irish past, such as Grattan's Parliament. Mary Hickson was the most hostile to Irish nationalism and Catholicism, but was significant for her use of primary sources and for defining a more public and polemical image for women historians through her involvement in the debate surrounding the 1641 depositions. The others were influential public historians as well, in the context of the time – Mary Ferguson because her popular book helped shape national perceptions and inadvertently provided historical justification for nationhood, Emily Lawless because she gained access to a powerful political figure who sought her out for her knowledge as he defined his Irish policy, and Eleanor Hull because of her leadership role in the Irish Texts Society and indirect influence on the formation of Celtic Studies programs in Irish universities. The careers of these women helped pave the way for the careers of later Irish female historians, some of whom wrote as advanced nationalists, entered the universities, and gained formal political power in the new Irish state.

2
Nationalist Women Historians, 1868–1922

Margaret Cusack and Alice Stopford Green were prominent Irish nationalist historians with international reputations in the period between 1868 and 1922. Though they came from Protestant unionist backgrounds like Ferguson, Hickson, Lawless, and Hull, they ultimately became committed political nationalists. Both were very public, influential historians who attained prominence for their involvement in social and political causes, as well as for their histories. This chapter discusses Cusack's and Green's careers as historians and considers their political commitments, contending that they were instrumental in constructing the persona of an Irish nationalist woman historian as a combative, politically engaged public historian. Their careers shed light on the opportunities for women associated with intellectual establishments outside the universities in the late nineteenth and early twentieth centuries. Cusack, as a member of a religious order, was affiliated with a powerful church that dominated education in Ireland, giving her a sphere of influence. Green was linked with intellectual circles associated with the rising Irish nationalist establishment, which contributed to her success and fame as a historian.

Margaret Cusack (1829–99)

Margaret Cusack set a precedent as the first Irish woman to write a complete history of Ireland, and the first to do so from a nationalist perspective. She wrote *An Illustrated History of Ireland* in 1868, the same year that Mary Ferguson wrote *The Story of the Irish Before the Conquest*. Cusack's considerable literary output included Irish history surveys and textbooks, local history, religious history, biography, and political and social commentary. Cusack stood out as the only nun among the Irish women historians of the period (there were several priests among the male historians), and the only one writing Catholic-oriented nationalist history.

Cusack was born into a wealthy Dublin Protestant family in 1829. Her father, Samuel Cusack, was a doctor. Margaret's parents separated in her early adolescence, and she and her mother, Sarah Stoney Cusack, moved to England, where Margaret was placed in boarding school.[1] Margaret Cusack was interested in social reform, and initially joined an Anglican sisterhood to further her goal, but, finding this unfulfilling, took the unconventional route of converting to Catholicism in 1858. She subsequently became a nun, joining the Poor Clares in 1859 and taking the name Sister Mary Francis Clare. Cusack returned to Ireland, and lived first at the Poor Clares convent in Newry, Co. Down. She moved to a new convent in Kenmare, Co. Kerry, where she lived from 1861 to 1881. Her role in Kenmare would be to write religious and other works to help financially support the convent.[2]

Cusack wrote prolifically while simultaneously promoting educational schemes for poor rural girls, raising funds for relief efforts in Kerry, and involving herself in Land League and ecclesiastical politics. She founded a new order, the Sisters of Peace, in 1884. Cusack's activities and forceful personality brought her into conflict with political elites and the Catholic hierarchy in Ireland, Britain, and the United States. They objected to her support of the Land League and her various fundraising efforts, which diverted funds from projects favored by the American Catholic hierarchy.[3] In 1889, demoralized by conflict, she left the convent and returned to Protestantism. She spent the last years of her life in England, where she supported herself by publishing her autobiography and polemics against the Catholic Church,[4] and died in 1899.[5]

Cusack's links with the Catholic Church and Irish antiquarian circles were central to her formation as a historian. As a nun, she had an institutional base in which to write and promote her works, and the clergy encouraged the reading of her histories by members of the Irish Catholic reading public and by students in Catholic schools throughout Ireland. Cusack, however, was also interested in reaching British readers, especially policymakers, as well as Irish-American Catholics and students in British and American schools. She operated a publishing company, Kenmare Publications, during the time she spent at the Poor Clares convent in Kerry. The company published approximately 200,000 volumes in ten years. Cusack's association with Irish antiquarian scholars was also significant. Like Mary Ferguson, whose history she admired, and other Irish women historians of the period, Cusack was interested in archaeology and new scholarship on early Ireland. Her acquaintance with prominent antiquarians, including William Wilde and the Fergusons, gave her access to manuscripts and books held in the Royal Irish Academy and in private libraries. They also helped promote her works, particularly her county history of Kerry, which relied on subscriptions prior to publication.[6]

Cusack' treatment of significant events and themes in *An Illustrated History of Ireland*, as well as in later versions of her history of Ireland which were pitched towards different readerships in Ireland and abroad, reflected her nationalist and Catholic stances. Like Mary Ferguson, she wished to refute notions of early Irish barbarism by stressing the spirituality and cultural and intellectual achievements of early Ireland. She cited the new scholarship of archaeologists and Irish-language scholars to support her claims. Cusack denounced the violence of the Vikings and the Normans, and condemned the fourteenth-century Statutes of Kilkenny, which sought to keep the Normans and Irish apart, arguing that they were unjust to the Irish and left a destructive legacy.[7] Her treatment of the Tudor period and the Reformation stressed Ireland's loyalty to the Catholic Church despite intense persecution by the authorities, and her discussion of the seventeenth century focused on the atrocities committed by the Cromwellian forces. Her account of the 1641 Rebellion stood in stark contrast to Mary Agnes Hickson's later assessments, especially in regard to the role played by the Catholic Church. Cusack believed the rebellion was justified due to the prior persecution of Catholics, downplayed the killing of Protestants, and cited instances of priests rescuing Protestants and urging the Irish to refrain from killing innocent Protestant civilians.[8] She denounced the Penal Laws in operation in the eighteenth century, which discriminated against Irish Catholics, and her treatment of the 1798 Rebellion stressed the atrocities committed by the militia and General Lake's forces, which she argued had been overlooked by earlier historians. She highlighted the role in the Rebellion played by a Wexford priest, Father John Murphy. Like other Catholic nationalist writers at the time who opposed republicanism, she stressed the role of priests who were driven to join their people in rebellion due to religious persecution, rather than highlighting the secular republicanism of the United Irishmen.[9] Turning to the nineteenth century, Cusack included a celebratory account of her hero Daniel O'Connell's political leadership and role in winning Catholic Emancipation through peaceful methods in 1829. She refrained from discussing the Young Ireland rebellion of 1848, in the midst of the Famine, or the 1867 Rising by the Irish Republican Brotherhood. She concluded with a discussion of Irish emigration to America in the nineteenth century, which she hoped would end when justice was done to Ireland.[10]

Cusack argued that an understanding of Irish history would reinforce her readers' Irish identities and strengthen their commitment to Catholicism, as they would be inspired by her presentation of Ireland's steadfast adherence to the Catholic faith. She was also concerned with defending the role of the Catholic Church throughout Irish history. In the medieval period, for instance, she defended the English Pope Adrian IV's support for the English monarch's claim to Ireland (expressed in Adrian's Bull), arguing that he sincerely believed that Ireland was in need of reform . Cusack's histories were filled with heroic Irish priests who were devoted to their people and suffered martyrdom for their faith, and who intervened to rescue Protestants in times of conflict. Her account of the origins of Protestantism, which presented Martin Luther and Henry VIII simply as depraved individuals,[11] reflected a sectarian understanding of the Reformation and lack of empathy for Protestants who were persecuted elsewhere in Europe at the time. Catholics were invariably presented as martyrs for their faith and innocent victims of Protestant violence; like Mary Agnes Hickson, Cusack was interested in demonstrating the innocence and moral superiority of her confessional community, and in countering historians and polemicists on the other side of the sectarian divide. Cusack sought, for example, to refute historian J.A. Froude's contentions in several of her works. She maintained that Protestant historians of Ireland had downplayed atrocities against Catholics, while Hickson was concerned about Catholic suspicion of the traditional Protestant narrative of the 1641 Rebellion.

Cusack was significant as a popular woman historian contributing to the genre of "faith and fatherland" history, and her works and career may be viewed within an Irish and a wider context. Her contention that the Irish had remained faithful to Catholicism despite centuries of persecution was a cornerstone of Catholic-oriented nationalist history. Faith and fatherland history, often produced by priests and nonprofessional male historians, was popular in late nineteenth-century Ireland, then undergoing a "devotional revolution" featuring an expansion of the institutional power of the Catholic Church.[12] This historical tradition continued into the Free State period in the works of Helena Concannon and other devotional writers. Cusack was not unique as a nun writing history; in other countries besides Ireland, "a culture of women writing and recording history, supported by the structures of the Catholic Church, existed among communities of sisters and nuns" prior to the 1960s, when the Second Vatican Council and feminist approaches to history and theology changed the ways in which nuns wrote history.[13] In addition, throughout late-nineteenth century Europe there were Catholic historians and devotional writers who wrote hagiographical works on the Catholic Church, and European nationalist historians who presented Catholicism as central to their national identities.

Cusack also produced local histories of Kerry and Cork, Irish history textbooks, and biographies, all of which link her to other women historians. Her work on Kerry likely influenced Mary Agnes Hickson, who would later edit *Selections from Old Kerry Records*. Several other Irish writers produced histories of counties and cities, including Wexford, Cork, and Galway in the late nineteenth and early-twentieth centuries. Just as *An Illustrated History of Ireland* contained sections on social and cultural history, which discussed customs, material culture, and literature, Cusack's history of Kerry also covered social history. In addition, there were sections on archaeology, geology, natural history, and industry, complementing the narrative of political and military history. Her textbooks, including *A Student's Manual of Irish History*, for students in England, and *A Compendium of Irish History*, for American schools, underscored her belief in inculcating young students outside of Ireland with the Catholic nationalist version of Irish history. Many other nineteenth-century women historians wrote history textbooks, which tied in with their role as instructors of children. Biographies were also a popular genre for female historians, and Cusack contributed to this genre by writing saints' lives and a biography of her hero, Daniel O'Connell, whom she admired for his nonviolent approach to achieving political justice.[14]

Cusack was known for her interventions in political debates, and reached audiences in Britain and the United States as well as in Ireland. She avidly read newspapers and journals, and often wrote letters to newspapers on social and political topics, like her fellow Kerry historian Mary Agnes Hickson. *The Present Case of Ireland, Plainly Stated* (1881), represents an attempt by Cusack to fuse history with political advocacy. Written when Irish tenant farmers in the Land League were protesting a downturn in conditions by withholding rent and boycotting evicting landlords, Cusack's book called for the British government to enact land reform legislation to benefit tenant farmers.

She added that the British governing classes and Irish landlords, believing that Irish people were generally prone to criminality regardless of the circumstances, favored coercive measures such as the 1881 Coercion Act. Appealing to history, she stated that "whenever Ireland rebelled ever so little against misgovernment 'coercion' was the remedy ... and because people have complained of the causes [of the 1879 famine] they are to be coerced again." She concluded by comparing Ireland to India, condemning the British government's record in both countries. British historians and journalists, she wrote, promoted "excessive pride ... in their government ... when [the English people] hear that a colony is discontented and living in smouldering rebellion ... they are certain it is the fault of the people" rather than holding British policy partly responsible.[15] While some criticized her books as polemics that might promote violent disaffection, Cusack favored Daniel O'Connell's approach of nonviolent activism. She was not an absolute pacifist, though, and believed Irish resistance to English political dominance in the past was justified due to religious persecution.

Margaret Cusack initiated the phenomenon of the Irish nationalist woman historian as a public figure contributing to political and intellectual debates, and shaping popular understandings of Irish history and an Irish national identity linked with Catholicism. In a time when "the public image of a historian was of a man of letters who combined scholarship with commentary on contemporary affairs, a role personified in Ireland by ... J.A. Froude and W.E.H. Lecky,"[16] Cusack stood out as a woman writing history and addressing social and political issues. Cusack was also unique among late nineteenth-century Irish female historians for writing history from a

Catholic nationalist perspective, and contributing to the tradition of confessional historiography. She reached audiences outside of Ireland, particularly in Britain and the United States, where editions of her books were published and widely reviewed. She gained influence through her writings, her forceful personality, and her membership in a religious order, and demonstrated that one did not have to be a "man of letters" or an academic historian to have an impact as a writer of history.

Alice Stopford Green (1847–1929)

Alice Stopford Green, the foremost Irish woman historian of the early twentieth century, was important not only as an innovative and influential historian of late medieval and early modern Ireland, but as a political figure with an international reputation. She shared an affluent Protestant background with the other Irish women historians of her era, but embraced nationalism and wrote history within a nationalist framework while challenging mainstream British and unionist traditions of writing about Ireland. An Irish nationalist with an international outlook, she was deeply involved in Irish and imperial politics. Her life illuminates the changing opportunities for women in intellectual and political life between the 1860s and the 1920s. As a young woman in the 1860s, she did not have access to a university education, but later studied and wrote history in a non-academic context and received honorary doctorates from the University of Liverpool and the National University of Ireland.[17] She faced political restrictions in an age when women were denied the vote, but became a politically influential hostess and campaigner, and gained access to political power in her own right in the 1920s as a Senator in the Irish Free State, by which time women had received the right to vote. She was empowered by the Irish nationalist movement both as a historian and as a political activist. The following examines Green's career as a historian and activist in a comparative context, arguing that she was significant as an influential scholar of late medieval and early modern Irish social history, and as a historian who reflected critically on historiography and challenged older conventions of writing about Irish history. Her career as a nationalist historian-activist anticipated the careers of younger Irish women historians in the Free State era.

Alice Stopford was born in Kells, County Meath on May 30, 1847 to Edward Adderley Stopford, the Archdeacon of Meath, and Anne Duke Stopford. The Stopfords and the Dukes were elite Irish Protestant families whose ancestors had settled in Ireland during the Cromwellian period. The Stopfords became prominent at Trinity College and in the Church of Ireland. Alice's parents sympathized with the evangelical tradition within the Church of Ireland, and she and her eight siblings were raised in a strict, religious, Victorian household. Her early life was not atypical for women historians of her era. Her affluent family valued education; in addition to instruction from governesses, Alice, an avid reader, had the advantage of her father's library. Other experiences that broadened her intellectual horizons in her adolescence and early adulthood included European travel and attending lectures at Dublin's College of Science, which required her to have a chaperone in order to attend. In 1874, Alice's father died, and she and her sister Louisa moved to England with their mother.[18]

Alice Stopford married J.R. Green, an Oxford-trained English historian and former Anglican clergyman, in 1877. John Richard Green, a social historian with radical democratic and libertarian views, was the author of the tremendously popular *Short History of the English People* (1874).[19] His social history was characterized by "a vigorous critical voice, by turns harsh, ironic, and humorous, that lashed out at injustices in English society past and present."[20] Green was not entirely unique as a social historian in his era, as the recent recovery of previously neglected English female historians demonstrates.[21] However, he stood out when compared with other Oxford historians, such as William Stubbs and E.A. Freeman, who focused on political and constitutional history.[22] He was particularly interested in medieval urban history, and believed that the freemen of the towns exemplified the English tradition of liberty.

Alice's marriage to J.R. Green was central to her formation as a historian, providing her with a supportive mentor, training in historical methodology, and access to an intellectual circle of friends connected with the world of scholarship. Prior to her marriage, Alice had written an unpublished novel, but no history. She conducted research for her husband's *The Making of England* and *The Conquest of England*, and co-wrote *A Short Geography of the British Islands*; J.R. Green wrote the parts on England and Wales, while Alice wrote on Ireland and Scotland.[23] The Greens' social circle included many historians and writers, and their home in London's Kensington Square was a popular site for intellectual discussion. Their friends included historians W.E.H. Lecky, E.A. Freeman, William Stubbs, and Mandell and Louise Creighton. Mandell Creighton was an ecclesiastical historian at Cambridge, and later the bishop of London. His wife Louise, who had once been romantically linked with J.R. Green, wrote, among other works, *A Social History of England*.[24]

Alice Green carved out her own identity as a historian after her husband's death from tuberculosis in 1883. She conformed to the expectations for widows of eminent men of letters by publishing collections of her husband's letters and essays. She also revised and added new sections to later editions of *A Short History of the English People*, which continued to generate royalties that left her comfortably off for the rest of her life.[25] Looking for further scope for her ambitions, Green applied for the position of mistress of Girton College, Cambridge, but was unsuccessful. She became interested in adult education, and she and her friend Louise Creighton taught history through the University Extension Service in the 1880s and 1890s.[26] Although she did not write *The Making of Ireland and its Undoing* until 1908, she was considering historical research on Ireland by the late 1880s. She turned to W.E.H. Lecky, whom she admired, for advice on historical sources. He responded by discussing the historiography of seventeenth- and eighteenth-century Ireland, offering assessments of the strengths and weaknesses of various books written from different perspectives, on topics such as the 1641 Rebellion, the Penal Laws, the Irish Parliament, and the 1798 Rebellion. He offered to help her with any questions about history that she might have.[27] Thus, Lecky was one of her early mentors in Irish history.

Before producing works of Irish history, Green wrote two books on English history, *Henry II* (1888) and *Town Life in the Fifteenth Century* (1894).[28] *Henry II* was written at the behest of her friend John Morley, who was editing a series of biographies called Twelve English Statesmen.[29] Green then turned to late medieval urban history, an interest she had shared with her husband, and made an original contribution with her two-volume *Town Life in the Fifteenth Century*. Contradicting the prevailing view that the fifteenth century had been a low point in English history, she highlighted political developments, trade, and the expansion of the urban middle class. Historian James Tait, reviewing her book, pointed out some flaws in her interpretation, but asserted that she was the first to have made "a serious attempt to estimate the importance of the part played by the English towns in the last critical century of the aspiring middle ages ... such a vivid picture of the life of the medieval English town will be indispensable to every student of the time."[30] Tait's comment on the vividness and picturesque quality of her writing would later be echoed by friendly and hostile critics of her Irish histories. Green reviewed two books for the *English Historical Review (EHR)* in the 1890s, demonstrating her expertise in aspects of medieval town life.[31]

While Alice Stopford Green remained close to friends she had made through her husband, she cultivated many new friendships on her own, which had implications for both her intellectual development and her role as a public figure involved in political and social causes. Her new friends included Irish nationalists, politicians, journalists, and humanitarians. She became close to John Francis Taylor, an Irish nationalist, barrister, and journalist, who urged her to focus on Irish history.[32] Taylor, whom she considered marrying in 1894, helped transform her understanding of her own national identity; by the 1890s she had come to see herself as distinctly Irish rather than British. Her renewed sense of Irish identity, in addition to her Liberal political views, deepened her commitment to Irish Home Rule.[33] Green's intensified Irish nationalist stance (as well as the "Little Englandism" she had shared with her husband) led her to empathize with nationalist movements within the British Empire, and increased her skepticism about imperialism.[34]

Alice Stopford Green and politics

Alice Stopford Green took an increasingly active role in British, imperial, and Irish politics by the turn of the century. This was to have implications for her historical writing, as her Irish nationalism was shaped within an imperial context, and the internationalist dimension to her nationalism was reflected in her writing. As a wealthy and socially prominent woman, skilled at social networking, she was involved in British politics as a hostess and lobbyist, illuminating the opportunities for well-connected women in politics prior to women's suffrage. She facilitated policymaking on Ireland by bringing English and Irish politicians together for discussion at her house in London.[35] Green also turned her attention to places far from the British Isles, particularly South Africa and the Congo. A critical thinker concerned about human rights and cultural autonomy, she had a complex relationship with imperialism, and believed in the idea of commonwealth.[36] Her Irish nationalist views grew more advanced by the War of Independence, although she was never a republican. She eventually became a Senator in the new Irish Free State, five years after women had won the right to vote in Ireland and Britain. The international cast to Green's political activism foreshadowed that of several other Irish women historians, such as Dorothy Macardle and Rosamond Jacob, who were interested in human rights worldwide and were involved in international organizations such as the League of Nations and the Women's International League for Peace and Freedom (WILPF).

Green became prominent as an outspoken political commentator during the controversial Boer War in South Africa, when she, like many other Irish nationalists, became associated with the pro-Boer camp.[37] She had become interested in African affairs through her friendship with the writer Mary Kingsley, who died in South Africa, where she had gone to nurse Boer prisoners of war, in June 1900. Kingsley had advocated West African cultural autonomy and made pragmatic criticisms of Britain's African policy.[38] Green went to St. Helena in September 1900 to investigate the conditions under which the Boer POWs were held. She discussed her findings in newspaper and journal articles,[39] and corresponded with British government officials regarding the privations and abuses in St. Helena's Deadwood Camp for Boer POWs. Overall, "pressure from outside, in the energetic form of Alice Stopford Green, was able to alleviate the conditions for the POWs, if not affect the penal policy itself."[40] After the Boer War she remained interested in the political status of South Africa, now under British rule. She wanted full self-government for both South Africa and Ireland within a British Commonwealth framework.[41]

Green's engagement with Africa continued through her involvement with the African society, which she co-founded in 1901 to honor the memory of Mary Kingsley. Green served as a vice-president of the organization, and edited the *Journal of the African Society*. The members of the Society came into conflict regarding the organization's agenda. Green favored a focus on African culture and ethnology, while others were primarily interested in imperial policy. Through the Society, she met the journalist E.D. Morel, who was active in exposing human rights abuses committed against Africans involved in the rubber industry in the Congo Free State, controlled by King Leopold II of Belgium. In 1904, she met Morel's friend and fellow human-rights campaigner, Roger Casement.[42]

Green's friendship with Roger Casement, one of the most meaningful in her life, reinforced her commitment to human rights and opposition to imperialism, as well as to Irish nationalism. Roger Casement, who came from an Ulster Protestant background, was a British diplomat who had interviewed Leopold II and investigated atrocities in the Congo Free State. He documented his findings in 1904 in *Administration of the Independent State of the Congo*, a report for the Foreign Office.[43] That year, Morel, supported by Casement, founded the Congo Reform Association and worked closely with Green to lobby members of Parliament and to promote public awareness of the situation in the Congo through the press. Green wrote to Irish party MPs, such as John Redmond and John Dillon, to obtain their support for the goals of the Congo Reform Association.[44]

Between 1904 and 1907, Green worked on Irish history and spoke on behalf of Irish nationalism, in addition to her public work in the Congo Reform Association.[45] In the autumn of 1904, she lectured on Ireland in the United States. She gained favorable publicity in the American press.[46] Green helped found and finance the School of Irish Studies in Dublin, working with Celtic scholars such as Kuno Meyer and Douglas Hyde. Thus, like Eleanor Hull, she was significant in helping to promote the institutionalization of Celtic Studies prior to the establishment of university departments.[47] In 1906 she joined the Historical Association based in London. Green also became more confident about confronting anti-Irish prejudice in the press, and wrote numerous letters to British and Irish newspapers. She found a humorous, ironic, sarcastic voice with which to do so in cases where history was invoked.[48]

Alice Stopford Green and history

Alice Stopford Green, as a historian, related to British, Continental European, and American women historians in various ways. Her research on medieval and early modern social and economic history had parallels with the research of British women historians, both "amateurs" and the new professionals. Women historians at the LSE and at Cambridge in the early twentieth century were particularly interested in economic history. Like Green, many of them were socially and politically active; they were feminists, labor activists, and peace campaigners.[49] Green differed from them, however, in that she did not write histories supportive of feminism or socialism; instead, she wrote to contest and overturn older assessments of early modern Ireland, first developed in a colonial context, and to demonstrate that Ireland had an advanced culture, trade, and political and legal system. Green resembled Continental European women historians in her nationalism. Their entry into national politics, like Green's, was often legitimated by taking part in an independence movement and writing nationalist-oriented history. Green's career has parallels with that of Tekla Hultin of Finland, who also wrote economic history, was involved in her country's independence movement, and served in Parliament from 1908 to 1924.[50]

Green's work also relates to histories written by white American women who empathized with the Native Americans, and tried to set the historical record straight and bring about justice and a change in the government's Indian policy. Although the two cases are by no means exact parallels, both the native Irish and the American Indians had been depicted as savages in historical works by writers from the dominant group, which both reflected and shaped discourses affecting policy. American historians Helen Hunt Jackson, Mari Sandoz, and Angie Debo, who wrote between the 1880s and the 1940s, were important in recovering and disseminating indigenous history. They turned to overlooked Native sources to reconstruct Native American history, just as Green promoted the value of Gaelic sources, to challenge contemporary thought and national policy. Green, like the three American historians, could be viewed as an "intercultural broker," as she wrote sympathetically about a group from which she did not descend. Sandoz and Debo, like Green, defied prevailing academic views on their subject and faced intense criticism from other historians, the tone of which was inflected by politics as well as scholarly disagreements.[51]

Green's major work was *The Making of Ireland and its Undoing, 1200–1600* (1908),[52] a social and economic history of late medieval and early modern Ireland. Her objective in writing was to recover an obscure history of late medieval Irish society and culture. This history, she maintained, had been falsified for political reasons by the English victors in the Tudor Wars. English historians, Green argued, had reshaped Irish history in a colonial context, contending that the

Irish were primitive, ignorant barbarians, when in fact they had much in common with the rest of medieval Europe.[53] Like Margaret Cusack, Green maintained that distorted histories of Ireland had been pressed into political service and shaped the thinking of British policymakers, with grievous results. She hoped that her book would restore national pride to the Irish people, and promote a truer understanding of Ireland in England, which would end contempt and prejudice towards the Irish and be reflected in an enlightened approach to British–Irish relations. The book's purpose related to Green's political support not only for Irish Home Rule, but also the commonwealth ideal based on the free association of equal nations, rather than an empire based on dominance and subordination. She argued that British rule in Ireland, while it revealed a tenacious will, rested on an insecure foundation of distorted history. This had broader implications for the British Empire, not just British rule in Ireland. With the historical record set straight, British–Irish relations could rest on a surer foundation, "the esteem and consideration that must form the only honourable relations between two neighboring peoples."[54]

The Making of Ireland, then, can be understood not only in light of Green's early twentieth-century Irish cultural and political nationalism, but also in the context of her criticism of imperial aggression and dominance, and her promotion of a commonwealth system based on cooperation and respect as an alternative framework. She was not an advocate of an Irish republic and complete separation. The book's message about the destruction of native cultures by conquering nations, followed by misrule stemming from lack of understanding, did not only apply to British–Irish relations, but more generally to the relationship between imperial nations and their territorial possessions. She worked on the book while arguing for self-government for South Africa and greater autonomy for Britain's African colonies, and raising questions about Belgian imperialism in the Congo. Her belief in political reform through education and working within the system marked her as a liberal reformist at this time.

Green highlighted Irish trade, social and cultural life, and education to enhance the political narrative and to refute long-standing pieties regarding the inherent inferiority of the Irish. She wrote that Irish trade with England and the Continent was extensive, citing records of Irish ships and goods in the State Papers as well as in Continental archives.[55] She recreated the texture of everyday life by describing houses, clothing, and entertainments,[56] as well as education and Irish achievements in science, medicine, literature, and the law.[57] She also discussed Irish agriculture and landholding arrangements.[58] Green contrasted the evidence she provided of medieval Irish life with still-current notions that the early modern Irish were unlearned, primitive nomads who shunned housing, settled agriculture, and trade in favor of shiftlessness and occasional plunder. She contended that the early modern English propagandists first wrote about Ireland in the context of the destructive Tudor Wars, when they mistook the abnormal social conditions for the norm. These misconceptions were later embraced by historians hostile to Ireland who accepted the accounts of the Tudor propagandists.[59]

Her controversial belief that the Normans and the Irish lived together harmoniously in the medieval towns and cooperated in commerce was central to Green's narrative. She had previously researched urban history in an English context, and now turned to the study of town records and statutes in Ireland. Most historians had viewed Galway and Dublin and other cities as exclusive Norman preserves in which the Irish were legally excluded. Green, as a social historian, was more interested in people's lived experience. She believed that the laws had often been violated, judging by frequent official exhortations to the Norman townsmen not to trade with the Irish or embrace Irish customs.[60] This contention about Norman–Irish cooperation was important to Green because of its implications for present-day relations between Irish Protestants and Catholics, whom she wished to see united in cultural and political aspirations.

Green argued that Tudor statecraft brought about the destruction of Ireland's advanced medieval society, and its international trade and intellectual traditions. Ireland's wealth and trade, Green maintained, attracted the attention of Henry VIII, who wished to seize Irish trade and profit from Irish resources. She located the Tudor policy within the context of European overseas expansion and rivalry between colonial powers in the sixteenth century, asserting that "the war to capture Irish trade was part of the commercial wars with Europe."[61] Social and economic changes within England came into play as well; English merchants shared Henry's interest in ending Irish commercial competition, and disinherited younger sons wanted lands of their own.[62] Economic motives, Green believed, were most important in the Tudor conquest. After the destruction of the Tudor

Wars, she contended, the myth of Irish inferiority was pressed into service by interested parties for centuries.

In an Irish context, Green's historical writing demonstrates that she not only bridged non-academic and academic history, but different traditions in antiquarianism and archaeology. Like past (unionist) antiquarians such as George Petrie and the Fergusons, she defended Ireland against its detractors who argued that Gaelic Ireland was barbaric and devoid of culture. Her interest in challenging works that denigrated the Irish would not have been inconsistent with certain strands of unionism, such as that embraced by George Petrie and the Fergusons, who were not invested in the barbarism thesis. Green's first Irish history dealt with the late medieval and early modern period, rather than early Ireland; it was far more confrontational and controversial to challenge stereotypes and support a nationalist interpretation in later periods. Her use of evidence challenged the thrust of colonial archaeology. Like earlier scholars, including patriotic unionists, she cited new archaeological scholarship to overturn a colonial archaeological discourse centered on pre-Norman barbarism.[63] While she was associated with new scholarly circles interested in Irish Ireland, whose leading figures included Irish language scholar Eoin MacNeill, nationalist antiquarian Francis Joseph Bigger, and archaeologist R.A.S. MacAlister, Green could also be located within a tradition of Protestant cultural leadership as the nature of that leadership was changing.

The Making of Ireland and its Undoing, 1200–1600, proved popular with Irish nationalist readers, though it met with a less positive response from more traditional historians as well as committed unionists.[64] Several reviewers objected to Green's nationalist standpoint and her contentions that the Statutes of Kilkenny were widely disregarded, that the Normans and the Irish had lived together in the towns and contributed equally to manufacture and trade, and that the Tudor Wars in Ireland were aimed at capturing Irish overseas trade, rather than pacifying Ireland to enhance England's national security.[65] The reception of *The Making of Ireland and its Undoing* revealed much about the political and ideological context in which the book was produced and received, and the ensuing debates underscored that neither unionists nor nationalists had complete dominance in the arena of historical scholarship. A nationalist historian like Green could be subjected to intense criticism, but unionists could not completely control historical production and prevent the dissemination of nationalist interpretations of Irish history.

Different levels of opposition were at work in critical assessments of Green's book. Primarily there were scholarly disagreements based on differing uses and interpretations of source material. As a non-academic woman historian who had never attended university, Green may have been viewed as an interloper on the scholarly territory held by men of letters and academic historians; as an Irish historian, her unflattering portrayal of early modern Englishmen was bound to cause offense.[66] Her academic critics were understandably opposed to a popular, nationalist female historian who used sources in a scholarly way and could not be easily dismissed due to her abilities and strong-willed, combative personality. There were also non-scholarly political opponents of Green's work; her iconoclasm offended the sensitivities of those who for various reasons were invested in notions of Irish inferiority from time immemorial. Writers of unionist apologetics who invoked history to substantiate their claims disliked being challenged in historiography during a time when they also faced political challenges posed by nationalists. Lastly, Green's nationalist partisanship may have seemed all the more striking to those unionist historians who perceived themselves as unbiased and who construed politically-driven bias as mainly an attribute of nationalists.[67] Although many historians did strive for impartiality, it was nearly impossible to escape the political context in which they produced and read history. Most were present-centered and partisan to some degree.[68] Green was aware of her own partisanship and about the polemical aspects of a work confronting deeply held preconceptions, and saw that others had biases as well.

Green was proud of her achievements, but did not think her work was infallible. She believed that she had successfully challenged orthodox historiography on Ireland, maintaining that henceforth history would have to be written differently. "Now when 'historians' talk of savages drinking blood and living naked in caves," Green wrote, "they will have to *prove* it. That will give them something to do."[69] While she responded to critics, and made corrections for the second edition, she felt that her critics were to a great extent politically motivated, and was pleased that her work had been affirmed by scholars she respected. She hoped other scholars would continue to work on Irish history along the lines that she had set out.[70] Green was gratified that her book had reached a popular audience in Ireland (the first edition was reprinted twice in 1908 and 1909), just as her husband's *Short History* had found a popular and non-elite readership in England. She received letters from readers in rural Ireland, who breathed a "sigh of relief at having the long reproach lifted off them."[71] Irish Catholic and nationalist readers responded to her book in much the same way they had responded in the late nineteenth century to Lecky's refutations of Froude and writings on eighteenth-century Ireland.[72] The fact that both Green and Lecky were elite Irish Protestants enhanced their credibility in legitimizing components of an Irish nationalist narrative.

A misstep made by opponents of Green's book enhanced its popularity. The Library Committee of the Royal Dublin Society turned down *The Making of Ireland and its Undoing* after one member proposed it for their Library. This decision was publicized and roundly criticized in the nationalist press. As Green wrote to Oliver Wendell Holmes, "I was used as a stone to sling at the Irish Tory giant, and questions were asked in the House of Commons [by Irish Party MP Tom Kettle], and sleepy Dublin was awakened to the fact that the book existed, and roused from their slumbers began to buy it, and the clamour grew till the Society held a special meeting and rescinded their order against admitting it. All of which was very useful to me."[73] Roger Casement, upon hearing of the Committee's rejection, mocked the Royal Dublin Society members in a sardonic letter to the *Freeman's Journal*.

> Having just come from Brazil, where I had read Mrs. Green's work and found that others had read it too, I brought with me some very curious specimens of ethnological interest, which I had hoped to give to the Royal Dublin Society for a museum situated in the capital of our country [Casement mistakenly believed the National Museum was managed by the Royal Dublin Society]. As it is evident, however, that the Royal Dublin Society must already possess, in view of this resolution of its Library Committee, living ethnological curiosities of no mean order, with which my poor survivals of a dead race could not hope to compete, I shall bestow my American examples of a defunct humanity upon some other non-Irish institution which has no live specimens of pre-historic man to offer to its students and visitors.[74]

Nationalists, both moderate Home Rulers and republicans, embraced *The Making of Ireland and Its Undoing*. Green's work, like Lecky's, came to be viewed as political, and good ammunition for Home Rule. Many in Ireland had a sense of being maligned in historical works by British writers, so Green's work struck a chord.[75] She achieved a measure of success in contesting stereotypes of Irish inferiority embedded in mainstream British and Irish unionist histories, and in promoting national pride and self-worth by showing Irish achievements in the past. As with Lecky, who had confronted Froude's denigration of the Irish, the notion of the Irish having been vindicated by elite, scholarly, Anglo-Irish Protestants whose work bolstered a nationalist interpretation came into play. From living in England and reading works on Ireland by British writers, Green seems to have developed a heightened consciousness about the Irish being denigrated in works of history. She was originally less familiar with the tradition of popular historical works by Irish nationalist writers, which would have shown there was always more of an exchange.

Another possible way to view the reaction to Green's work in 1908 would be within the framework of the "Irish art of controversy" discussed by Lucy McDiarmid. Green, with her humor, sarcasm, theatrical sense, and charismatic personality, effectively galvanized Irish public opinion through the press and well-placed friends. Her skill at public relations helped her to come out ahead. Green's unionist opponents, although not without a sympathetic audience of their own as they sparred with nationalists, did not have as much popular support in Ireland, so they could not always operate as effectively in popular culture. Issues of power as well as Irish identity were at stake in these controversies, and the contemporary context heightened the emotive aspects of debates about historiography.[76]

There were conceptual differences about who controlled the dissemination of history. Both unionists and nationalists felt their opponents dominated politics and historical writing, although they were powerful in different areas. Unionists had power in British universities, literary circles, and in the government, where their historical narrative found acceptance, as well as popular support in Ulster and in Britain. Nationalists were a minority in the British government, but nationalist history had considerable support in Irish popular culture and in the Irish educational system. While nationalists struggled to have their interpretation of history accepted by academia, the world of letters, and the British public, unionists had heightened fears about Irish schoolchildren reading nationalist textbooks, and knew that unionist-oriented history lacked popular support within the Irish Catholic reading public.

Green's second book was *Irish Nationality* (1911), a short survey of Irish history that made a strong impression on nationalists.[77] While it proved to be the most popular of all of her books, it was also the one she took the least seriously. Green wrote *Irish Nationality* in three months at the behest of the editors of the "Home University Library of Modern Knowledge" series, H.A.L. Fisher, Gilbert Murray, and J. Arthur Thomson, who wanted "an historical account of Irish Nationalism in a very brief shilling book."[78] *Irish Nationality* was consciously written in a popular style to appeal to a wide readership.

Irish Nationality covered Irish history from the prehistoric period to the late nineteenth century. Green emphasized themes such as the advanced Irish legal system, culture and intellectual achievement, and trade, as well as the propensity of foreigners such as the Vikings and the Normans to assimilate into Irish society. She attributed conflict to outside interference by England, rather than stressing internal conflict between the Old English and the Irish in the late medieval period, or between Protestants and Catholics from the sixteenth century onwards. She downplayed the explosive issue of sectarianism by stressing that Protestants were part of the national narrative, and that they played an important role in nationalist political and cultural leadership. For example, she discussed the Protestants in the 1782 Parliament and the Protestant role in the nineteenth century antiquarian movement and Irish cultural revival.[79] She favored peaceful agitation rather than violence to promote political and social democratization, and praised the nonviolent Daniel O'Connell highly as "perhaps the greatest popular leader that any country has known. As a leader of democracy he had outdistanced them all."[80]

When Green wrote *Irish Nationality*, she had faith in political methods to achieve Home Rule, and the book was not a separatist-republican text. Irish nationalists may have written canonical status onto *Irish Nationality* after independence. It was first published in 1911, and then went through second, third, and fourth impressions between 1919 and 1922. Thus it appears to have been most popular during the War of Independence, rather than right after its publication a decade earlier. A conservative "Free State ending" which offered closure was added to later reprints in the 1920s, when Green was a Free

State senator defending the new state against its republican challengers. "The long tradition of foreign rule has been broken," she wrote. "The story of national life has been resumed ... [and under the new representative government] is free to develop as it may."[81] The implication was that if Ireland were to advance further towards a republic, it would do so through political means, as Green agreed with Michael Collins that the new government could be a "stepping-stone" to complete independence.

Green's *The Old Irish World* (1912) was significant for its critiques of unionist historiography, and because it demonstrated that the older traditions of writing about late medieval and early modern Ireland were being seriously deconstructed and challenged by nationalist historians who had studied the sources. In Green's first chapter, "The Way of History in Ireland," she questioned the impartiality of mainstream unionist historians, and the foundational claims of professional history.[82] She reiterated an earlier point that "the words partial and impartial have a recognized technical meaning. Impartial means a strong bias to Imperial and English interests [the status quo] – partial signifies a regard for the special interests of Ireland."[83] Green criticized the scholarship of unionist historians such as J.P. Mahaffy, C.L. Falkiner, Robert Dunlop, and Goddard Orpen. She was particularly concerned about their apparent embrace of dubious theories of innate Irish inferiority as explanatory factors in Irish history, as well as their seeming eagerness to highlight and distort the testimony of early modern writers in Ireland (European travelers as well as English statesmen), who commented negatively on the Irish.[84] She also punctured the triumphalist approach to Irish history that denigrated the Irish as primitive savages: "English writers have forgotten a grave disadvantage to themselves ... in [their] version of Irish history the Englishman's triumph remains a poor thing, destitute of interest or value, where the fame of the victor is abased and confounded by the worthlessness of his foe."[85] She believed that her approach to history could free the Irish from the disabling effects of a historiographical tradition in which the Irish were denigrated, and promote national self-respect. Then the Irish would no longer be "made to stand before Europe with the appearance of defeat, ruin, and rebuke."[86]

The last chapter, "Tradition in Irish History," was written as a response to Robert Dunlop, who had condemned *The Making of Ireland and its Undoing* in a review. Green presented herself as an interrogator of received wisdom, who had provoked the wrath of the orthodox gatekeepers of history. Anticipating some of the later twentieth-century revisionist historians of Ireland, she announced her subversiveness in challenging the orthodox historical narrative. This was hardly surprising. "Nationalist historiography," Terry Eagleton notes, "was itself the first great revisionist school in Ireland, which took what were then the official imperial narratives of native history and rewrote them with breathtaking boldness from below, with all the courageous imagining, false continuism, historical truth, Manichean ethics, generous devotion to the dispossessed and triumphalist teleology which that involved."[87] Green affirmed the importance of native Irish sources in addition to State Papers, and critiqued Dunlop's own use of sources. She concluded that his criticisms did not alter the main body of her work.[88]

Green used humor as a device to undercut what she viewed as the self-righteous tone of histories that were hostile to the Irish, and had a relatively mature understanding of historical bias. She believed that the older tradition of historiography would be exposed by historians determined to recover native Irish history by going back to the sources. "History is no sooner driven out the door than it comes in through the window," she maintained. She provoked laughter at a dinner in London when she satirized the triumphalist understanding of Irish history: "emissaries of Providence ... showed as much humanity as was possible under the circumstances. They used, in fact, no more force than was necessary to slay half the inhabitants and they only took all the land and all the trade ... it seems wonderful to have invented a story so dull. An intelligent people might have done better."[89] She understood that few historians were free of bias, and contended that those who supported the status quo were more often affirmed as objective and impartial by important political and intellectual establishments. Green facetiously stated, "I have indeed known people who boasted of being open and impartial, without any bias. I never knew one of them who did not turn out to be an inveterate Tory."[90] Her understanding of bias would resonate with later historians who wrote from alternative perspectives that did not support powerful establishments. As feminist historian Mary Cullen wrote in the 1990s:

> History written from the perspective of groups distant from the centers of power, such as women's history ... is often labeled as

> political or liable to bias. The pitfalls of bias are real … But historians who believe themselves to be value-free and "neutral" are in more danger [than historians of non-elite groups who recognize their own bias]. An assumption that the current political or intellectual status-quo or orthodoxy is usually "right" and those who dissent from it likely to be "wrong" is as political a perspective as a feminist or Marxist one, and, if unconsciously held, more likely to distort the way history is written.[91]

Green proved to be an influential historian. Her emphasis on trade, intellectual and social life, and Irish interaction with Europe in *The Making of Ireland and its Undoing* reinforced an alternative approach to the study of the economic and social history of late medieval and early modern Ireland. She influenced a younger generation of historians who engaged with her work during the 1920s through the 1940s, including Ada Longfield, who wrote *Anglo-Irish Trade in the Sixteenth Century*, and Mary Donovan O'Sullivan, who wrote a social and economic history of late medieval Galway.[92] Ada Longfield completed graduate work in history at the LSE in the 1920s, where research on economic history with a focus on late medieval trade had strong institutional support. She wrote on Irish trade during the Tudor period, a topic Green had addressed, and had similar assessments about economic motivations for the Tudor conquest. While O'Sullivan had political and intellectual differences with Green, and believed, for instance, in Norman exclusiveness rather than close Norman–Irish relations in late medieval Galway, her work resembled Green's in its emphasis on scholarship and Irish interaction with the Continent.

Academic historians in the middle decades of the twentieth century showed less interest in Green's approach and in medieval social and economic history. By the 1970s, however, there was renewed interest in social and economic history, and historians such as Kenneth Nicholls, Wendy Childs, and Timothy O'Neill wrote important studies of medieval Irish economic and social history and foreign trade.[93] *The Making of Ireland and its Undoing*, then, was an important contribution to Irish historiography in the early twentieth century, and while not all of its assessments have stood the test of time, it remains valuable for the sections on commerce and foreign trade,[94] and on Irish scholars in Europe through the early modern period. Professional historians today, in part because of Green, do not depict the medieval Irish in the terms used by the writers Green challenged a century ago.

Politics, 1914–29

Green's Irish nationalism took a more radical turn in response to the growing militancy of the Ulster Unionists, who had formed the UVF (Ulster Volunteer Force) to resist Home Rule in 1912. The Irish Volunteers were formed in 1914 in response to the formation of the UVF, and were led by Green's close friend Eoin MacNeill. Green supported the Irish Volunteers, believing that nationalist Irishmen outside Ulster had the right to self-defense if the UVF, confident of the British army's non-interference, turned to armed struggle against Home Rule. Green addressed a meeting in Dublin under the auspices of Cumann na mBan, the women's auxiliary of the Irish Volunteers, to raise money for arms for the Volunteers.[95] The decision of the Irish Volunteers to purchase guns from Germany in 1914, prior to the outbreak of the First World War, was made at her house in London. Her friends Erskine and Molly Childers sailed to Germany in their yacht and smuggled the rifles to Ireland.[96]

The First World War years were a turning point in Green's life. She was dismayed by the outbreak of the war in 1914, but was not a vocal opponent of the war. While she opposed the Easter Rising in 1916, she was more upset by the execution of fifteen insurgents. Green believed Irish Party leader John Redmond favored the executions to do away with advanced nationalist rivals.[97] Her friend Roger Casement was executed for treason in August 1916, as he had been caught trying to smuggle arms from Germany to Ireland. Green tried her utmost to save him from the death penalty, but to no avail.[98] She was devastated by his death and appalled that the British government had chosen to publicize Casement's diaries to destroy his reputation. Green returned to Ireland in 1918, and lived at 90 St. Stephen's Green in Dublin. She soon became involved in the anti-conscription movement, writing that opposition to the extension of conscription to Ireland was organized by laypeople rather than the Catholic hierarchy, and that it was legally and morally defensible.[99]

Ireland's War of Independence, or the Anglo-Irish War, began in early 1919, following the electoral victory of the republican Sinn Fein party in the 1918 elections. The conflict took the form of guerrilla warfare by the IRA, outnumbered as they were by the British forces. Irish public opinion now favored a radical alternative to constitutional nationalism. The Government of Ireland Act of 1920 partitioned Ireland and established Parliaments in Belfast and Dublin. The war ended in 1921 with the Anglo-Irish Treaty, which gave dominion status rather than complete independence to the twenty-six counties comprising the Irish Free State. Northern Ireland, which consisted of six Ulster counties, retained political links with Britain.[100]

Green supported the War of Independence, between 1919 and 1921. Prominent IRA men, including Michael Collins, sometimes hid in her house in Dublin when on the run. They used the overgrown back garden of her unionist next-door neighbors as an arms dump. Green's secretary, Maire Comerford, was a republican and active member of Cumann na mBan. Because Green's house was a center of republican activity, it was raided several times in 1921, which hindered her writing as the British special forces, the Black and Tans, sometimes confiscated her papers. There were numerous ambushes in the St. Stephen's Green area as well. Green, a member of the managing committee of the Irish White Cross, a republican-oriented relief association, publicized instances of the Black and Tans' brutality towards civilians. She used her political contacts in London throughout the War of Independence, appealing to Herbert Asquith to negotiate with imprisoned Irish republican hunger strikers, such as Terence MacSwiney, in 1920. She tried to work for peace negotiations, and was upset by Tom Barry's ambush in Cork in November 1920, in which a number of British Auxiliaries were killed, as she feared that would undermine peace efforts.[101]

The Anglo-Irish Treaty polarized Ireland. The Free State supporters accepted the new settlement, while republicans still favored a fully independent, thirty-two county Irish republic. The Irish Civil War ensued in 1922. The Free State, pro-Treaty forces were led by Michael Collins, while the anti-Treaty side, linked with the Irish Republican Army, was led by Eamon de Valera. The IRA's guerrilla war tactics were now aimed at Ireland's new political authorities. The Civil War ended in 1923, with the Free State government victorious. Prime Minister William Cosgrave of the Cumann na nGaedheal party presided over the socially conservative new state until the 1930s, when his leadership was supplanted by that of Eamon de Valera and his Fianna Fail party.[102]

Green supported the Treaty and the Free State troops during the Civil War, agreeing with Michael Collins' view that the Treaty could be used as a steppingstone to full independence. Her pro-Treaty stance led to estrangement from some of her friends, such as the Childers.[103] Maire Comerford, now Cumann na mBan's director of propaganda, also opposed the Treaty, and spent time in prison in 1922 and 1923.[104] Green had little regard for the IRA and its leaders, arguing that they deepened the alienation of Ulster unionists and that they lacked political skills. She especially disliked Eamon de Valera, whose "political incapacity [was] augmented by his supreme vanity."[105] She was on good terms with her new next door neighbor, the republican leader and newspaper editor Sean T. O'Kelly, although she disliked his newspaper, the *Nation*.[106]

The highlights of Green's career in the 1920s, the last decade of her life, included her election to the Senate and the publication of her last book. A widely recognized and respected public figure, Green was elected to the Senate in 1923, five years after women had won the right to vote in Britain and Ireland. (Ironically, she had once opposed women's suffrage).[107] This made her one of the first women to serve in a national government anywhere in the world, and highlighted the opportunities available to nationalist women activists and writers in a newly independent state in which women could vote. She set the stage for another nationalist female historian-senator, Helena Concannon, and served in the Irish Senate at the same time as a nationalist Finnish woman historian, Tekla Hultin, served in the Parliament of the newly independent state of Finland. Green promoted education and Irish culture, and favored civil rights over the coercive measures advocated by William Cosgrave's government to deal with political disorder in the 1920s. Her opposition to the outlawing of divorce, which linked her with her fellow senator W.B. Yeats, demonstrated that she was at odds with the more conservative and religious aspects of Free State culture.[108] Green was interested in the workings of a political group formed to monitor affairs in the Dominion states, as this had political relevance for Free State Ireland, and gave articles on Ireland from South African newspapers to the Department of External Affairs, demonstrating her continued engagement with international issues.[109]

During the 1920s, Green worked on her last book, in addition to writing short historical studies for students in the Free State schools.[110] *History of the Irish State to 1014* (1925), dealt with early and medieval Irish history. This book synthesized and popularized Eoin MacNeill's work for a wider audience, focusing on the church in the early Christian period, education, the social structure, the legal system, and art and industries. This continued an older tradition in Ireland in which women writers "presented in a lucid and readable style the more scholarly but less accessible research of antiquarians, archaeologists, and historians."[111] *History of the Irish State to 1014* was written when she was in her seventies, and she struggled to complete it during the revolutionary years. She believed it was important, despite its difficulty, as it "put an end to a lot of bad trash, and opened an entirely new history ... it has baffled completely the old-fashioned reviewers."[112] Green's last book received more positive reviews in scholarly journals than her earlier books. Medievalist F.M. Powicke, for example, called her book "the best account of many aspects of early Irish life yet written."[113] G.P. Gooch added that "the book aroused less controversy than its predecessor, for the period lay further off and the tone was less polemical."[114] By 1925, then, it was no longer revolutionary to present early Ireland as an advanced culture to audiences outside of Ireland.

History of the Irish State to 1014 was criticized by later historians for its idealization of early Ireland and its anachronistic depiction of Ireland as a united, centralized state. The depiction of a united Ireland under the rule of a high king in the medieval period seemed to be shaped by "the desire to establish a legitimate continuity for Irish separatism."[115] It was not only a political history, however; Green, as usual, wished to show that the Irish had an advanced culture, which would undermine older stereotypes and inspire national pride. There was also a more conservative dimension to the *History of the Irish State to 1014*, when viewed in the context of the Free State in the 1920s, when the book was first read. Green was never a republican who wanted complete separation from Britain, and if she linked the Free State with an ahistorical medieval Irish state, it could be read as defending the Free State against republican opponents who contested the new government's legitimacy. Her emphasis on the universal acceptance of the law in medieval Ireland had conservative implications as well in the 1920s.[116]

The History of the Irish State to 1014 had an unfortunate effect on Green's reputation in later years. It shaped an image of Green as solely a popularizer of Eoin MacNeill's early Irish history, who was herself "ill-acquainted with the primary sources" and "lacking in historical criticism."[117] Green was not a specialist on Celtic Ireland or a Irish-language scholar, and openly acknowledged that she used MacNeill's work in *History of the Irish State to 1014*. Assessments of Green as only a follower of MacNeill, however, wrote out her earlier, critical, source-based scholarship on late medieval Irish social and economic history. One facet of Green's identity as a writer, the synthesizer and popularizer of new research on early Ireland, was emphasized at the expense of her legacy as an original scholar of late medieval and early modern Ireland. Historians examining the development of Irish nationalist views of history singled out Green and her last book, as well as *Irish Nationality*, as having played a central role in what they saw as the debasement of history for nationalist ends. Green was characterized as an insecure Protestant who overcompensated with excessive nationalism,[118] and as a promoter of a mythical nationalist version of Irish history in the schools, and in the culture more generally.

The image of Green as merely a popularizer and simplifier of MacNeill's scholarship was reinforced by the tendency of historians critical of earlier nationalist histories to limit their analysis by overlooking *The Making of Ireland and its Undoing*, the historiographical debates at the time, Green's important contributions to underexplored topics in social and economic history, and the questions she raised about the practice of historiography. In discussions of early twentieth-century historiography by Irish historians in the 1980s and early 1990s, the biases of unionists were often downplayed in favor of an emphasis on the shortcomings of nationalist historians, who were often construed as "racialist" and sectarian, which made it difficult to see how Green was responding to unionist-oriented history and polemics, and the ways in which unionist commentators invoked history to support their political agenda. There was always more of a dialogue between the two opposing camps, and nationalist historians were not invariably on the offensive. Lastly, the more conservative aspects of Green's history, as well as her liberal, nonsectarian, internationalist politics, received little attention.

By the 1990s, Green's legacy came in for scholarly reassessment.[119] Medieval and early modern historians acknowledged the value of Green's discussion of Irish merchants and Irish trade with Europe in

The Making of Ireland and its Undoing, and noted her use of a range of sources, both English and continental European, as historical evidence.[120] A new interest in women's history, women historians, Ireland in an imperial context, Roger Casement, and the human rights legacy he shared with Alice Stopford Green all helped facilitate a more positive assessment of Green. Historians noted how Green's achievements were remarkable for someone who, because of the restrictions faced by women of her generation, had not received university training in history, and recognized similarities between Green and other women historians writing in the early twentieth century.[121] There is now a more nuanced understanding of the context of the cultural and historiographical debates in early twentieth-century Ireland, and a recognition that nationalists were not simply on the offensive, but in debate with unionists and each other.[122]

Alice Stopford Green died in Dublin on May 28, 1929. She was among the leading Irish female intellectuals of her time, as well as one of the most influential and popular Irish historians. One of the two leading Irish female nationalist historians writing between the 1860s and the 1920s, she differed from Margaret Cusack in that the former wrote from a Catholic nationalist perspective, and shaped notions of an Irish identity linked with Catholicism, while Green reinforced an inclusive understanding of an Irish national identity centered upon shared identification with the Gaelic cultural past. She helped shape the image of the Irish nationalist female historian as an outspoken, socially and politically engaged public historian, and later as one who gained access to state power through the writing of nationalist history. She reached audiences outside Ireland, and was involved in international politics and human rights advocacy. Her scholarship and political concerns can also be placed in a wider context, as they relate to those of female historians in Britain, the United States, and Continental Europe.

Openly acknowledging her wish to refute the negative view of Irish history, Green raised important questions about the practices of historiography, in addition to making an original contribution to the study of late medieval Irish history. Though she was not a university-trained historian, and was associated with an alternative establishment linked with Irish cultural nationalism, she reached academic historians and elite men of letters. She related to the unionist women historians of her time in terms of her affluent

Protestant background and educational opportunities, but diverged from the cultural nationalists or "patriotic unionists" who had favorable views of early Ireland while opposing Irish self-government. Green's recognition by the state, her social and political engagement within Ireland, and her international activism anticipated the Free State historians Helena Concannon, Dorothy Macardle, and Rosamond Jacob, while her work on late medieval and early modern Irish social and economic history influenced Mary Donovan O'Sullivan and Ada Longfield.

In conclusion, Margaret Cusack and Alice Stopford Green were the foremost Irish nationalist women historians of the late-nineteenth and early twentieth centuries. They took different paths to nationalism, and embraced different nationalist narratives. Both were raised in affluent Irish Protestant families, like their unionist counterparts, and were well-educated, though they did not have the opportunity to attend universities due to the restrictions faced by women of their era. Cusack and Green shared an interest in new scholarship on early Irish civilization and in reaching students and popular audiences. Cusack converted to Catholicism and as a nun was affiliated with a powerful church that facilitated her writing and research and helped promote her work. She wrote "faith and fatherland" history in which Catholicism was central to Irish identity. Ironically, she later wrote polemical works against the church she had once glorified and defended. Green, a secular Protestant, was affiliated with Irish nationalist cultural and intellectual circles, which helped facilitate her career, although she was also influenced by new approaches to social and economic history developed in Britain. Both Cusack and Green were politically active and reached audiences outside of Ireland. They had confident, forceful personalities and were unafraid to defend and promote their work. Their careers helped shape the parameters in which Irish women historians could combine historical writing and political activism in the Free State years.

3
Women Historians in the NUI, 1922–1949

Academic history in the Irish Free State

Four women taught history in the National University of Ireland (NUI) in the first half of the twentieth century.[1] Mary Hayden became the Professor of Modern Irish History at University College Dublin (UCD) in 1911, Mary Donovan O'Sullivan was appointed the Professor of Modern History at University College Galway (UCG) in 1914, Sile Ni Chinneide became a Lecturer in History at UCG in 1927, and Pauline Henley became an assistant lecturer in history at University College Cork (UCC) in 1931. All had received their degrees from the NUI,[2] and only Ni Chinneide had initially specialized in history. The educational backgrounds of the NUI women historians diverged from those of other academic women historians, particularly in the United States, Britain, Finland, and Scandinavia, who tended to have studied history as undergraduates or as graduate degree candidates.[3]

The women's success in obtaining positions in history departments in the NUI colleges in these years may be attributed to several factors. These include the low status of modern history relative to other disciplines (such as Classics and Philosophy), the greater openness of a new institution, the scarcity of credentialed academics in Ireland at the time, the lack of interest in recruiting faculty from outside Ireland, and the fact that the women were all Catholics, like the vast majority of the students and staff within the NUI, who tended to be nationalists as well. Irish women, by the interwar period, had made notable gains in academia compared to both British and Continental women. In 1930, there were eight female professors (3% of the total) and sixty female lecturers (21% of the total) in Ireland.[4]

While Mary Hayden taught in Dublin, where she had been raised and educated, Mary Donovan O'Sullivan, Sile Ni Chinneide, and Pauline Henley taught history in regional NUI colleges during the Free State period. O'Sullivan had been educated at UCG, while Ni Chinneide and Henley had attended University College Cork (UCC). O'Sullivan and Ni Chinneide were based at University College, Galway, a highly unusual institution in that its history department consisted solely of women for many years. O'Sullivan and Ni Chinneide supervised many more graduate students than Hayden, while Henley was primarily an undergraduate teacher. The NUI women historians often combined teaching and research with social and political engagement. Although Hayden had the highest political profile of the academic women historians during the 1920s and 1930s, O'Sullivan and Ni Chinneide were also public historians involved in political and social causes, who occasionally wrote for newspapers and journals of opinion as well as historical journals.

The four historians wrote a range of works. Mary Hayden, the most politically active of the four, wrote an Irish history textbook as well as a number of articles. Pauline Henley, who was apolitical during the 1930s and 1940s, wrote *Spenser in Ireland*, which challenged mainstream English scholarship on Spenser. Mary Donovan O'Sullivan was the most politically conservative of the four Catholic women historians in the NUI. She had been a Home Ruler, rather than a republican, and a feminist in the years prior to the Free State's creation. However, after 1922 she wrote polemical articles denouncing aspects of the Free State. Unlike many of the leading male historians in the 1930s and 1940s, she focused on medieval and early modern urban, economic, and social history, rather than political and administrative history. Sile Ni Chinneide's situation was different; her nationalism coincided with that of the Irish Free State, as she was too young to have been deeply involved in prewar political movements. While she was closer in age to the members of the new historical establishment, she had been trained differently from them and did not publish scholarly monographs. By the 1950s, however, she became a public figure who was appointed to various boards and councils by the government, like some of her male counterparts in the profession. During this time she also questioned revisionist interpretations of Irish history.

Modern history became consolidated in Irish universities in the early twentieth century. A chair in modern history and a lectureship in modern Irish history were established at UCD in 1909; the first meeting of the Special Committee of the School of History and Political Science at Trinity College occurred in 1912; the history, English, and philosophy department at UCG split and became separate departments in 1914; and James Hogan was awarded a chair in history at UCC in 1920. The leading male academic historians in the 1920s and early 1930s included Eoin MacNeill, John M. O'Sullivan, and George O'Brien at UCD;[5] Edmund Curtis and Walter Alison Phillips at Trinity;[6] and James Hogan at UCC.[7] O'Sullivan, Phillips, and Hogan were professors of Modern [European] History. MacNeill, Ireland's leading Celtic scholar and a committed nationalist, taught early Irish history in the UCD Celtic Studies department. The Oxford-educated Curtis, a respected medievalist, had taught at the University of Sheffield before joining the Trinity College history department in 1914. George O'Brien, who had been trained as a lawyer, taught in the UCD Economics department and wrote on Irish economic history.

Like the NUI women academics, these men did not believe that being a professional historian precluded political engagement. MacNeill, who had been imprisoned in the aftermath of the 1916 Rising, and O'Sullivan both served in the Free State (Cumann na nGeadheal) government in the 1920s as Ministers of Education. O'Sullivan also served in the Dail (Lower House of Parliament) as a Cumann na nGeadheal/Fine Gael TD between the 1920s and the 1940s.[8] George O'Brien was appointed by the Free State government to serve on the Commission on Banking, Currency, and Credit, established in 1934,[9] and was elected to the Senate in 1948. Both Phillips and Hogan wrote polemical political works.[10] Hogan, in addition, was a veteran of the War of Independence and the Civil War, in which he served as Director of Intelligence for the pro-Treaty side. He joined the Blueshirts in 1933, and in 1936 unsuccessfully ran for the Dail.[11]

Academic Irish history began to move in new directions in the late 1930s. Two young academic historians, R.D. Edwards[12] of UCD and T.W. Moody[13] of Queen's University Belfast and later Trinity College, founded the professional journal *Irish Historical Studies* (*IHS*) in 1938.[14] Both historians completed graduate work at the University of London's Institute of Historical Research. Their goal was to professionalize Irish history by promoting objective, empirical, documents-based historical research and writing, free of the blatant sectarianism and political partisanship that had plagued Irish history in the past.[15] Moody and Edwards wrote that their goals were "constructive and instrumental."[16] They wanted to promote innovative research and overturn popularly held views of the past (such as popular, sentimental Irish nationalist versions of history) that were based on deficient understanding. Moody and Edwards and their younger colleagues showed their professionalism in the late 1930s and 1940s by being neither stridently supportive of the government nor extremely critical and subversive, which would also compromise neutrality and professionalism. They rejected the old-fashioned model of the historian as a political figure with close ties to the government. Moreover, they chose not to write propagandist Irish history that would celebrate the republican tradition.[17]

The ideas and objectives of Moody and Edwards, the founders of the new critical or "revisionist" school of Irish history, were shaped during their graduate school experiences in London, though they were redefined in an Irish context. The school they developed was influenced by the "new history" current in Britain and the United States in the 1930s. The New Historians believed that while complete detachment was impossible, historians should try to be as objective and accurate as possible in their empirical study of archival documents. In addition, the use of interpretive frameworks from the social sciences, such as economics, could help historians realize their objectives. Moody and Edwards were also influenced by the views of Cambridge historian Herbert Butterfield, expressed in *The Whig Interpretation of History* (1931). Butterfield charged that English historians held an overly deterministic view of their country's past; they perceived a linear progression towards political liberty. Moody and Edwards, in an Irish context, rejected a "whig-nationalist" perception of Ireland inevitably moving towards national independence as the final outcome of its history. Overall, the historical journal and the associated school founded by Moody and Edwards stand alongside the *Annales* school in France and the school associated with the *Economic History Review* in Britain as one of the significant historical associations to emerge in interwar Europe.[18]

The changing social and political contexts of the university history departments in Ireland between 1922 and 1949 informed the careers of the academic women historians. Mary O'Dowd argues that the nature of professionalism, as understood and practiced by the new historical establishment, served to exclude many of the academic women historians who began teaching prior to the 1930s, and that their ambivalence towards "scientific history" meant that their contribution to Irish history in the new academic context was limited. The Irish academic world, she contends, "remained a male club, from many parts of which women were still excluded" well past the 1930s. This had parallels elsewhere; for example, women historians in interwar France experienced marginalization in the "male club" of French academic history, and their contributions to the *Annales* school went unrecognized for years.[19] The NUI women historians resembled the male academic historians who entered the NUI prior to the 1930s more than they did the Moody–Edwards school. The parameters of Irish historical discourse and practice from the late 1930s onward were set by men who had received PhDs in England. Most of the women academics had been trained differently; they had been educated in Ireland and had received master's degrees rather than doctorates. Some, such as Hayden, were overtly political and emotionally engaged with their scholarly work. Women faced other professional disabilities, such as pay differentials, and, at Trinity College, exclusion from the Senior Common Room and from Fellowship until the 1960s.[20] Women historians in Ireland and elsewhere also faced exclusion in informal socializing among male historians. These exclusions are not trivial, because of the significance of collegiality and networking in academic life. In the United States, the exclusion of women from social functions at the annual American Historical Association conventions provided an impetus for the founding of the Berkshire Conference of Women Historians in 1930.[21] In Ireland, women academics defended their interests through the Women Graduates' Association, while the Irish Women Writers' Club was a source of intellectual support for Dublin-based academic historians Mary Hayden and Constantia Maxwell, as well as non-academic historians Dorothy Macardle and Rosamond Jacob.

Hayden, O'Sullivan, Ni Chinneide, and Henley

Mary Hayden (1862–1942)

Mary Hayden was not only significant as one of the first Irish female academic historians, but as one of the most prominent feminists in the Irish Free State. She was the most politically active of the female academic historians both before and after the formation of the Free

State. Hayden was a Home Ruler rather than a republican prior to independence, and a defender of the Free State from the 1920s onwards. Her decades of feminist activism encompassed suffragist politics and the promotion of women's education in the 1880s, to protests against restrictions on women's rights in the 1920s and 1930s. She was involved in university politics as well, as a member of the UCD Governing Body and the NUI Senate. Hayden is also significant for writing an influential Irish history textbook that was used in universities for decades.

Hayden was born in Dublin in 1862 to middle-class Catholic parents. Her mother, Mary Anne (Ryan) Hayden, died when Mary was eleven. Her father, Dr Thomas Hayden, a professor of medicine, died when she was nineteen. Hayden attended convent schools for her secondary education, and then studied at Alexandra College, which enabled her to obtain a BA in 1885 from the Royal University of Ireland (RUI). In 1887, she earned an MA in modern languages from the RUI. Hayden began her career in women's colleges in Dublin and taught at both St. Mary's University College, which was run by Dominican nuns, and Alexandra College.

A committed feminist and believer in coeducational universities, Hayden was involved in early campaigns for women's suffrage and for equality in higher education.[22] At the turn of the century, women could not enter Trinity College or the Catholic University College, and women were discriminated against in the allocation of teaching fellowships. While male teaching fellows could work in the women's colleges, women could not teach male students. Hayden faced this discrimination when she applied for a teaching fellowship at University College in 1900 and in 1901.[23] Ultimately, the 1908 Irish Universities Act reorganized higher education and mandated equal access for women in the three constituent colleges of the NUI. Hayden was instrumental in securing the admission of women to what became UCD in 1908, when the Catholic University College was dissolved. She remained active in the NUI Women Graduates' Association, which she helped establish in 1902 to advance the educational interests of women.[24]

Hayden's career at UCD

Mary Hayden taught at UCD from 1909 to 1938, in addition to serving on the UCD Governing Board and the NUI Senate. In 1911 she was promoted from a lectureship in history to the first Professorship of Modern Irish History. The other candidate for the position was the medievalist Edmund Curtis, who became a professor at Trinity College in 1914. Hayden's only other colleague in History was John M. O'Sullivan, Professor of Modern History. However, Eoin MacNeill, in Celtic Studies, taught early and medieval Irish history, and George O'Brien of the Economics Department wrote on Irish economic history.[25] Between 1909 and 1938, when Hayden retired, there were four other female senior staff members at UCD. Mary Macken was a professor of German, Maria Degani was a professor of Italian and Spanish, Agnes O'Farrelly lectured in Irish before becoming a professor in 1932, and Mary Kate Ryan lectured in French. Thus, 1932 represented a high point for women professors at UCD.[26] Women may have been more successful obtaining professorships in history and modern languages in the early days of the NUI when there were fewer credentialed academics competing for positions. In addition, these subjects were considered less prestigious than higher status, established disciplines such as classics and philosophy.[27] This was to change by the late 1930s.

The class lectures Hayden gave focused primarily on early modern and modern Ireland, from the Tudor period to the early twentieth century. She gave three lectures a week to students doing an Honors course in modern Irish history. During the 1920s, her courses covered the years 1485 to 1654, and 1654 to 1870. She used books by nationalists and moderate unionists. In addition to her own *A Short History of the Irish People* (co-written with George Moonan), she used Alice Stopford Green's *The Making of Ireland and its Undoing, 1200–1600*, Thomas Davis's *The Patriot Parliament*, W.E.H. Lecky's *A History of Ireland in the Eighteenth Century*, and Philip Wilson's *The Beginnings of Modern Ireland*.[28]

Hayden's lectures concentrated on political history from a nationalist perspective, and paid close attention to the treatment of Irish Catholics, particularly under the eighteenth-century Penal Laws. Her lecture, "Some Aspects of Dublin Life in the Early 18th Century," conforms to the themes outlined in her book, *A Short History of the Irish People*. She emphasized the oppression of Irish Catholics, the group with whom she identified, the harshness of the criminal justice system, and the extremes of wealth and poverty.[29] Other lecture topics included the "Flight of the Earls," the Stuart Pretenders, the Catholic

Committee, the Irish Parliament, "Emmet's Insurrection," "From O'Connell to Parnell," and "The 1848 Movement."[30]

Drafts of history examinations also indicate the scope and emphases of Hayden's courses. One Modern History examination, covering European and Irish history, gave students the option of answering the question, "How far do you consider that Ireland before the Norman invasion might claim to be a nation?" Other essay questions concerned the Tudor plantation policy ("What advantages did the English government of the Tudor period seek to gain of its plantation policy in Ireland?"), the treatment of Irish Catholics by King James I, and King Louis XVI and the French Revolution. The students were also asked to identify and briefly explain concepts and historical figures such as the High Kingship, King Henry II and the Normans, the Statutes of Kilkenny, Erasmus, John Knox, Napoleon, and Thomas Davis.[31]

Only a small number of graduate students earned MA degrees in any field of history during the first twenty years of UCD. Eoin MacNeill directed one MA dissertation in early Irish history, John M. O'Sullivan worked with two MA students, and Mary Hayden advised three MA candidates. In comparison, twenty MA degrees were obtained by graduate students in the English department, nineteen in Economics, and fifteen in Classics. Donal McCartney attributes the paucity of MA candidates to MacNeill and O'Sullivan dividing their time between UCD and the government, in which they both served terms as Ministers of Education between 1922 and 1932, and to Hayden's limited involvement in archival research.[32]

Two MA students Hayden supervised were Dora Casserley and Robert Dudley Edwards.[33] Casserley, the daughter of a Church of Ireland clergyman from Donegal, was one of the few Protestant students to attend UCD in its early decades. She received an MA in history in 1929 for her thesis, entitled "Primary Education in Ireland in the Eighteenth Century." She taught for years at Alexandra College, and wrote *History of Ireland*,[34] a primary school textbook for Protestant schools.[35] Edwards earned his MA at UCD in 1931 for a thesis on the impact of the Penal Laws on Protestant Dissenters.[36] He went on to the University of London's Institute of Historical Research, where he earned a PhD in 1934 for a dissertation entitled "The History of Penal Laws Against Catholics in Ireland From 1534 to the Treaty of Limerick (1691)."[37] When Edwards returned to Ireland, Hayden gave him advice on how to get a teaching position at UCD. She offered to ask Eoin MacNeill to discuss Edwards' case with UCD's president, Dr Denis Coffey, as she believed MacNeill had greater leverage with Coffey. She also asked her colleague John M. O'Sullivan to help.[38] Edwards became a lecturer in Modern Irish History at UCD in 1938, the year Hayden retired, and later the chair of the department.

Hayden's social and political activism

Mary Hayden's activist life demonstrates the continuity of the tradition of Irish female historians acting as engaged intellectuals. She challenged the discriminatory treatment of women by the government, academia, and society both before and after 1922. She challenged the marginalization of women in higher education by founding the Women Graduates' Association in 1902, serving as president of the NUI branch of the Association from 1913 to 1942. Hayden found further scope for her leadership abilities by serving in the NUI Senate and the UCD Governing Body. As a member of the nonmilitant Irish Women's Suffrage Federation, which was formed in 1911, she used constitutional methods to press for the vote.[39] Hayden also favored the use of constitutional means to achieve Home Rule. An opponent of republicanism, she joined the short-lived, centrist Irish Dominion League in 1919 to press for Irish self-government within the British Empire.[40] When the Free State was established, she supported William Cosgrave's Cumann na nGeadheal government.

Hayden remained active on behalf of women during the Free State years, and was frequently critical of the government's policies towards women. Her feminism and pacifism took on an international dimension when she joined the Women's International League for Peace and Freedom (WILPF). Hayden and other Irish feminists advocated social welfare measures, such as children's allowances, that would help women and their families. As the president of both the National Council of Women and the National University Women Graduates' Association, she provided an articulate feminist voice in the debates about the Civil Service Regulation (Amendment) Bill in 1925, the Conditions of Employment Bill in 1935, and the 1937 Constitution. The two bills gave the government the right to restrict women's participation in the workforce, while the Constitution's clauses on women appeared to feminists to restrict women's citizenship and confine women to the home. Feminists successfully lobbied for the defeat of the 1925 Bill, but failed to stop the ratification of the 1935 Bill and the 1937 Constitution. However, they did get some sections of the Constitution removed.[41]

One of Hayden's last articles was a defense of feminism. It was written as a response to an article by Hunter Guthrie, S.J., who had argued that mothers were to blame for not teaching their children morality or obedience to authority, while feminists were denounced for spurning domesticity and passivity.[42] Hayden, in her rebuttal, appealed to recent history to validate feminism, noting that since 1918, when women in Britain and Ireland won the vote, several acts had been passed by Parliament that benefited women and children. Politically active women, she suggested, had helped make society more just and humane. Hayden discussed the suffrage movement and its turn to militancy in the prewar era in conjunction with Irish nationalist activism. Militancy was "regrettable, as [were] the methods by which amelioration of the Irish Land Laws and the dissolution of her Legislative Union with England ... were obtained."[43] She defended working women, the majority of whom worked low-paid jobs to support themselves and their families. She added that many men in Ireland chose not to marry, and therefore bore some responsibility for the perceived decline of marriage and the family.[44]

A Short History of the Irish People (1921, 1927)

Mary Hayden's major work was *A Short History of the Irish People*, co-written with George A. Moonan and first published in 1921. A synthetic narrative, it was intended as a textbook for university students. Moonan wrote part I, covering the prehistoric era through the fifteenth century, as well as brief sections on language and literature. Hayden wrote part II, the bulk of the book, covering the reign of Henry VIII through the establishment of the Free State. *A Short History* concentrates on the political narrative, and minimizes social, cultural, economic, and women's history. The authors conceded that they wrote "from a frankly national stand-point ...[but] made every effort to attain accuracy and avoid prejudice."[45] *A Short History* found a niche as the most popular Irish history textbook in the National University system and in secondary schools until the 1960s. During these years, the book exerted a considerable influence in shaping Irish students' perceptions of their history.[46] By the 1960s, the book seemed outdated, and new textbooks were written to incorporate new research in history.

This section assesses *A Short History* by examining its narrative framework and treatment of key themes and events. Moonan's treatment of early and medieval Ireland conformed to the pattern of early twentieth-century nationalist historiography. Like Alice Stopford Green and Eoin MacNeill, he emphasized positive aspects of early Irish history, such as the spirituality of the Celtic Church, art, literature, intellectual life, and the complex legal system.[47] He condemned the violence perpetrated by the Vikings[48] and Normans, as well as the discriminatory Statutes of Kilkenny. He maintained, though, that both foreign groups assimilated and brought innovative practices to Ireland.[49] Moonan's praise of early Irish culture and lack of emphasis on internal political conflict may have been intended to reinforce the MacNeill-Green view against older, but still current, unionist depictions of early Ireland as a turbulent, barbaric society prior to the Norman conquest.

Mary Hayden's section of *A Short History* covered themes and events from the sixteenth through early-twentieth centuries that were still controversial. She wrote from a Catholic nationalist perspective, and clearly sympathized with the historic Irish Catholic community, presenting their perspective in accounts of conflicts. Nevertheless, an analysis of her presentation of Irish history demonstrates that she avoided some of the weaknesses attributed to nationalist historians by their critics.[50] For instance, while she observed historical continuities, she did not invariably deploy a simplistic "whig-nationalist" conceptual framework. She never embraced the view that all Irish risings foreshadowed the republican-led War of Independence and the establishment of the Irish Free State. Hayden noted, for instance, that the 1534 Rebellion of Silken Thomas Fitzgerald "cannot be considered a National rising. The object of its leader was merely ... to assert the uncontrolled feudal independence of his House."[51]

Hayden condemned the Tudor and Cromwellian wars and detailed various atrocities committed by English soldiers, but tried to maintain balance in her account of early modern warfare by denouncing atrocities committed by Catholics, such as the murders of Protestant settlers in the 1641 Rising.[52] Her treatment of the eighteenth century conforms to a traditional nationalist perspective, with some modifications. She strongly condemned the violation of the 1691 Treaty of Limerick, which led, in part, to the Penal Laws against Irish Catholics. Hayden wrote that although many excuses were made for the breach of the Treaty and subsequent Penal Laws, such as European-wide sectarian animosities, the persecution of Huguenots in France, and England's fear of Continental Catholic powers, "the fact remains that what was done was in itself indefensible and disgraceful."[53] She maintained that the discriminatory Penal Laws were intended to crush Catholic political power and maintain Protestant power, rather than eradicate Catholicism, an assessment with which later scholars concurred. Hayden, along with her contemporaries, believed that the Penal Laws were strictly enforced until they fell into abeyance in mid-century, when enforcement was in fact beyond the capacity of the eighteenth-century state.[54] This weakness in Hayden's work stems from a general failure of early twentieth-century historians to investigate social history and the lived experience of ordinary people to see how laws passed by political elites affected their daily lives.

Hayden concluded that the Penal Laws helped shape the characters of Protestants and Catholics alike. The landed Protestants, she wrote, became decadent and irresponsible, much given to drinking and dueling, while Catholics became obsequious, dishonest, and lazy. Hayden displayed a need to rehabilitate the Irish Catholics, who were often stereotyped and maligned for the qualities she cited, but could not reject the practice of stereotyping itself. She insisted that these alleged traits were not innate, but a response to a social and political system that placed considerable legal obstacles in their way. To prove her case, she pointed to the achievements of Irishmen in Continental Europe and in America. The stereotype of eighteenth-century landlords was still current in 1920s Ireland, but Hayden stated that there were landlords with a sense of social responsibility.[55]

While Hayden did not glorify warfare, she thought that the 1798 Rebellion, led by the United Irishmen, was justified under the circumstances. She maintained that widespread maltreatment and torture of the peasantry by the militia, with the intention of forcing them to reveal arms depots, led many to join the insurgency. Moreover, advocates of reform and Catholic emancipation were thwarted by the government. This led many Catholics to believe that peaceful methods would never secure reforms. Hayden praised the rebels, Catholics and Protestants alike, and condemned the militia's atrocities, but also denounced murders of prisoners by the rebels. She commended Wolfe Tone, the United Irishman, for his intelligence and resourcefulness.[56]

The Repeal Movement, the Famine, and the Home Rule Movement dominate Hayden's account of nineteenth-century Irish history. Hayden praised Daniel O'Connell's nonviolent political activism, and lauded Thomas Davis of Young Ireland.[57] Her treatment of the Famine conformed to traditional nationalist historiography in several respects. She sympathized with the victims of the Famine and dramatically depicted their suffering. This contrasted with later scholarship on the Famine by some academic historians, who tended to downplay its catastrophic nature.[58] She criticized insufficient relief measures enacted by the British government, and added that the government did not prevent the export of food from Ireland during the Famine years.[59] Despite her criticisms of the British political leadership as callous, prejudiced, and inept, she did not adopt the genocide thesis of the Young Irelander, John Mitchel, who believed the British government had deliberately withheld food to decimate the Irish population and clear the land.

Hayden's discussion of Home Rule champion Charles Stewart Parnell and the Land League of the 1870s and 1880s underscored her mainstream nationalism. Parnell, a Protestant landlord, was commended for his political leadership. She thought that the goal of the Land League, the reform of the land system for the benefit of the tenant farmers, was justifiable. Hayden favored the Home Rule bill first pushed by the Irish Party and Prime Minister William Gladstone in 1886, and lamented its defeat. Revealing her social class prejudice, she attributed British opposition to the bill to the machinations of unionists, "who well understood the art of appealing to the prejudices of millions of ignorant men on whom the Franchise Act of 1884 had conferred the vote."[60] She ended this section by praising Gladstone's activism on behalf of Ireland.[61]

The final chapters of the 1927 edition of *A Short History of the Irish People* cover the revolutionary period, 1916 to 1923. Hayden gave the 1916 Rising a cursory, factual overall treatment, rather than glorification. She asserted that Patrick Pearse, whom she had met in the Gaelic League, and his fellow insurrectionists were mostly "cultured and highly intelligent men ...[and] all died bravely."[62] Hayden criticized the tactics of the British special forces, the Black and Tans, and their treatment of Irish civilians during the War of Independence, although she did not glorify the violence of the IRA.[63] She may have thought it important to validate the experiences of these civilians by recording them in her book; during the war many British authorities had refused to countenance stories about the Black and Tans victimizing innocent civilians.[64] Hayden condemned both the IRA for killing fourteen British officers in November 1920 and the British forces for killing fifteen unarmed civilians on the same day.[65] She favored the victorious, pro-Treaty Free State side in the Irish Civil War, and deplored the actions of IRA "Irregulars" who continued to fight after the ratification of the Treaty. Hayden gave her book a "Free State ending" by stating approvingly that both Stormont, the Northern Irish Parliament, and Dail Eireann, the Free State Parliament, were more representative than Henry Grattan's eighteenth-century Irish Parliament, and suggested they should both be judged on the basis of their future achievements.[66]

A Short History of the Irish People was essentially the work of a Catholic constitutional nationalist and Free State supporter, who favored William Cosgrave's government in the 1920s, rather than the IRA and revolutionary republicanism. When Hayden began working on her book, the ideal of Irish independence lacked the sanction of the state.[67] Her textbook represents the transmission of a marginal, alternative history into an orthodox, state-sanctioned national narrative that would later be attacked by revisionist historians. *A Short History* was part of the post-1922 consolidation period. Writing as a university historian, Hayden became an important voice by giving the new state a meaning and an interpretation that was widely disseminated to secondary school and university students.[68] Her book was attacked by republicans in the 1930s, once Fianna Fail came to power. A letter-writer to the *Irish Press* in 1935 objected to Hayden's defense of the Free State forces in the Civil War and her characterization of the IRA men as "gunmen" and "irregulars," contending that this was an "insult to the patriot dead."[69]

Hayden identified with the Irish Catholics of the past, and was frequently critical of English policy in Ireland, but tried to avoid egregious prejudice and imbalance.[70] For example, she praised English leaders such as Gladstone, and English people who behaved benevolently, such as those who contributed to Famine relief efforts. She also criticized some instances of violence by Irish Catholics, such as the murders of Protestants in 1641. Hayden did not adopt the extreme "whiggish" view of the Irish Free State as the inevitable outcome of over seven hundred years of struggle against English invaders, noting that many struggles had goals far more limited than Irish independence.

Hayden was criticized by later historians for writing an unimpressive textbook, rather than scholarly monographs.[71] Modern historians of Ireland might fault Hayden's old-fashioned moralizing, overt nationalist identification and emphasis on the oppression of Catholics, and occasional emotional engagement with the material. Moralizing, however, was not uncommon among historians of Hayden's generation. Many drew lessons from history, and Irish nationalists were by no means unique in the tendency "to legitimize, to praise and to blame."[72] Surveys of national history informed by the writer's nationalism were not confined to Ireland in this period, as chauvinistic nationalism remained a force in Europe after the First World War. Educators in interwar Britain who called for a more internationalist history curriculum with less of an emphasis on military history encountered considerable resistance.[73] History textbooks have rarely been known for being critical or "unpatriotic," especially in discussions of military history and foreign policy, and frequently display a conservative bias. Strategic as well as ideological considerations play a role in this, as these textbooks are geared towards the academic market.[74]

Hayden's almost complete omission of women's history was also not unusual in European and American textbooks at the time. Nevertheless, the absence of a discussion of significant aspects of Irish women's history – such as Anna Parnell and the Ladies' Land League, the women's suffrage movement, Constance Markiewicz and other nationalist women in the 1916 Rising, and the winning of the suffrage in 1918 and consequent election of women to the Dail and Seanad (Senate) – is striking, since Hayden herself was part of this history. She may have decided to concentrate mainly on the people and events that would appear on examinations.

Hayden's journal articles

Mary Hayden wrote journal articles that dealt with women's and social history, and demonstrated that she was familiar with contemporary scholarship by women historians outside Ireland, particularly in England. A 1913 article, "Women in the Middle Ages,"[75] resembles medieval women's history written by prewar feminist historians in England, who wrote on medieval England to frame contemporary arguments about women's education, work, and their legal and political rights. They were particularly interested in medieval convents as communities of educated women who sought an alternative to marriage, and in independent tradeswomen in the towns.[76] Hayden wrote comparatively about women in different medieval European societies, using literary sources and legal texts as evidence. She maintained that women enjoyed certain legal rights relating to property and inheritance, though they were still subordinate to men.[77] Hayden, an unmarried Catholic laywoman who had worked closely with Dominican nuns when she taught at St. Mary's University College, viewed medieval convent life as a positive development. She described early medieval nuns as scholarly, spiritual, accomplished in the arts, and charitable.[78]

Hayden made specific references to early Ireland to bolster the contemporary arguments of Irish feminists demanding greater equality in educational opportunities. She maintained that in Ireland, "learning seems to have been equally honoured in both sexes. We are told that in the 2nd century, A.D., there was at Tara a Woman's College."[79] Hayden concluded her article by asserting that even modern feminists are surprised by the many rights enjoyed by some medieval women, and stated that if women ever enter the government or the legal profession, society "will see nothing which has not often been seen before."[80] In sum, Hayden's present-centered article, using new scholarship on medieval women, resembled the work of her feminist counterparts in England, who also appealed to medieval tradition to make radical new ideas palatable to the public. Hayden added an Irish dimension to this project by invoking Celtic Ireland to appeal to nationalists, who often construed feminism as an English import rather than an authentically Irish movement.

A posthumously published article, "Charity Children in 18th-Century Dublin," resembled the social and economic history written by British women historians during the interwar years. Their work sometimes focused on women and children, and dealt with the early modern and modern period rather than the medieval era. For some interwar-era women historians, writing social history tied in with their pacifist commitments; an emphasis on social history, they maintained, could undercut the impact of traditional political and military history, which stressed conflict and seemed to promote favorable attitudes to war.[81]

Hayden's article related to her experience as the founder of a charity for Dublin slum children, the St. Joan's Club.[82] She provided a survey of the experience of poor children in the Foundling Hospital, workhouses, and charity schools, using institutional records and reports of Parliamentary Commissions sent to investigate these places.[83] Hayden condemned the physical abuse of children in workhouses, and the general apathy of the public in the face of institutional inhumanity. She mentioned female reformers who tried to improve conditions, anticipating later academic studies of Irish female philanthropists. She concluded on a present-centered note. Combining historical study with her social activism on behalf of poor children and orphans, she stated that although life in institutions was still difficult for children, it was not as dreadful as it was in the eighteenth century. Hayden's two articles demonstrate how she, like earlier Irish female historians, fused history and political engagement, and how she chose to write women's and social history in periodicals reaching those outside of academia.

Conclusion

Mary Hayden died in July 1942. A member of the first generation of female academic historians, she left a more substantive legacy as an activist and teacher than as an innovative historian. Hayden, a lifelong campaigner for women's rights who became an important feminist voice of protest in the Free State, combined political activism with a demanding teaching career well into her seventies. She was also an important feminist voice in UCD and the NUI. A somewhat defensive and emotionally engaged nationalist, Hayden reflected on bias in historical scholarship, recognizing that she wrote within a nationalist framework, and that there were competing frameworks in which to write history. Her textbook remains significant as an artifact of the Free State in the 1920s, as it put forth a historical narrative that was acceptable in a post-revolutionary state whose legitimacy was questioned by more radical nationalists.

Mary Donovan O'Sullivan (1887–1966)

Mary Donovan O'Sullivan was the first female professor at UCG. She came from a less affluent background than the other NUI women, and was the only married female academic historian of the Free State period. She was also unique as a pro-British Catholic woman historian and critic of the Free State, which shaped her historical writing and political journalism. She was important as an undergraduate teacher and as a supervisor of graduate students, and the UCG history department became notable for its encouragement of research, largely due to O'Sullivan's efforts. Finally, she did much to promote a learned society outside of academia, the Galway Archaeological and Historical Society.

Mary Donovan was born in Galway in 1887 to lower-middle-class Catholic parents. Her father had served in the Royal Navy, and her family identified with the British state and its military. Donovan attended secondary school at the Dominican College in Galway and graduated at the top of her class. She then went to Queen's College Galway, where she earned a First-Class Honors BA in Modern Languages in 1908 and a First-Class Honors MA in the subject in 1909. She also studied some history with Professor W.F. Trench. Donovan studied at the University of Marburg before returning to Galway to take up an assistantship in the college, now called UCG. The Professorship of English, History, and Mental Science [Philosophy] was divided into three chairs in 1914, at which time Donovan was appointed Professor of History, "with special reference to Irish history." She taught for over forty years and retired in 1957. She was a fellow of both the Royal Historical Society and the Royal Society of Antiquaries of Ireland, and a member of the Royal Irish Academy.[84]

Donovan was politically active as a young woman. She acted on her feminist convictions by joining the Connaught Women's Franchise League, a regional group affiliated with the Irish Women's Suffrage Federation. Her early feminism was largely motivated by her frustration at professional women being paid less than men for the same work.[85] She wrote a newspaper article in 1913 entitled "Why I am a Supporter of Women's Suffrage," in which she criticized gender discrimination and lower pay for women in the workplace. The following year, the First World War broke out. Irish Parliamentary Party leader John Redmond urged Irish support for the war, which divided Irish feminists. Donovan's enthusiasm for the war, exemplified by her presidency of the Galway Ladies' Recruiting Committee,[86] would have been popular in British, Irish unionist, and Redmondite circles, but placed her in opposition to pacifist Irish feminists and advanced nationalists.[87] Donovan was a supporter of John Redmond and constitutional nationalism, a stance that was not incompatible with a favorable attitude towards British imperialism. She retained her pro-British stance throughout her life.

O'Sullivan's career at UCG

O'Sullivan's career at UCG was unusual both in an Irish and international context. She was the only Irish female academic historian during the Free State years to combine marriage and a career, as she married Major J. O'Sullivan after her appointment to the professorship. Most academic women historians in Britain and North America were single in the interwar period, as were many in Continental Europe, and some other married women academics, like O'Sullivan, were childless. The history faculty at UCG was remarkable in that it consisted of two women for many years, as Sile ni Chinneide joined O'Sullivan when she was hired as a lecturer in 1927. G.A. Hayes-McCoy became the history professor in 1958, after O'Sullivan retired.[88] Other women on the UCG staff during the Free State years were Catherine Donnellan (English), Margaret Heavey (Ancient Classics) and Kathleen Mulchrone (Celtic Studies).[89]

O'Sullivan played an important role as a mentor, supervising many more graduate students than Mary Hayden or Constantia Maxwell. Her students included MA candidates G.A. Hayes-McCoy and James Lydon, who later earned PhDs in Britain, and PhD candidates Michael Cafferky, Frederick Jones, Sheila O'Malley, and Diarmuid Murtagh, all of whom researched topics in medieval or early modern Irish history.[90] Sheila O'Malley, who received her PhD in 1954, was one of the first women to earn a PhD in history at an Irish university. Hayes-McCoy, an early modernist, received a PhD at Edinburgh and worked at the National Library of Ireland before being awarded the Chair of History at UCG. Lydon, a medievalist, earned a PhD from the University of London and began teaching at Trinity College in the early 1960s, becoming the Lecky Professor by 1980.[91] One student in the early 1940s who especially impressed O'Sullivan was Frederick Jones, a Redemptorist priest, who later published a revisionist work on Lord Mountjoy based on his MA thesis.[92] Describing Jones as "one of the most brilliant minds I have ever met," she believed few graduate students at UCG were the intellectual equals of the Galway scholars of the era prior to Irish independence.[93]

O'Sullivan as a public historian

The Galway Archaeological and Historical Society, and an attempt to establish a municipal art gallery in Galway, also engaged O'Sullivan's attention, and illustrated the wider role she played as a public historian and intellectual in her community. O'Sullivan served as secretary of the Society and editor of its journal from 1932 to 1951. She invited speakers such as archaeologist R.A.S. Macalister to address the Society and the wider public, thereby popularizing historical scholarship outside of academia.[94] O'Sullivan formed the Galway Art Gallery Committee in 1943, which in 1946 held an exhibition of Irish paintings donated by art collectors at UCG. While the Committee members were unsuccessful in realizing their goal of a municipal art gallery, they were instrumental in building up UCG's art collection and providing greater cultural offerings for the people of Galway.[95]

O'Sullivan was a controversial figure politically in Free State Ireland. A pro-British opponent of republicanism and complete independence, she often played the role of a right-wing, oppositional intellectual. Standing somewhere between Catholic supporters of Cumann na nGeadheal, like Mary Hayden, and ex-unionist Protestants, like the Trinity College women historians, O'Sullivan resembled the Catholic ex-Redmondites and imperialists who felt alienated by the democratic, republican ethos of 1930s Ireland.[96] Like the ex-unionists linked with Trinity College, the ex-Redmondites felt they were fighting a rearguard action during the Free State years, especially after Fianna Fail gained power. They resented what they viewed as Fianna Fail supporters' parochialism and chauvinistic, anti-British nationalism.[97]

Although the Irish political landscape changed dramatically between 1913, when O'Sullivan made an early venture into the political sphere by advocating women's suffrage, and the mid-twentieth century, a strong identification with power, specifically the power of the British state and its military, was to remain central to O'Sullivan's political thought. This stance derived from family tradition and her personality and prerogatives.

While O'Sullivan was the most politically conservative of the Catholic historians under consideration, she was liberal in religious matters. She attended UCG despite the fact that the Catholic hierarchy at the time inveighed against this "godless" college.[98] O'Sullivan later spoke out against sectarianism in the Free State, particularly in regard to the Letitia Dunbar Harrison case, in which the appointment of a Protestant librarian in Mayo led to protests and boycotts by the county council.[99] Her liberalism was also revealed in her opposition to censorship.

Political articles and letters written by O'Sullivan in the 1930s and 1940s shed light on her social and political outlook, and demonstrate how at odds she was with the ethos of de Valera's Ireland. Senia Paseta contends that "by the early 1930s, the voice of pre-Independence constitutional Ireland had all but disappeared from the public stage,"[100] but echoes of that voice can be found in O'Sullivan's writings. In April 1930, she wrote an article for a conservative British journal, reviewing developments in Ireland since 1922. She opened the article by commenting on the demand of Indian nationalists for independence, identifying with Britain in viewing this activism as a threat to be skillfully contained in order to preserve the Empire. O'Sullivan, who was dubious about Indian popular politics, presented herself as an adviser to British statesmen, believing her discussion of Ireland could help British leaders to formulate an advantageous Indian policy.[101] She differed from advanced Irish nationalists on India. Many republicans followed newspaper coverage of independence movements in the British Empire, and felt themselves in solidarity with nationalists in India and elsewhere. Shortly before O'Sullivan's article appeared, for example, Eamon de Valera was quoted as saying, "I wish the people of India speedy success in their efforts to secure Independence."[102]

O'Sullivan's article offered a tactical, rueful critique of British policy towards Ireland, presenting it as a series of regrettable missed opportunities. She wished Britain could have worked towards a settlement with the Irish Dominion League in 1919, rather than with the more radical Michael Collins and Arthur Griffith in 1921. An opponent of Partition, she favored a united federal Ireland linked to the British Commonwealth and loyal to the Crown.[103] She praised the Cosgrave government for its fiscal conservatism and devotion to law and order, but criticized its censorship and compulsory Irish policies in education.[104] While O'Sullivan had once promoted the expansion of democracy by advocating women's suffrage, she now questioned whether universal adult suffrage in Ireland was desirable. She strongly condemned republicans, claiming they drew their support from irresponsible, politically illiterate young and lower-class people with no stake in the country.[105] Since O'Sullivan had little faith in the Irish masses and was dismayed by the practical experience of democracy in Ireland, closer ties to a strong British state must have seemed more and more appealing. She concluded by advocating a new party made up of ex-unionists and ex-Redmondites to stem the tide of republicanism and prevent what she viewed as an unparalleled disaster, the taking of office by de Valera, "which most sensible people in the country could only regard with the utmost misgiving."[106]

Her article, then, demonstrated her inability to understand that the more republican Fianna Fail program had genuine popular support, and that the majority of Irish people favored greater sovereignty and a revision of the Treaty to further that aim, rather than strengthening ties with Britain. Stephen Quinn condemned her article in an angry, unfocused piece in the *Catholic Bulletin*, in which he highlighted quotes from her article that he found particularly obnoxious.[107]

"Minorities in the Free State," written in 1932, discussed the position of Irish Protestants in the decade following the establishment of the Free State. While O'Sullivan had a genuine belief in religious tolerance, she also seemed interested in possible ways in which a higher political profile for Protestants could strengthen the position of pro-British Catholics like herself. Reviewing the religious history of Ireland, she sounded a rueful note as she asserted that until the introduction of Reformation-era legislation, the Roman Catholic Church, with its great influence in Ireland, had been "absolutely loyal to the English interest in Ireland ... [and] one of the pillars of government there."[108] This legislation, in her view a tactical error, had prevented the growth of an Irish Catholic nationalism based on loyalty to England, the type of non-revolutionary nationalism embraced by O'Sullivan.

The article continued with a critique of sectarianism in the Free State. Attempts to discriminate against Protestants, O'Sullivan stated, were "the work of individuals who exploit religion at the expense of Christianity, and who seek to enact in the Free State the very things which they affect to despise most in the life of Northern Ireland."[109] While she praised the Cosgrave government's overall treatment of Protestants, she condemned its abolition of the right of appeal to the judicial committee of the Privy Council, which was of special interest to Protestant ex-unionists, as well as to pro-British Catholics. These groups opposed ending the right of appeal because it further eroded links with Britain and gave Ireland greater sovereignty. In addition, some Protestants had hoped that the right of appeal would safeguard their civil rights in the event that the Free State courts did not.[110] Stephen Quinn again submitted an erratic, loosely argued attack on her article to the *Catholic Bulletin*, expressing his anger at O'Sullivan for "enlighten[ing] the ranks of Toryism on the doings of her own people."[111]

O'Sullivan revealed her anger and frustration with the policies of Eamon de Valera and his Fianna Fail government in a 1935 article entitled "Anglo-Irish Relations," which appeared in a British journal. She reiterated her complaint that the Irish people were politically illiterate and unable to handle the responsibilities of universal suffrage. O'Sullivan condescendingly declared that "the Irishman has always accepted his teachings ready-made for him, and it has never been one of his characteristics to question and criticize ... the absence of a healthy public opinion has ever been the bane of Irish life."[112] De Valera, in her view, had gained adherents among an intellectually limited populace with simplistic, emotive appeals to nationalism. This highlighted her reluctance to take more advanced forms of Irish nationalism seriously. Insisting "that loyalty to the Free State is not inconsistent with loyalty to the Commonwealth,[113] she condemned de Valera for taking steps that further eroded the links with Britain, such as abolishing the Oath of Allegiance and downgrading the Governor-General's office. While many Irish nationalists who accepted the Anglo-Irish Treaty viewed it as a steppingstone to full independence, O'Sullivan urged that the Treaty be strictly observed, rather than revised.[114]

In sum, these three articles reveal the frustration of a middle-class Catholic ex-Redmondite in 1930s Ireland. An upholder, rather than a critic or victim, of British imperialism, she could not understand why the majority of Irish people favored separatist policies. Although she supported parliamentary democracy, she regretted that universal suffrage had been extended to Ireland, where the lower classes did not vote the way she wished. She looked to the British state to protect conservative, affluent Irish people from the consequences of greater democratization. Concerns about class were central to O'Sullivan's political thinking about England as well as Ireland, as will be demonstrated further.

O'Sullivan expressed her wholehearted support for Britain and the Allies during the Second World War, but did not state whether or not she disagreed with Ireland's policy of neutrality. In letters to her friend Sir D'arcy Wentworth Thompson, a professor in Scotland, she wrote about how she anxiously followed the Allied campaigns. O'Sullivan expressed her horror and anguish at the massive suffering endured on the battlefields, saying it reminded her of the First World War, "with its struggle, yard by yard and colossal losses."[115] This reinforces how for her, unlike Irish republicans, the reference point for wartime suffering was the First World War, not the War of Independence and Civil War.[116] Again, her politics of empathy, shaped by family tradition and personal pro-British views, would always lead her to identify with and care about soldiers and civilians who had suffered and died on the Allied sides in the world wars, rather than with those who fought for Irish independence or who were victimized by British forces during the 1919–21 period.[117]

O'Sullivan became less enthusiastic about England after the Second World War, during the period of Clement Attlee's Labour government. She thought postwar England was depressing because of rationing and deprivation, and felt sympathetic towards English people for having to face these conditions after the sacrifices they had made in the war. More ominously, she feared the working class was gaining the upper hand by the late 1940s. Writing to Thompson about postwar economic crises in England, she first drew attention "to the shortcomings of a socialist government." She then indignantly denounced "selfish" English workers for "demanding a 44 hr. or a 40 hr. week. As if we all don't work a lot more than that! What would one of these workers say if a doctor refused to come out and attend him [because] he had already worked his 44 hrs. for that week?"[118] The anxious postwar mood, she wrote, "was not the spirit that made England great."[119] When she observed the British political landscape, fears about lower class empowerment informed her political judgments, just as they had when she considered the situation in Ireland. As late as 1949, she asserted that Ireland still lacked an "intellectual middle class ... the mainstay of every nation ... which has given the world the best things in its civilization." Because many college graduates emigrated, there was no "educated public opinion" to challenge and restrain the politicians.[120] She may have been grieved that in 1949, educated middle-class people sharing her political views had been unable to prevent Ireland from officially becoming a fully independent republic.

O'Sullivan's books and articles

O'Sullivan's scholarly work consisted of two major books, *Old Galway: The History of a Norman Colony in Ireland* (1942), and *Italian Merchant Bankers in Ireland in the Middle Ages* (1962). The most productive scholar of the NUI women historians, she also wrote numerous articles on early modern Irish social, economic, and urban history, most of which dealt with Galway and appeared in the *Journal of the Galway Archaeological and Historical Society* as part of her larger works in progress. O'Sullivan believed herself to be an unsentimental, scientific historian, contrasting herself and her friends with romantic nationalist antiquarians and historians who had idealized Celtic Ireland.[121]

O'Sullivan's *Old Galway* was an important contribution to Irish urban, social, and economic history in the early 1940s.[122] It also opened a window on to O'Sullivan's present concerns. Like unionist historians of medieval and early modern Ireland, O'Sullivan favored the "civilized," loyal Norman colonists over the rebellious native Irish. She was similarly impressed with the outward signs of wealth, trade, law and order, and elite culture in the Norman colony, and believed this indicated their cultural superiority.[123] However, while unionist medievalists such as Goddard Orpen viewed loyal Anglo-Irish Protestants as the inheritors of the Norman mantle,[124] O'Sullivan's work could be read as reappropriating the Normans as the predecessors of loyal, elite Irish Catholics like herself. The idea of a small, urbane, pro-English outpost in the midst of the Gaelic west of Ireland appealed to her imagination, since her own identity was bound up with Galway and loyalty to the Crown. The spirit of rueful, pragmatic criticism of English policy found in her political articles appeared in her book as well. She lamented that the Tudors, Stuarts, and Cromwellians had chosen to view all Catholics in Ireland as a political threat, when the "Old English" or Norman-descended Catholics were traditionally loyal to the Crown.

In the early modernists' debate as to whether Irish churchmen and laypeople initially accepted the introduction of the Reformation, O'Sullivan contended, in contrast to most Protestant historians such as G.V. Jourdain, that the evidence showed that Galway remained both faithful to Catholicism and staunchly loyal to England. The Old English were rewarded for their centuries of allegiance to the Crown by being linked with rebellious Gaelic Catholics as enemies of the English interest.[125] O'Sullivan ended part I of her book, "The History of the Town," on an elegiac note, lamenting the passing of the old Norman elite in the Cromwellian period. The once proud, loyal city of Galway, with its wealth and culture, "was left derelict and in decay ... the policy of the Commonwealth ruin[ed] Galway irretrievably without accomplishing its object of making the place a stronghold of Protestantism."[126]

The second part of the book, "Life Within the Town," covers the social history of Galway from the thirteenth through the seventeenth centuries. O'Sullivan was unusual in the Irish academic context of the time for working on social, economic, and urban history, as Irish medievalists and early modernists tended to focus on constitutional history. Mary O'Dowd notes that O'Sullivan's work resembled that of interwar-era English female historians who favored social and economic history,[127] though unlike Eileen Power and Alice Clark, for example, O'Sullivan was not drawn to social history through sympathy with non-elites or involvement in the international peace movement, with its strictures against triumphalist military history. She stressed the wealth and cosmopolitanism of late medieval Galway, evidenced by its European-wide trade contacts and the complimentary reports of foreign visitors, perhaps attempting to undermine notions of Irish insularity and parochialism, which she criticized.[128] Her commendation of the affluence, culture, and intellectual life in a late medieval Irish town related to the emphasis found in Alice Stopford Green's work.

An important controversy O'Sullivan entered into concerned the extent to which the Normans in Galway mixed with the native Irish. She disagreed with Alice Stopford Green, who minimized ethnic exclusiveness and argued that the Irish took part in the town's social, cultural, and economic life. O'Sullivan's reading of the evidence led her to concur with English and unionist historians that the Normans, believing themselves superior to and threatened by the Irish, segregated themselves and kept the Irish out of Galway. As a social historian, however, she recognized that there was often a gulf between discriminatory statutes against the Irish and their actual enforcement, and that that may have led to greater cultural interchange and intermarriage between the Normans and the Irish than had previously been thought.[129]

Old Galway received a positive early reception. O'Sullivan told Thompson that "[her] book got a very good press both here and in England. I was perfectly amazed at the friendly reception it got and the way it sold," adding that UCG was awarding her a DLitt.[130] "P.F.," writing in the *Dublin Magazine*, praised O'Sullivan for placing Galway in its European context, and concluded that "this is History as professors in Irish universities should write it."[131] "Colm's" review in the *Irish Book Lover* praised O'Sullivan's "natural style of grace and lucidity" and called her a "legitimate successor" to James Hardiman, who had written a major history of Galway in 1820.[132]

Admiration from her scholarly peers was less forthcoming. *Old Galway* was among the first books by an Irish female historian to be reviewed in *IHS*, established in 1938. O'Sullivan would appear to have been less of an outsider in the academic, male-centered world of the Irish Historical Society than other Irish women historians at this time. She was an academic historian who used primary sources critically and accepted the ethos of detachment and objectivity. Nevertheless, as Mary O'Dowd asserts, the English medievalist H.G. Richardson, in *IHS*, wrote "a highly critical, and in many ways unfair, assessment ... [making] use of the review to demonstrate his superior knowledge of the history of medieval Galway."[133] Richardson believed that discussions of Galway's European context hindered considerations of the town's unique features: "if all town histories were written on this plan, they would have a great deal in common."[134] Unlike O'Sullivan, he maintained that the evidence showed the Reformation had made some progress in Galway. He believed that her discussion of early modern Galway was stronger, though not flawless. In his conclusion, Richardson asserted that the book's flaws would not "trouble the general reader, who will find the book lively, entertaining, and enthusiastic and will take the author's learning on trust."[135] While he made a number of scholarly criticisms, it is also possible that as an academic historian writing constitutional medieval history for a small audience, Richardson was suspicious of readable books such as *Old Galway* that would reach a wider audience, perhaps viewing these books as less serious. Ironically, he also seemed to misread O'Sullivan as a grievance-oriented nationalist who exaggerated and dramatized English atrocities.[136]

O'Sullivan approached her second book with enthusiasm in the mid-1940s. She was fascinated by her research on the Italian merchant bankers in medieval Ireland, and believed she would make a real contribution to scholarship.[137] The book was not published until 1962, four years before her death. The Italian merchant bankers may have appealed to her because, like the Normans, they represented wealth and elite culture. In addition, their presence in the country demonstrated Irish contacts with the wider European world. O'Sullivan also thought it was important to address social and economic history, since few Irish medievalists focused on these subfields.[138] Her short second book received a more positive review in *IHS* than her first. Trinity historian Jocelyn Otway-Ruthven declared that *Italian Merchant Bankers* was "more than welcome as a pioneering contribution in the almost untouched field of medieval Irish economic history."[139]

O'Sullivan died on July 21, 1966.[140] A woman whose social and political outlook was shaped in the years prior to the First World War, she lived to witness the fiftieth anniversary of the Easter Rising. She did not feel always feel at home in post-1922 Ireland, particularly after Fianna Fail assumed power, and antagonized Irish nationalists by openly expressing her less than popular political views. Her Irish identity was informed by an attachment to traditionally loyal Galway, where she spent her life, and her scholarly engagement with Galway was lifelong. The only female Irish academic historian to combine marriage and a career during the Free State years, her considerable accomplishments included writing two books and numerous articles, editing a journal, mentoring graduate students, and popularizing historical knowledge through the Galway Archaeological and Historical Society.

Sile Ni Chinneide (1901–80)

Sile Ni Chinneide, O'Sullivan's colleague in the UCG history department, was very different from O'Sullivan in terms of background, political outlook, and intellectual interests. Their differences precluded a close collegial relationship; in fact, they barely spoke to each other.[141] Yet, like O'Sullivan, Ni Chinneide believed in a wider role for academic historians. This section discusses her social and educational background, teaching career at UCG, role as a public historian, and her scholarship and its influence. She was significant as an academic woman historian who benefited from the nationalist orientation of the Free State's educational and Irish language policies, and received state recognition.

Sile Ni Chinneide (Sheila Kennedy) was born in Waterford in 1901, the daughter of a doctor. Unlike O'Sullivan, Ni Chinneide was raised in a Catholic family with republican sympathies, rather than pro-British ones. Ni Chinneide, as a committed nationalist, embraced the language movement and became a fluent Irish speaker. She attended University College Cork, receiving a BA in 1923 and an MA in history in 1925 for a thesis on "The Plantation of Ulster," supervised by James Hogan. Thus, she differed from Hayden and O'Sullivan in having an academic background in history. Ni Chinneide was hired by UCG to teach history through the medium of Irish in 1927. A lecturer for nearly forty years, she was promoted to an associate professorship in 1965, and retired in 1970.[142]

Ni Chinneide's career at UCG

Sile Ni Chinneide had an advocate in the Dail in the form of Helena Concannon, Fianna Fail Dail Deputy (TD) and fellow historian and Galway resident. Concannon explained the purpose of the UCG Irish lectureships in the subjects of history, economics, and mathematics. They were created in 1927 "as a definite advance in the policy of Gaelicisation ... to each of these lectureships a salary of four hundred pounds was attached."[143] Later, three more Irish lectureships in Education, Greek, and Latin were added, at an annual salary of 500 pounds, and Concannon urged that the salaries for the first three lectureships be raised. She gave some details about the UCG lecturers, describing Ni Chinneide as "a brilliant woman [who] is engaged on a history of Ireland in Irish, which will fill a claimant need."[144] Concannon appears to have been mistaken about Ni Chinneide writing a history of Ireland. However, in 1947 Ni Chinneide produced a European history textbook for college students, written in Irish, entitled *An tSean-Eoraip*.[145]

Ni Chinneide was an effective and interesting teacher who taught a wider range of courses than Mary Donovan O'Sullivan. She offered classes on Irish and European history from the early Christian period to the modern era. Ni Chinneide's classes emphasized Ireland's connections with Europe, particularly eighteenth-century France. She made an impression on her students by her approach to the French Revolution. A liberal Catholic, she taught the French Revolution in a non-judgmental way, rather than condemning it as anti-Christian, as more conservative educators were inclined to do at this time. She also told students that it would do them no harm to read certain works on the Vatican Index of Forbidden Books, such as those by Voltaire. Some of her students found this intellectually liberating, and felt they were now free to read anything.[146]

Ni Chinneide supervised fewer graduate students than O'Sullivan during the 1930s through the 1950s. It was not until 1953 that her first research student, Maire Immaculata Nic Eoin, received an MA.[147] Most of her students worked on eighteenth-century Irish topics, such as Irish trade with France, as well as biographical studies of figures such as Thomas Russell and Charles O'Conor of Belnagare (some of whose diaries were edited by Ni Chinneide).[148] She was innovative in the 1950s in encouraging topics in economic history; leading academic Irish historians at the time remained dubious about economic and social history, maintaining that sources were scarce.[149]

Ni Chinneide as a public historian

Ni Chinneide sought to communicate historical knowledge to a wider audience outside of academia. She co-edited two journals during the 1950s and 1960s: the *Journal of the Galway Archaeological and Historical Society*, and *Galvia*, a historical journal she helped establish, which featured articles in Irish. She published articles in newspapers and non-academic journals, as well as giving radio broadcasts.[150]

Like her colleague in the UCG history department, Ni Chinneide wrote several political articles in the 1930s. She contributed to the Fianna Fail newspaper, the *Irish Press*, and to *Ireland To-day*, a short-lived liberal journal, rather than conservative British journals.[151] Ni Chinneide's first article for *Ireland To-day*, entitled "The Foundations of Modern Ulster," appeared in 1936. As a republican, she hoped that Partition would soon end and that Ireland would become a nonsectarian, thirty-two county Irish republic. O'Sullivan also opposed Partition, but hoped to end it by strengthening links with the Crown. Ni Chinneide argued that the historical evidence pointed the way to the realization of the ideal of a united Ireland. The Scots settlers in Antrim and Down, she wrote, had united with the Irish in the sixteenth century, and were therefore viewed as a threat by Queen Elizabeth. While Ni Chinneide argued that the seventeenth-century Plantation of Ulster was brutal, unjust to the Irish, and a practical failure, she maintained that not all the planters were corrupt: "religious persecutions [in Scotland] forced quite decent men to take part in this plantation scheme."[152] Ulster Scots Presbyterians and Irish Catholics had both joined the United Irishmen and taken part in the 1798 Rebellion. Therefore, it was not inconceivable that Northern Protestants could once again unite with Irish Catholics and end Partition once and for all. She attributed the continuation of sectarianism in Northern Ireland to a divide and rule strategy of Belfast employers who followed in the footsteps of the nineteenth-century landed ruling elite.[153]

This article, then, revealed the perspective of an optimistic, liberal Irish republican in the 1930s, who believed that sectarianism had been fostered by powerful elites and could therefore be easily overcome, rather than being entrenched in popular consciousness. Her underestimation of the strength of Northern unionist opposition to a united Ireland was widely shared by other republicans at the time and later.

A letter and an article published in *Ireland To-day* in 1937 highlighted Ni Chinneide's strong belief in the revival of the Irish language. She resented that some commentators were urging that compulsory Irish in the schools be scaled back. While she seemed to acknowledge that the language policy had its limitations, she tried to minimize popular resentment towards compulsory Irish. Appealing to recent Irish history, she asserted that Irish political rebels had always disturbed the complacency of the comfortable classes. Ordinary people, however, had supported the political revolution, and would support the nationalists in the language revival, the "most drastic and difficult of all Irish revolutions."[154] In the matter of compulsory Irish, then, she sided with those in power who were enforcing an unpopular policy. In "Our Western Seaboard," she wrote about the poverty in the Connemara Gaeltacht, or Irish-speaking region in the west, and about the historic failure of government schemes to promote viable industries there and stave off emigration. Ni Chinneide argued in support of the government's new migration scheme, whereby poor farming families from Connemara were resettled in the richer lands of English-speaking Meath, forming a "Meath Gaeltacht." The settlers could earn a better living and promote Gaelicization in an anglicized Leinster county, outcomes she maintained were well worth the public funds spent on them.[155]

Ni Chinneide was a public historian in that she served on various government-appointed bodies in the 1950s and 1960s. These included the Department of External [now Foreign] Affairs' Cultural Relations Committee, the Television Commission, and the Bureau of Military History. She was chosen by the Department of External Affairs to attend a Council of Europe conference on universities in Rome in 1953.[156] As a committed nationalist and language lobbyist, she was viewed as a congenial academic by the Fianna Fail government then in power. Ni Chinneide was one of two women on the Television Commission, but not the only academic historian, as T.W. Moody was on the Commission as well.[157] The Military History Bureau collected oral testimony from witnesses to events in the 1916–23 period, demonstrating the participating historians' interest in oral and social history to complement official and limited military and political histories. The Bureau then denied the historians access. Ni Chinneide, like the other academic historians, felt frustrated by the policies of the Military History Bureau, maintaining that "to prevent researchers who lived through any part of the period from working on the material in question is to deprive future historians of a valuable key to the past."[158] In 1954, Ni Chinneide unsuccessfully ran for the Senate as an NUI candidate. Had she been elected, she would have been the third Irish woman historian in the Senate, following Alice Stopford Green and Helena Concannon, who died in 1952.

Her relationship with the Irish historical profession, in contrast to the political sphere, was more problematic. While Ni Chinneide published articles based on archival research and edited journals and eighteenth-century diaries, her major strengths were in teaching and supervising MA students, rather than in the publication of monographs. The only book she wrote was a European history textbook in the Irish language. This was at odds with the standards of the new critical school of Irish history, which valued original research and publication over undergraduate teaching and textbook writing. Given her commitment to the language movement, Ni Chinneide may have felt it was more important for her to write an Irish-language textbook and edit *Galvia* than to publish her thesis on the Plantation of Ulster, or to write a monograph on another one of her major scholarly interests, eighteenth-century French travelers in Ireland. She more closely resembled Constantia Maxwell in her interest in eighteenth-century Irish social and economic history than she did the dominant figures in the modern school of history who stressed administrative and political history. Ni Chinneide was innovative in moving away from Anglocentric histories and placing Ireland in a European framework, by considering Irish–French relations. It was not until the 1970s, 1980s, and 1990s that other Irish academic historians produced major studies of eighteenth-century Ireland and France.[159]

The fact that Ni Chinneide was based in Galway precluded greater involvement in the Irish Historical Society (IHS), the professional body of Irish university-based historians. The IHS was Dublin-based, and dominated by Moody and Edwards in the late 1930s through the 1960s. It would have been difficult for Ni Chinneide to attend, for instance, the monthly meetings of the IHS in 1938–39 and 1939–40, in which academics read papers based on their current research.[160] The IHS was predominantly male, and there were no female committee members of the Irish Committee of Historical Sciences (the national affiliate of the International Committee of Historical Sciences) until 1973.[161] Towards the end of her career, however, Ni Chinneide was appointed to the Advisory Board of the New History of Ireland project.[162]

Ni Chinneide articulated a critique of the prevailing trends in historical scholarship in the late 1950s. She reviewed a book by J.G. Simms of Trinity College on the confiscations of Catholic lands after the war of 1689–91.[163] Simms' study of the legal proceedings led to his conclusion that Catholics were able to retain more of their lands than had been previously thought, and that the Williamite settlement was relatively mild. While Ni Chinneide found much of his book worthwhile, she felt "the apologia is carried a little too far. One cannot help feeling that the book would be read with complete satisfaction by one of the forfeitur trustees, while the reactions of the vanquished claimants would probably be unprintable ... a more balanced picture ... would emerge if material were drawn from the records of the dispossessed as well as those of the confiscators."[164] This foreshadows later critiques made by Irish social historians who have examined "history from below," and who have argued that academic historians have focused too heavily on the records of elites.

In "The Gaelic Contribution to Irish Nationalism," Ni Chinneide wrote that paying attention to Gaelic sources, particularly poetry, enhances understanding of Irish history and offers alternative perspectives. "State-paper historians" had ignored "a valuable source of historical evidence, the only key we hold to the inner life of eighteenth-century Ireland."[165] She was concerned that as professional historians reacted against popular Irish nationalist history, they might move too far in the opposite direction and arrive at erroneous conclusions. Revisionist historians argued, for example, that Irish nationality was a relatively recent development, but Ni Chinneide contended that examining Gaelic sources would reveal a different picture.[166]

Ni Chinneide's activities began to converge with those of her male counterparts towards the latter stages of her career, in the 1950s and early 1960s. Like them, she was a public but not an oppositional historian and intellectual at this point. By the 1950s, male academic historians were developing closer relationships with the state and the media, and were neither dissidents nor polemical defenders of the state. For example, T.W. Moody of Trinity College was a friend of Erskine Childers, who became president of Ireland in 1973. In the early 1950s Childers was the Fianna Fail Minister of Posts and Telegraphs; his department oversaw Radio Eireann and later RTE, the state television service. Moody was appointed a member of the Irish Broadcasting Council in 1953. Like Ni Chinneide, he was also appointed by the government to the Cultural Relations Committee in 1949 and the Television Commission in 1958.[167] Moody and other male academic historians broadcast the "Thomas Davis Lectures," a series of history lectures, on Radio Eireann beginning in 1953.[168] Desmond Williams, professor of Modern History at UCD, edited the *Leader* in the 1950s.[169] Though tensions ultimately emerged when government officials and historians worked together on historical endeavors, the state had sought to reach out to the new academic historians earlier, in the mid-1940s, when Eamon de Valera proposed a collection of essays to mark the centennial of the Famine. Maurice Moynihan, the secretary of the Department of the Taoiseach (de Valera's department), was a friend of R. Dudley Edwards, and worked with the historians on the collection, which was published in 1956.[170]

Sile ni Chinneide died in 1980, ten years after her retirement.[171] She had a complex relationship with the Irish historical profession. As an academic historian, she did not entirely fit in with the new school, as she published only articles based on her archival research, rather than major monographs. She was most effective as a teacher and mentor to research students. Ni Chinneide also held overtly nationalist views and critiqued the direction in which Irish historiography appeared to be moving. Like other women historians, she wrote political as well as historical articles for popular publications in order to reach a wider audience in the 1930s. Ni Chinneide differed from older Irish women historians in that her nationalism coincided with the Irish Free State and the Republic. While her ideal was a united Irish republic, she accepted the Free State and was not a dissident republican. Significantly, she owed her job to a state policy, that of Gaelicization. The government was favorably impressed by Ni Chinneide, and appointed her to various councils dealing with educational and cultural matters. She differed from her younger academic colleagues Jocelyn Otway-Ruthven of Trinity and Maureen Wall of UCD in that both wrote groundbreaking publications and were taken more seriously by the academic historical establishment in Ireland.

Pauline Henley (1883–1973)

Pauline Henley taught history as an assistant lecturer at UCC from 1931 to 1948. She had less of an impact than the other women historians in the NUI system both as a teacher and as a public figure, and little information pertaining to her survives. Henley, however, was important in that she wrote a pioneering interdisciplinary work, *Spenser in Ireland* (1928).

Pauline Henley was born into a Catholic family in Cork in 1883. She attended secondary school at an Ursuline convent in Waterford, and received a BA from UCC in 1913.[172] She was involved in the Gaelic League in Cork, where she met and became friendly with Terence MacSwiney and his sisters.[173] MacSwiney became an IRA leader in Cork, as well as Lord Mayor, and starved himself to death in London's Brixton Prison in 1920. Henley, who had written to MacSwiney in prison, was deeply affected by his death, and saved all of his letters.[174] Despite her friendship networks, Henley supported the Free State rather than the IRA in the 1920s.[175]

Henley worked at Stranmillis Training College in Belfast for several years before returning to Cork to work on an MA in history, which she received in 1926. She taught in the Education Department of UCC in the late 1920s. From 1931 to 1948 she was an assistant lecturer in the history department, mainly teaching first-year students.[176] Her colleagues in the history department in the early 1930s included the Professor, James Hogan, who had supervised her MA, and D.J. Leahy, the lecturer in history through Irish. Leahy was replaced by Seamus

Pender in the late 1930s. When Henley retired in 1948, two other faculty members had joined Hogan and Pender: Denis Gwynn, the Research Professor of Modern Irish History, and Rev. Flanagan, who taught Ecclesiastical History and Palaeography.[177] Two prominent academic historians, Margaret MacCurtain of UCD and John A. Murphy of UCC, were taught by Henley as undergraduates at UCC.[178]

Henley's only publication was *Spenser in Ireland*, a book based on her MA thesis. Her innovative book discussed the political career of English poet Edmund Spenser, who served as secretary to the Lord Deputy of Ireland during the Elizabethan period. Like Alice Stopford Green, Henley raised questions about the English (and Irish unionist) historiography of early modern Ireland. *Spenser in Ireland* confronted mainstream English scholarship on Spenser, and revealed another facet of the revered Elizabethan poet. Henley sought to place Spenser's political ideas in the context of early modern England and Ireland as she described the gulf between Spenser the poet and Spenser the advocate of extreme measures to pacify Ireland.[179] She stated that English admirers of Spenser tended to get defensive when writers with alternative perspectives questioned the tactics Spenser advocated in *A View of the Present State of Ireland*, and that they assumed that the sixteenth-century Irish were as barbaric as Spenser claimed.[180] Henley argued that the Irish were in fact "a brave people [fighting] for their religious liberty and their Gaelic civilization."[181]

Spenser in Ireland was reviewed by the Irish unionist historian Goddard Orpen in a short notice in the *English Historical Review*. He sympathized more with the Elizabethan statesmen in Ireland than with the Irish, and felt that Henley had viewed Spenser and his world "too exclusively through Gaelic spectacles, and no allowance is made for the difficulties of the rulers in carrying out the primary duty of preserving order."[182] However, Orpen thought Henley's discussion of how Spenser's time in Ireland helped shape his poetry was "instructive."[183] Renewed interest in Spenser's Irish context was shown by historians of early modern Ireland and literary scholars in the 1980s and 1990s.[184] Less interest was shown in Henley herself, who was acknowledged as having written a pioneering study in 1928.[185]

Afterword: Maureen Wall (1918–72)

The late 1940s was the last time there would be a significant number of female faculty and graduate students in Irish universities until their numbers increased again in the late 1960s.[186] Maureen MacGeehin Wall was one of the most outstanding female graduate students researching history in the NUI in the late 1940s, and one of the most successful Irish women historians prior to the 1970s.[187] A consideration of her career reveals the possibilities open to talented women trained in the methodology of the Moody–Edwards school in the mid-twentieth century. She was mentored by Robert Dudley Edwards at UCD, and earned an MA at UCD in 1952 for a thesis entitled "The Organisation and Personnel of the Irish Catholic Committee." She wrote pioneering articles on eighteenth-century Irish social and political history, and her reinterpretations of the Penal Laws and of the social and economic position of the eighteenth-century Catholic community were extremely influential.[188] Wall also wrote important revisionist articles on the 1916 Rising, though she was not a twentieth-century specialist.[189] She worked as a research assistant and later as a tutor and lecturer at UCD from the early 1950s until her death in 1972, and was recognized as a gifted, enthusiastic, and committed undergraduate teacher.[190]

Maureen Wall's success as a historian is attributable to her intelligence, perseverance, and confidence, as well as to her position as a protégée of the powerful department chair R. Dudley Edwards. Like Jocelyn Otway-Ruthven of Trinity College, she had "scientific" historical training and conducted innovative historical research, and was taken more seriously by the Irish academic historical establishment than earlier women historians. She did, however, experience discrimination at the hands of the UCD authorities, as she was asked to resign upon her marriage to Tom Wall in 1954. A marriage ban on non-statutory female staff members in the NUI had been in place for years, but Wall refused to resign. Promotions from assistant lecturer to college lecturer and finally to statutory lecturer were slow in coming.[191]

Conclusion

This chapter has sought to analyze the careers of NUI-based women historians within the contexts of the academic world of Irish history and of Irish politics, society, and the state, as well as in comparison with female academic historians in other countries. As academic historians, they supervised and mentored students, identified research topics, and sometimes articulated critiques of historiographical approaches. Of the NUI women historians, O'Sullivan and Ni Chinneide were much more involved in promoting graduate student research than Hayden and Henley, who were primarily undergraduate teachers. Political and social activism informed the lives and scholarship of the NUI women. Overall, nationalist women historians tended to be more politically and socially engaged than the unionists, and in that sense resembled the Irish male academic historians of the 1920s and 1930s who combined an academic career with political engagement, as well as progressive British academic women historians of the interwar era. The academic women's nationalist stances ranged from ex-Redmondite to republican; O'Sullivan was the most critical of the Free State, while Ni Chinneide held the most advanced republican views. Like the women historians of the 1868–1922 period, the NUI women were comfortable taking on the roles of political and social activists and of public, engaged historians.

4
Women Historians at Trinity College, 1922–1949

Several women taught in the Trinity College history department between 1922 and 1949. Constantia Maxwell, Olive Armstrong, and Jocelyn Otway-Ruthven, who had the longest teaching careers, were all Irish Protestants and unionists, as well as Trinity College graduates.[1] With the exception of Maxwell, an eighteenth-century specialist, all were medievalists. Constantia Maxwell's academic career will be given the fullest consideration, as she was the most prolific writer, and because she taught at Trinity during the entire period between 1922 and 1949. The distinguished academic career of Jocelyn Otway-Ruthven lies beyond the scope of this chapter, as most of the important milestones in her career as a writer and academic took place during the 1950s through the 1970s. In addition, her experience in the profession was fundamentally different from the other women historians under consideration.

Constantia Maxwell (1886–1962)

Constantia Maxwell, like Mary Hayden, was a prominent member of the first generation of Irish academic women historians. She was a prolific writer who specialized in eighteenth-century Irish history and a dedicated teacher of undergraduates. Her career is instructive about the challenges faced by the first female professors at Trinity College, an older, more traditional university than the National University of Ireland (NUI). This section discusses Maxwell's career as a teacher and writer, arguing that she was important not as a feminist campaigner and political activist, like her University College Dublin (UCD) counterpart Mary Hayden, but as a prolific and popular historian who reinforced an alternative narrative of Irish history in the Free State. She was an academic who helped pave the way for other women at Trinity College.

Constantia Maxwell was born into a middle-class Protestant and Unionist family in Dublin. Her mother, Elizabeth Maxwell, was originally from England. Her Scottish father, Patrick Maxwell, was a doctor, and her sister Euphran became a doctor as well.[2] Constantia received her secondary education at St. Leonard's, a rigorous, elite girls' school in Scotland founded by feminist educators. She studied modern history at Trinity College from 1904, the year Trinity admitted women, to 1908. She graduated first in her year with a Senior Moderatorship and a gold medal.[3] Maxwell spent a year at Bedford College in London, and returned to Trinity in 1909 as an assistant to Professor Wardell of the History School, becoming the first woman on the university staff. Wardell soon became ill and Maxwell essentially ran the History School on her own until Edmund Curtis joined the faculty in 1914, though she continued to carry a heavy teaching load.[4] In 1939, Maxwell was awarded the Chair in Economic History, becoming the first woman at Trinity to be awarded a chair, and in 1945 was appointed the Lecky Professor of Modern History. She retired from Trinity in 1951 after more than forty years of service.[5] A far more prolific writer than her UCD counterpart Mary Hayden, she dedicated herself to scholarship rather than to political and social activism.

Maxwell's career at Trinity College

Maxwell's career at Trinity spanned the years from 1910 to 1951.[6] Women who taught in other departments at Trinity during Maxwell's time included Eleanor Knott in Celtic Languages, Frances Moran in Law, Meta North in French, Anita Little in Education, Thekla Beere in Statistics, Ruth Duthie in Zoology, and Margaret Dixon in Anatomy. The history department changed significantly in terms of the history curriculum and faculty during Maxwell's tenure. The first meeting of the Special Committee of the School of History and Political Science took place in 1912, and was attended by Maxwell and Professors Weaver, Goligher, Bastable, and Purser. W.A. Phillips and Edmund Curtis joined the faculty in 1914. The minutes note that in 1920, Maxwell's annual salary was raised to 150 pounds, because her teaching load was increased to six lectures a week in modern history, "together with a special course of lectures to Junior Sophister students to be given in the Hilary term each year."[7] The Moderatorship in Modern History and Political Science was restructured in 1922. Students were required to complete papers in six subjects: General Medieval and Modern History, a special period in Modern History, Constitutional History, Political Science, Economic History, and English and Irish History. New books in Irish history were introduced in 1923, including Robert Dunlop's *History of Ireland*, Maxwell's *Irish History From Contemporary Sources*, Edmund Curtis's *History of Medieval Ireland*, Eoin MacNeill's *Phases of Irish History*, and Book IV of Hayden and Moonan's *A Short History*, revealing that books by unionists and nationalists were used. Maxwell's influence was evident in a 1934 decision to include questions in social and economic history, as well as political history, in the entrance examination.[8]

The late 1930s were especially notable for changes in the Trinity College history department that had far-reaching consequences. Maxwell was no longer the only woman in the department, as Margaret Griffith and Olive Armstrong joined the faculty in 1936, and Jocelyn Otway-Ruthven in 1938, the year Margaret Griffith left. T.W. Moody came to Trinity from Queen's University, Belfast in 1939.[9] Moody is significant not only for his role in founding the modern school of Irish history with R.D. Edwards, but also for the major role he played in gradually bringing Trinity out of its unionist isolation into the mainstream of modern Ireland. During the Free State years, unionism was still a force at Trinity, particularly among older professors such as Maxwell,[10] though others were sympathetic to nationalism, such as Edmund Curtis.[11] Maxwell was promoted to a personal Chair in Economic History in 1939. At this time, she also supervised a PhD thesis on eighteenth-century Ireland by R.B. McDowell, who later became a history professor at Trinity and a prolific writer, and a B.Litt. by Brian Osborne on "Social and Economic Aspects of the Irish Famine."[12] Maxwell succeeded Edmund Curtis, who died in 1943, as the Lecky Professor of History in 1945. Maxwell retired in 1951, and Moody's former student F.S.L. Lyons joined the history faculty.[13]

An undergraduate in the late 1930s, May Darlington, took copious notes on Maxwell's lectures, and her notebooks help reconstruct Maxwell's courses and reveal aspects of the professor's personality and outlook. In the 1930s, Maxwell taught classes on European History, 1494–1598 and European History, 1598–1716, both of which incorporated political, religious, cultural, and economic history. The first course focused on Spain and its overseas expansion, sixteenth-century economic developments, and the Reformation, while the second focused on early modern France. Maxwell outlined pragmatic motivations of historical actors and tried to be even-handed. The historical figures and movements she favored included Protestants, enlightened tolerant Catholics, the Renaissance, the Reformation, and the Enlightenment. She also liked rulers who promoted strong government, law enforcement, intellectual life, the creation of wealth, and Enlightenment principles such as religious toleration and civil liberty. Maxwell disliked religious extremism, the excesses of the Counter-Reformation, the extremes of despotism and anarchy, and economic backwardness.[14] A secular Protestant, she lectured that the Reformation had multiple causes, political and intellectual as well as religious. Though she presented Protestantism as more modern and rational than Catholicism, she added that the Reformation did not lead to intellectual freedom and democracy, as it appealed to new authorities, and because Lutheranism and Calvinism stood for political conservatism.[15]

Maxwell was particularly interested in early modern France, the focus of her class on European History from 1598 to 1716. The recommended books included David Ogg's *Europe in the 17th Century*, Willard's *Henry IV*, Armstrong's *French Wars of Religion*, Lavisse's *Sully*, and Baird's *The Huguenots and the Revocation of the Edict of Nantes*. Much attention was devoted to French foreign, economic, and religious policies. Maxwell admired Henry IV, a politique who promoted religious toleration, and the economic minister Colbert. The one instance where she seemed emotionally engaged with the material was in her discussion of the persecution of the Huguenots, or French Calvinists, whom she viewed in much the same way as Mary Hayden regarded the Irish Catholics. Maxwell praised the Huguenots' success in trade and industry, then detailed the atrocities they suffered, which led to their mass exodus from France.[16]

During the 1940s, Maxwell worried about retirement and receiving an adequate pension, and shared these concerns with the Provost of Trinity College. She wrote in 1940 that she hoped to retire after the war, as she was in indifferent health. A pension was important to her, because "at one time [she] had a certain amount of private means, though never enough to keep [her] without working, but these have of late considerably diminished."[17] The Board fixed her pension at 300 pounds a year. Maxwell wrote another letter to the Provost in 1945 to accept the Lecky Chair and to ask if her pension could be raised to 350 pounds, as the cost of living had increased due to the war. She asked the Provost to consider her work record. From 1914 to the 1930s, she wrote, "by far the greater part of the lecturing work fell to my share. To illustrate this I may say that for a great many years I was giving 11 lectures a week to Professor Phillips' 4 and Professor Curtis's 5 or 6."[18] Maxwell asked the Provost to take into consideration the fact "that my salary has always been very small [which would affect the amount of her pension]. This has, I daresay, been largely my own fault, for I have always been reluctant to trouble the Board."[19] She subtly implied that she felt exploited, but had never made demands on the Board by asking for a raise. The Provost agreed to put the matter before the Board and the Salaries Committee, and added that he thought the matter would receive "sympathetic attention."[20]

Maxwell's books and journal articles

Maxwell wrote two history textbooks early in her career, *A School History of Ireland* (1914) and *A Short History of Ireland* (1914). This placed her in the tradition of other female historians who wrote textbooks for schoolchildren.[21] Maxwell, a southern unionist, did not represent a political or ideological threat to the government or the Commissioners of National Education in 1914, unlike children's textbook writer Helena Concannon, and her books were sanctioned for schools prior to the creation of the Free State. The Presbyterian Church gave Maxwell an award for *A School History*, but Catholic educators disliked this primary school textbook. Nevertheless, it was sanctioned as a textbook by the Free State's Department of Education.[22]

Maxwell's *A Short History* is the work of a moderate southern unionist, and can be usefully compared to her UCD counterpart Mary Hayden's textbook, the work of a moderate nationalist. Maxwell's preface stated that she wished to provide "a clear and impartial account of the chief features of Irish history ... [in her] elementary school textbook."[23] While Hayden and Moonan's preface acknowledged that they wrote from a nationalist perspective but sought to be accurate and unprejudiced, Maxwell believed she was objective and non-partisan.[24] Maxwell, like Hayden, concentrated on the political narrative, leaving out women's history and minimizing social and economic history, an understandable approach as she was writing a short book for younger students. Though Maxwell wrote within unionist parameters, just as Hayden wrote within a nationalist framework, she sought to be even-handed. For example, she recounted atrocities committed in wartime by both sides, and stated the grievances of Irish Catholics. Her tone was somewhat different from Hayden's. While Maxwell was also didactic and moralistic, she was less emotive and defensive.

Maxwell's unionist approach to Irish history was reflected in her treatment of early and medieval Ireland. She introduced several key themes that were repeated later in the book, including Ireland's lack of national consciousness and unity, primitiveness, turbulence, and isolation.[25] While nationalist historians believed that Irish national consciousness had existed since the earliest times, Maxwell emphasized fragmentation and disunity. Up until the sixteenth century, "there was no Irish nation, and no central government, but only separate and independent tribes."[26] It was the impact of the Counter-Reformation and shared Catholic grievances that forged a sense of Irish identity.[27] Maxwell maintained that early Irish legal systems, land tenure, architecture, warfare, and agriculture were all very primitive, but she praised metal work and the illumination of manuscripts.[28] Maxwell appeared concerned with strong government, law and order, property rights, trade and industry. Like Goddard Orpen, Maxwell believed that because early Ireland had no strong central government, the laws were unenforceable, and therefore chaos reigned and threatened life and property.[29] She downplayed the extent of early Irish trade and contact with the Continent, asserting that the Norse settlers in Ireland were mainly responsible for trade and cultural interchange with Europe. Maxwell praised Brian Boru, the victor in the Battle of Clontarf in 1014, because she believed he represented strong leadership and law enforcement.[30]

Maxwell wrote that the Irish did not recognize Norman rule as legitimate, but maintained that the Normans improved Ireland by promoting law and order, trade, and progressive agriculture until they were undermined by the machinations of English officialdom and their own "degeneracy," or intermarriage with the native Irish and greater immersion in Irish culture. The result was feudal anarchy, which was not alleviated by the unenforceable Statutes of Kilkenny.[31] Maxwell and Orpen, whose work on the Normans she relied upon, identified with the Normans and English, not the Irish; however, critiquing past English policies on pragmatic grounds was not incompatible with a southern unionist viewpoint.[32]

Maxwell viewed the political and military events of early modern Ireland largely through the prism of England's national security considerations. Like Hayden, she outlined pragmatic political motives that factored into policymaking. Though Maxwell had unionist sympathies, she tried to be fair by acknowledging atrocities committed by English and Irish Protestants, just as the nationalist Hayden had acknowledged atrocities committed by Irish Catholics. For example, Maxwell described the brutal treatment of Protestant settlers in 1641, but added that Catholics were retaliated against in kind. Cromwellian atrocities were condemned, but Maxwell alluded to the fate of the Huguenots, the general barbarity of early modern warfare, and England's national security priorities.[33] Maxwell favored William of Orange and the Protestants in the war of 1689–91, though she condemned the Irish Parliament's repudiation of the relatively generous terms the Treaty of Limerick had offered to Irish Catholics. She then referred to Catholic persecution of Protestants throughout Europe, and asserted that Louis XIV broke treaties.[34]

Maxwell discussed the Penal Laws and the 1798 Rebellion in her section on eighteenth- century Ireland. She criticized the Penal Laws on pragmatic grounds, asserting that they hurt the Irish economy and that the persecuted Catholic Church paradoxically grew in strength.[35] While she admired Enlightenment ideals, she was dismayed by eighteenth-century republicanism and the 1798 Rebellion, as it spiraled out of control. She noted that atrocities were committed by the militia, as well as by the insurgents. While Hayden was defensive about the maligned Irish Catholics, Maxwell sought to defend the eighteenth-century Protestant Ascendancy against stereotypes, a recurring theme in her later books. She wrote that members of the Ascendancy were wealthy and public-spirited; "they did not spend all their time in dueling, drinking, gambling, and cock-fighting, as is often supposed."[36] The Ulster Presbyterians, Maxwell felt, "were more industrious and intelligent than any others in the country."[37]

The final chapter of *A Short History* briefly deals with some events of the nineteenth century. Maxwell praised Daniel O'Connell and his nonviolent activism on behalf of Catholic Emancipation. Her treatment of the Famine differed from that of Hayden and other nationalist historians, as she was completely uncritical of British government policy, emphasized the generosity of the English people and of Irish landlords, and left out emotive descriptions of starvation and evictions.[38] Maxwell was dubious about Home Rule and appeared to favor the constructive unionist policy of diffusing nationalism by addressing socioeconomic grievances and enacting land purchase legislation.[39]

Overall, then, Maxwell's *A Short History* revealed the viewpoint of a moderate southern unionist of the era prior to 1916, and shared certain similarities as well as important differences with Hayden and Moonan's *A Short History*. Maxwell's survey resembled Hayden's in that both concentrate on the political narrative, acknowledged past misdeeds of their confessional community, demonstrated an awareness of pragmatism in policymaking, and shared a tendency to moralize. Maxwell differed from Hayden in her unionist stance; as a unionist, she focused on early Irish primitiveness and isolation, and empathized with England and the Irish Protestant community, while the nationalist Hayden identified with the Irish Catholics. Hayden was defensive about Irish Catholics, while Maxwell was anxious to dispel stereotypes about the Irish Protestant community. Maxwell prioritized strong government, law and order, property, commerce, religious tolerance, and civil liberty. This went hand in hand with her political unionism, since she believed those prerogatives would be safeguarded under British rule. Mary Hayden, a middle-class Catholic nationalist, had similar priorities, but believed they could be upheld by affluent, educated Catholics in a Home Rule Parliament. Maxwell and Hayden both had misgivings about extensive democratization.

During the revolutionary years 1916–23, Maxwell wrote two important articles for historical journals and edited a substantial book of documents, *Irish History From Contemporary Sources, 1509–1610* (1923). "The Colonisation of Ulster," was published months after the 1916 Rising. This article conformed to Maxwell's schema of prioritizing England's national security concerns as they related to Ireland, and criticizing English policy in Ireland, often on pragmatic grounds, while highlighting mitigating factors. She stressed the primitiveness of Irish society, but thought English attempts to reorganize the Irish land system were wrong, as this policy generated discontent and conflict.[40] She outlined the pragmatic reasons behind England's colonization of Ireland in the sixteenth century, stressing strategic and economic concerns rather than ideals or the "civilizing mission" often invoked by British imperialists. Like T.W. Moody, she noted the limitations and failures of the Ulster plantation policy.[41] Maxwell ended this article on a presentist note, writing that "the suppression of Irish culture and the confiscation of the land were not only a gross injustice, but an error which has influenced adversely the subsequent course of Irish history ... Irish problems would more often repay a psychological or economic treatment than a policy of purely political import."[42] She went further than some unionist writers in condemning English policies of the past, though she may have thought it safer and more convincing to criticize on tactical rather than solely moral grounds. "The Plantation of Ulster at the Beginning of James I's Reign" unfolds similarly, but in this article Maxwell offered a more critical analysis of the reports of English officials in Ireland than she usually did, juxtaposing their reports with evidence from the State Papers.[43]

Maxwell was remarkable for writing or editing more than ten books in light of her heavy teaching load. Her two most popular books were *Dublin Under the Georges, 1714–1830* (1936) and *Country and Town in Ireland Under the Georges* (1940),[44] both of which were engaging and readable, and included reproductions of eighteenth-century prints and paintings According to the *Times*, "the justly famous *Dublin Under the Georges*, a pioneer essay in social history ... made her possibly the best-known Irish historian of her generation."[45] Both books focus on the eighteenth-century Irish Protestant elite and stress their contributions to Irish cultural and intellectual life and economic development. Sections on the predominantly Catholic urban and rural poor are included. Maxwell stated that although she wrote from the standpoint of "an admirer of the Age of Reason and in defense of the Anglo-Irish gentry" (revealing a perspective, rather than complete impartiality), she was "naturally aware of the deplorable fact that the civilization of the rich during this period in Ireland as elsewhere was built up on the poverty of the masses."[46]

The two books were innovative in placing social, cultural, and economic history at the forefront, rather than politics. Maxwell's sources included a range of published traveler's accounts, memoirs, letters, economic surveys, and journals from the eighteenth century, whereas the new Irish academic historians of the 1930s favored the use of State Papers and unpublished government documents. While

Maxwell was interested in economic history, she did not engage in a sustained economic analysis. She mainly relied on travelers' accounts and secondary works on economic history by A.E. Murray and George O'Brien for assessments of Irish trade and agriculture.[47]

Mary O'Dowd relates Maxwell's books to the social and economic histories written by women in interwar Britain,[48] but Maxwell's purpose was different. Unlike some of the British women historians, she was not committed to feminism or the peace movement, and did not write social history to undercut military and diplomatic history with their stress on conflict. Instead, Maxwell wrote to rehabilitate the eighteenth-century Protestant landed elite during the Free State era, challenging stereotypes and outlining their contributions to Irish culture. Irish Protestants could then be seen as an integral part of the modern Irish nation, rather than an isolated minority fighting a rearguard action in predominantly Catholic Ireland. She asserted that "for long the Protestant Ascendancy ... has been in bad odour in Ireland, but its cultural heritage is now at last being valued, and will, one sincerely hopes, soon become completely absorbed in the national tradition."[49] Maxwell was not completely uncritical of the eighteenth-century elite, and tried to be fair to the Catholic lower classes, though stereotyping and condescension sometimes characterized her discussion of them. Still, her book was significant in an era when some Irish Protestants felt marginalized due to the Catholic nationalist ethos of the Free State.[50]

Maxwell's two books on eighteenth-century Ireland were reviewed in scholarly journals. *Dublin Under the Georges* was reviewed in *History* and the *English Historical Review* in 1937, and the revised third edition received a "Short Notice" in *Irish Historical Studies* in 1959. Maxwell's friend Dorothy George, an LSE-trained historian who worked at the British Museum, called *Dublin Under the Georges* "one of those rare books of picturesque description which are firmly planted in their historical setting" and "a well-balanced account of the different aspects of the town."[51] An *EHR* reviewer also praised Maxwell's discussion of Dublin's rich and poor, assessing the book as "a fascinating and comprehensive study ... [written] in a learned and exceedingly readable way."[52] The ability to write in an "exceedingly readable way" was an elusive goal for some of the new academic historians whose works also appeared in the late 1930s. For example, T.W. Moody's exhaustive study, *The Londonderry Plantation* (1939), included a "twenty-two page bibliography," and "dullness was the price paid at times for this objectivity," according to Robert Dudley Edwards.[53] J.G. Simms, writing in *IHS*, simply noted the readability of Maxwell's book and its status as the essential book on eighteenth-century Dublin.[54]

Country and Town in Ireland Under the Georges received longer and more mixed reviews. T.W. Moody, Maxwell's new colleague at Trinity, reviewed the book in the *EHR*, rather than *IHS*. Moody thought she produced a balanced assessment of the strengths and flaws of the "Ascendancy," and praised her judicious care in presenting evidence derived from a range of sources. He also wrote that the book was weak on cohesion, synthesis, and analysis of social structures.[55] A writer named "M.B.," reviewing the revised edition of the book in the *Journal of the Galway Archaeological and Historical Society*, was more critical. "M.B." stated that *Country and Town* was a lively narrative written with enthusiasm, which brought eighteenth-century Ireland to life. While it moderated the stereotypes of the Irish elite by presenting cultured and enlightened individuals, throughout the book "exceptions to the rule are given prominence, perhaps unduly in some places."[56] The reviewer added that Maxwell was less strong in analyzing the soundness of the evidence provided by travelers in Ireland, citing the assertion in her preface that "English authorities are usually suspect in Ireland—unjustly, I think, for bias may be discounted."[57] "M.B." felt that Maxwell tried to be impartial in her sections on the peasantry and the Catholic clergy, but thought she was unfamiliar with the Irish sources on these groups. The reviewer concluded that the book was "entertaining and informative," but not a "first-class work on Irish history."[58]

Constantia Maxwell died in Penbury, Kent, England on February 6, 1962. She left a varied legacy. She was the first woman on the Trinity faculty, and the only woman on the history staff until the 1930s. By writing books that conveyed notions of an alternative Irish identity to a wide readership, Maxwell sought to rehabilitate the Irish Protestant community and relocate them within the national tradition. Like Mary Hayden, she was indirectly important as a popular (though not populist), dissonant voice in history that the new professionals felt compelled to write against, though her books were never as harshly criticized as Hayden's book would later be. Maxwell was more detached than Hayden, and wrote from a moderate unionist rather than an Irish nationalist perspective. Nevertheless, she remained outside the new critical school because her social histories were based on printed sources and were weak on structural analysis and hard economic data. However, she was again indirectly influential in that she mapped out new areas of research in Irish history. These include eighteenth-century Irish social, economic, and intellectual history, all of which attracted more researchers from the 1960s onwards. Her reassessment of the eighteenth-century Irish elite was continued by, among others, her student R.B. McDowell and later by S.J. Connolly.[59]

Olive Armstrong (1892–1958)

Olive Armstrong, who was trained as a medievalist, lectured at Trinity from 1934 to 1957, in addition to teaching history at Alexandra College. The daughter of a Church of Ireland clergyman, she was raised in Dublin and attended Alexandra School and College. She graduated from Trinity College in 1913 with a Senior Moderatorship, or Honors BA, in History and Political Science.[60] Armstrong was notable for her involvement in the Dublin University Women Graduates' Association (DUWGA), which she helped establish in 1922. A pressure group affiliated with the Joint Committee of Women's Societies, the DUWGA members joined other Irish women in monitoring legislation affecting women and lobbying the government. The DUWGA was also associated with the Irish Federation of University Women and the International Federation of University Women.[61]

Armstrong's major publication was *Edward Bruce's Invasion of Ireland* (1923), which dealt with fourteenth-century Ireland. In her preface, she stated that people needed to learn moral lessons from history; overall, the tone of the book is didactic and moralistic. History taught "that when men are brave and strive to be just, they prosper, but when they depart from these high standards, they fall into distress and wrong."[62] Armstrong's overview of medieval Ireland was written within a unionist framework, contending, like Goddard Orpen's work, that because Ireland lacked a centralized government, anarchy prevailed and laws were not enforced. Armstrong believed the Normans were superior to the Irish because of their feudal institutions.[63] The invasion by Edward Bruce of Scotland in 1315 devastated much of Ireland and destabilized the loyal Norman colony there, paving the way for Irish uprisings which further diminished the power of the Norman colonists and English institutions in Ireland. Unionist historians viewed the regaining of power and territory by the Irish as a return to anarchy, whereas nationalist historians viewed the Irish resurgence as a positive development. Armstrong concluded the book by placing Ireland in historical context, explaining that the early fourteenth century was a time of major political and social upheaval throughout Western Europe.[64]

Goddard Orpen discussed Armstrong's book in a letter to Edmund Curtis of Trinity College. Both medievalists had helped her with her research, but had mixed feelings about the end result. Orpen wrote that Armstrong had ability, and he admired the way she placed Ireland in perspective by viewing the Bruce invasion as part of a wider unraveling of the medieval order in Europe. Nevertheless, he maintained that "Miss Armstrong has shown a want of discernment, or misconceived her authorities, in her narrative of the invasion," and wondered whether "so slight a work ... is deserving of a degree of LittD."[65] While Armstrong and Orpen both approached medieval history from a unionist perspective, Curtis was an Irish Protestant nationalist who tried to view the Normans and the Irish in dialogue with one another.[66]

Armstrong joined the Trinity College faculty as a lecturer in Political Science in 1934 and taught there until the 1950s. The Political Science faculty worked closely with the School of Modern History, initially called the School of Modern History and Political Science. The texts Armstrong used in her course in the early 1940s included Aristotle's *Politics*, Hobbes' *Leviathan*, Michael Oakeshott's *Social and Political Doctrines of Contemporary Europe*, Marx's *Communist Manifesto*, the Statute of Westminster, and the Constitutions of Eire, France, and the Soviet Union. Armstrong resigned from Trinity due to health reasons in 1957, and died on December 16, 1958.[67]

Armstrong, like Constantia Maxwell, was pro-British and held ambivalent feelings about the Free State and its institutions. Her professional life centered on Anglo-Irish and Protestant institutions, such as Trinity College, Alexandra College, and the Church of Ireland. She was also a member of the politically active alumnae and pressure group, the DUWGA. Armstrong's influence was, in the main, limited to the academic environments in which she spent her life, although as a member of the DUWGA, she was not disengaged from contemporary politics.

Jocelyn Otway-Ruthven (1909–89)

Jocelyn Otway-Ruthven, a medievalist, taught history at Trinity College for over forty years and wrote an important book on medieval Ireland. She was born in Dublin in 1909 into a landed Protestant family whose ancestral home, Castle Otway, was in County Tipperary. Her father, Captain Robert Otway-Ruthven, was killed in the First World War. Her mother, Margaret (Casement) Otway-Ruthven, was related to Roger Casement, who was executed for treason in 1916. Otway-Ruthven attended the Hall School, a Protestant school in Monkstown, Co. Dublin, and studied history at Trinity College with Edmund Curtis. She received a gold medal in history and a research prize upon graduating with a BA in 1931. Otway-Ruthven completed graduate work in medieval history at Girton College, Cambridge under the supervision of Professor Helen Maud Cam, who later became the first female professor at Harvard. In 1937, she received her PhD in history.[68]

Otway-Ruthven's PhD set her apart from other Irish academic women historians in the 1930s and 1940s, and underscored how differently she had been trained from her older female colleagues. Her graduate education in England resembled the experiences of her male contemporaries, the new professional historians R. Dudley Edwards and T.W. Moody, who had both received PhDs from the University of London in the 1930s, as well as Cambridge graduate Desmond Williams of UCD. She differed from many of her female contemporaries in the 1930s and 1940s in that she, like the men in the emerging new historical profession, concentrated on political, administrative, and constitutional history, rather than social and economic history.

Otway-Ruthven began her career as a lecturer in Medieval and Modern History at Trinity in 1938. In the early years of her career her colleagues were Maxwell, Armstrong, Curtis, and T.W. Moody. Though Otway-Ruthven and Moody were close in age and had similar graduate educations, they did not relate well to one another due to differences in personality and outlook. Otway-Ruthven was more traditional and conservative than Moody, who was a moderate Irish nationalist and an academic modernizer.[69] Nevertheless, both were involved in the new Irish Historical Society. Otway-Ruthven was also a fellow of the Royal Historical Society and a member of the Irish

Manuscripts Commission in the 1940s. She supervised only one PhD student in the 1940s, Clara Crawford, whose thesis dealt with "Feudal Tenures in Ireland in the Thirteenth Century."[70] Thus, Otway-Ruthven was not initially as involved as Moody and Edwards in promoting graduate student research. In 1951, when Maxwell retired, Otway-Ruthven became the new Lecky Professor of Modern History. In that year, she also became a member of the Royal Irish Academy. Later highlights in her academic career included becoming the first dean of the Faculty of Arts and the treasurer of the Academic Staff Association.[71] She was one of the first women to be elected a Fellow of Trinity College when Fellowship was opened to women in 1968.[72]

Otway-Ruthven, like Maxwell and Armstrong, was far more dedicated to her career than to social and political activism in the late 1930s and 1940s. Unlike Maxwell, she did not write popular books and articles for non-academic journals that might have shaped or reinforced alternative Irish identities and historical memories in the 1930s through the 1950s. Otway-Ruthven, an erudite scholar and consummate professional, avoided popularizing history. However, she took on the role of a public historian when she joined Edwards and Moody in conducting historical research for the Foyle and Bann Fisheries Case, a High Court case in the 1940s.[73] She also decided early in her career to work for justice and equal treatment for women at Trinity College, who still faced discrimination and exclusion from Fellowship. Her successful three-fold strategy involved demonstrating her worth as a scholar and her loyalty and dedication to Trinity, and persuading others to support change. The status of women at Trinity changed significantly after 1968, when they were admitted to Fellowship.[74]

Otway-Ruthven wrote two important books and numerous scholarly articles based on her archival research. She initially focused on medieval English history. Her first book, *The King's Secretary and the Signet Office in the Fifteenth Century* (1939), was based on her Cambridge PhD thesis. When she returned to Ireland to teach at Trinity, she wrote articles on medieval Ireland and edited manuscripts while continuing to research English and Welsh history. An early article she wrote for *IHS*, "The Native Irish and English Law in Medieval Ireland,"[75] was significant for contextualizing the legal systems and the status of the Irish in the period following the incomplete twelfth-century Norman conquest. Rather than viewing Irish administrative history in isolation, she noted that after the Norman conquests of England and Wales, the common law came into conflict with English and Welsh customary law, as it later would with Irish law. She added that in Ireland, as well as elsewhere in medieval Europe, there were free and unfree classes, and that the latter lacked legal rights.[76]

Otway-Ruthven's major work, *A History of Medieval Ireland* (1968) was widely acclaimed by medievalists as an outstanding scholarly achievement. She produced a history of the Norman colony and its institutions, rather than a history of the interaction of Norman and Gaelic Ireland.[77] Otway-Ruthven's approach to medieval history resembled that of her predecessor Goddard Orpen and contemporaries Olive Armstrong, H.G. Richardson and G.O. Sayles, rather than nationalist historians such as Alice Stopford Green, Eoin MacNeill, and Edmund Curtis, who were interested in medieval Gaelic culture and institutions. Otway-Ruthven's scholarship anticipated later work that placed medieval and early modern Irish history within the framework of the "new British history," with its comparative approach.[78]

In conclusion, then, Jocelyn Otway-Ruthven's historical training and early career set her apart from the other women historians of the 1930s and 1940s. She held a PhD from Cambridge, embraced the new ethos of professionalism as defined by the historical establishment, wrote political and constitutional history, avoided partisan political engagement, and did not to write for a popular readership. She impressed people with her outstanding intellect and strong, powerful personality. James Lydon, Otway-Ruthven's colleague in medieval history at Trinity in the 1960s and 1970s, later remarked that "As an historian, working through record evidence, she was just unbeatable. Her contribution to Irish history at that level will never be surpassed."[79] She was taken seriously as a scholar by male academic historians in mid-twentieth century Ireland. Otway-Ruthven was a transitional figure in that her career anticipates those of women historians who entered academia during and after the social and political changes of the late 1960s. Her successors also entered the university system with graduate training similar to that of their male counterparts, and were better equipped to undertake original scholarship than the women academics of the Free State years.

Conclusion

Constantia Maxwell, Olive Armstrong, and Jocelyn Otway-Ruthven were significant as Irish Protestant and unionist women writing history in an academic context in the period between 1922 and 1949. Maxwell wrote on eighteenth-century Irish social history, and reached a wide audience, while Armstrong and Otway-Ruthven reached academic readerships with their medieval histories. All came from relatively affluent families and attended elite secondary schools, and benefited from the recent opening up of Trinity College to women. Otway-Ruthven was unique in earning a doctorate in history at Cambridge. As women at Trinity College prior to the changes of the 1960s, they faced exclusion and discrimination, but Jocelyn Otway-Ruthven lived to see the changes she had worked to bring about. The women did not feel felt entirely at home in the independent Ireland of the 1930s and 1940s, but still found sources of support within the Protestant and unionist community. Sibling relationships were important to Maxwell, who lived with her sister Euphran, and to Armstrong, who was close to her sister Persis and her brother Claude. Alexandra College was also an important source of community for Armstrong. Maxwell had a circle of academic female friends in England, and was particularly close to Myra Curtis of Newnham College, Cambridge.[80] Jocelyn Otway-Ruthven was mentored by the eminent medievalist Helen Maud Cam, and maintained her friendship networks with other Girton scholars. The Trinity women were not politically engaged to the extent that the NUI women were. For the ex-unionists Maxwell, Armstrong, and Otway-Ruthven, Trinity College provided an academic home among others who shared their ambivalent feelings about independent Ireland.

5
Non-Academic Women Historians, 1922–1949

A substantial number of women who wrote about Irish history did not pursue academic careers in the Free State period. Although most had obtained a university education, they took different career paths as writers, journalists, teachers, archivists, and museum professionals. As writers of innovative works on women's, religious, early modern, and contemporary Irish history, they were significant in demonstrating the diversity of historical scholarship in Ireland, produced in both academic and non-academic contexts, at a time when the Irish historical profession was undergoing modernization and consolidation in the universities. The careers of these women show parallels with those of women historians outside of Ireland in the interwar period in terms of their influences, research interests, and social and political engagement.

Three of the most prominent of the non-academic Irish women historians, Helena Concannon, Dorothy Macardle, and Rosamond Jacob, were active in the nationalist movement that led to the establishment of the Irish Free State in 1922. All three were prominent public figures in Ireland in the 1920s and 1930s, when they wrote their major historical works. Helena Concannon, who held an MA in modern languages, was a politician as well as a prolific writer of women's history, religious history, and textbooks. Dorothy Macardle earned a BA in English from the National University of Ireland (NUI), worked as a teacher and journalist, and wrote plays and fiction as well as *The Irish Republic* (1937), a work of contemporary political history written from a republican perspective. Rosamond Jacob, the only non-academic Irish woman historian of her generation who did not attend university, focused on eighteenth-century Irish political history. Like Macardle, she worked as a journalist and novelist in addition to writing history. Her major historical work was *The Rise of the United Irishmen, 1791–1794* (1937), written from a leftist and republican perspective. All three historians were engaged in some of the crucial political and cultural dialogues of the interwar period. Macardle and Jacob's political and social activism linked them with other female historians of their era, as they were not only nationalists, but also feminists and internationalists who supported social and political organizations with a global scope.

Isabel Grubb, Grace Lawless Lee, and Ada Longfield are significant as trained historians who worked in archives and museums rather than in universities during the 1920s and 1930s. Unlike Concannon, Macardle, and Jacob, these women had not been involved in the independence movement, nor were they active in Free State politics. Their work demonstrates that professionally trained female historians outside of academia made important scholarly contributions to Irish religious and early modern social and economic history. Isabel Grubb, who held an MA in history from the University of London, wrote books and articles on Quaker history and worked as an archivist at the Society of Friends' Historical Library in Dublin. Grace Lawless Lee, who earned a BA in history from Trinity College, wrote *The Huguenot Settlements in Ireland* and worked as a writer and archivist in England for many years. Ada Longfield, who studied history at Trinity College and earned an MA in history from the London School of Economics, wrote *Anglo-Irish Trade in the Sixteenth Century* (1929) and worked as a museum professional until compelled to resign from the National Museum of Ireland due to her marriage.

Helena Concannon, Dorothy Macardle, and Rosamond Jacob

Helena Concannon (1878–1952)

Helena Concannon was unique as a woman historian and politician who wrote women's history and Catholic religious history during the Free State era. Her career was facilitated by the new educational opportunities for women at the turn of the century, as well as by the Irish independence movement and the political enfranchisement of women. Her books, like those of Margaret Cusack, were significant for reinforcing a specifically Catholic Irish nationalist historical narrative, as well as for writing women into that narrative. Concannon's histories were influenced by European Catholic social thought and interwar-era discourses on women, in addition to her Irish nationalism. Her work as a historian and politician shows points of convergence with historians of women, confessional historians, and politically active women in interwar Europe.

Helena Walsh was born in Maghera, Co. Derry on October 28, 1878. She was one of seven children. Her parents, Louis Walsh and Lizzie Donnelly Walsh, owned Walsh's Hotel in Maghera. The Walshes were middle-class Catholics and nationalists, and thus belonged to Ulster's minority community. Helena's father was in the Land League, and her mother was in the Ladies' Land League. Her brother, Louis J. Walsh (1880–1942) became a writer, a member of Sinn Fein, a character in James Joyce's fiction, and a district justice, while another brother became a priest, and a sister became a nun.[1] Helena completed her secondary education at the Loreto Convent in Dublin, where she was awarded prizes and a scholarship to study modern languages. She received a BA with first class honors from the Royal University of Ireland in 1900, and an MA in 1902.[2] Her training in modern languages rather than in history, then, links her with Mary Hayden and Mary Donovan O'Sullivan.

Helena Walsh's outlook was shaped in an early twentieth-century European cultural context, as well as by Irish cultural nationalism. She spent time studying abroad at Continental universities with her friend Mary Macken before completing her MA, gaining exposure to the intellectual life and social thinking of Continental Catholicism, which helped shape her outlook as a historian and politician. She later studied Irish in Dublin with Patrick Pearse under the auspices of the Gaelic League, which reinforced her nationalist commitment.

Helena Walsh was open to combining marriage with an academic career in Dublin. She married Thomas Concannon, a Gaelic League member and National Health Insurance Inspector, in 1906.[3] After her marriage, she successfully applied for the lectureship in Italian at University College Dublin (UCD), but before she could take up the position, the offer was withdrawn and a joint lectureship in Italian and Spanish was given to Maria Degani.[4] Having been denied the opportunity to work in an academic setting, she wrote history at her home in Galway, where she and her husband, who had no children, lived for many years. She wrote over twenty books, including textbooks, women's history, and religious history.[5]

Helena Concannon's life reveals how a woman could be empowered by nationalism and political enfranchisement in twentieth-century Ireland. She began her career as an advanced nationalist opponent of British rule, and became a political insider in the new Irish state after 1922. Concannon supported Eamon de Valera, whom she may have met in the Gaelic League, and the anti-Treaty side during the Civil War. She later joined de Valera's Fianna Fail party. De Valera, assessing Concannon as a valuable asset to Fianna Fail, urged her to run for office as a National University of Ireland candidate. He believed that having a devoutly Catholic, popular writer of hagiographical historical works in his new party would enhance Fianna Fail's image in the eyes of the Catholic Church, and generate support from the clergy.[6] As a TD and Senator, Concannon supported the Free State and its institutions against the IRA, although, as a Catholic nationalist from what became Northern Ireland, she strongly opposed Partition.

Concannon's books and journalism

Concannon produced Irish history textbooks for schoolchildren and wrote on women's and religious history, gaining notoriety in the era before independence and considerable praise and renown from the 1920s onwards. She wrote in a popular style and reached a wide readership in Free State Ireland. Concannon was significant as the only Irish women historian of her era to substantially contribute to the field of women's history, and her work is important for showing the state of Irish women's history at the time as well as the presentist concerns that animated Concannon's writing on Irish women of the past. Her career as a historian of women invites comparisons with other women's historians outside of Ireland, and her Catholic religious histories show links with both Irish and European traditions of confessional historiography. Her histories tended to reinforce certain constructions of ideal womanhood as well as an Irish identity in which Catholicism was a central component.

Concannon's historical textbooks for schoolchildren included *Makers of Irish History* (1918) and *Irish History for Junior Grade Classes, 1460–1660: Defence of Our Gaelic Civilization* (1921). Both reflected Concannon's strong Catholic nationalist beliefs. In *Makers of Irish History*, Concannon lauded famous leaders such as Brian Boru, who defeated the Norsemen in 1014, and the Volunteers of the late eighteenth century. Her book ended with an enthusiastic account of

Daniel O'Connell and Catholic Emancipation.[7] *Makers of Irish History* was denounced by William Starkie, the Commissioner of National Education in the era immediately preceding Independence. He complained in his diary that it "[gave] colour to Sinn Fein principles ... I can't understand how these publishers can think we can sanction such books."[8] Nationalist history books were regarded with suspicion during the First World War, particularly after the 1916 Rising.

Irish History for Junior Grade Classes frightened the authorities more, and was banned in the tense days of the War of Independence, or Anglo-Irish War, only to be revived in the Free State era. In this textbook, Concannon maintained that the Irish had historically been a "fit race" and the women of Ireland "fit mates of such men, and fit mothers of a numerous progeny of soldier sons."[9] She justified Irish armed resistance to English and Protestant rule by citing a 1580 statement by Pope Gregory XIII.[10] A major lesson from her study of early modern Ireland was that the Flight of the Earls after the Elizabethan wars was a mistake; Ireland should always keep its soldiers at home.[11] Her textbooks later attracted criticism from scholars researching the teaching of Irish history. One writer, for example, called them "blatantly ahistorical" and characterized by a "fulsome and emotional" style.[12] Concannon's textbooks illustrated Gabriel Doherty's assessment that "the dominant theme of history teaching in Ireland was the belief in an inner spirituality of the Irish people, demonstrated by their abiding fidelity to the twin ideals of Catholicism and political freedom."[13]

Concannon was unique in that she wrote several books on Irish women's history during the interwar period, including *Women of '98* (1919), *Daughters of Banba* (1922), *The Poor Clares in Ireland* (1929), and *Irish Nuns in Penal Days* (1931).[14] She carried on an older tradition of Irish women writing biographies of famous women and nuns, whose lives could be shaped to meet nationalist or religious priorities,[15] but she also shared research interests with American, Norwegian, Danish, and British women, who were more likely to write on women's history than Irish women. A number of the Scandinavian and British historians of women were feminists, while Concannon, a conservative Catholic, was ambivalent about feminism. Concannon's *Women of '98* (1919) related to historian Ragna Nielsen's *Norwegian Women in the 19th Century* (1904) in that both works addressed the role of women in nationalist movements in Ireland and Norway respectively, and also shared similarities with works by American women historians on well-known women of the colonial and revolutionary periods. Her religious histories focusing on nuns, though based on substantial research, reflected the priorities of Catholic confessional historiography in Ireland and elsewhere, and resembled earlier hagiographical works on Irish nuns written by women. They stood in contrast to the critical, archives-based histories of convents and religious women by academically trained British women historians who wrote on nuns from the late nineteenth century through the interwar period.[16]

Women of '98 shared many of the conventions of the nationalist women's histories produced in Europe and the United States during the late nineteenth and early twentieth centuries, in which the lives of supportive women associated with male revolutionaries were celebrated. Concannon's book, like other works in this genre, reflected present-day concerns about the role of women in the nation. She wrote *Women of '98* to inspire and sustain nationalist women during the War of Independence with the ideal of republican womanhood, and urged them to emulate Irish women who had sacrificed their men in a previous struggle for Irish independence.[17]

Written in a melodramatic style, *Women of '98* featured biographical sketches of the mothers, wives, sisters, and lovers of famous men in the 1798 Rebellion. The women tended to be idealized as beautiful, saintly, and self-sacrificing. Overall, *Women of '98* was heavily prescriptive. For example, Concannon stated that "a nation is what its women make its men" and proceeded to describe Mrs. Teeling as an ideal "mother of '98" for "exercising the sweet and lovely rule of the mistress of a Catholic home, training her children to the noblest ideals of life and conduct, [and] directing her servants with gentle authority."[18] She added, in a presentist mode, that if "the era of persecution is to open again-ah! then it is that Ireland will need her Mary Teelings to stand by their husbands' side while 'they suffer persecution for justice's sake'."[19] Descriptions such as these underscore the centrality of the ideal of the republican mother and wife for Concannon. While she did not oppose women's suffrage, and realized that some women would remain single and work outside the home, she felt that the future of her ideal Irish republic depended on at-home, Catholic nationalist mothers raising virtuous future citizens. She later attributed "success for the long fight we have had for our faith and nationality ... to Irish mothers and Irish homes,"[20] although some women had in fact ventured outside their homes in the struggle for Irish independence. The book was a success, and went through several editions.

Concannon's *Women of '98* shared some of the ambiguities of other women-centered histories written in the nineteenth and early-twentieth centuries. Several of the nineteenth-century British women historians were conservative, yet their works could be read as promoting an expanded role for women in historiography and in contemporary society. These historians found a niche in "picturesque" or romantic history, where they first established the significance of previously sidelined women in the national narrative. Rosemary Mitchell notes that these women writers "stressed the domestic virtues and benign social influence of their subjects," in relation to "home and family, but also – and more ambiguously – to the semi-public spheres of moral and religious issues, and social and cultural developments." The term "influence" rather than "power" was frequently deployed, "with its implications of unobtrusive persuasion."[21] Julie des Jardins writes that feminine histories by nineteenth-century American women "reveal the growing inclination of women to present their contributions to national progress as distinct from yet equal to those of remarkable men."[22] The domestic, maternal role of women was stressed for its wider political implications for the nation. A "dutiful mother did more than act as an agent of moral progress; she directed the path of a heroic man and thus changed the course of national history."[23] Twentieth-century women historians writing in a more explicitly feminist mode stressed women's individual agency and contrasted the status of women in the past and in the present, sometimes arguing that women had more power in the past. Nationalist women historians emphasized the powerful role they believed had been played by women in societies as diverse as Celtic Ireland, Norway during the Viking era, or ancient Greece.[24] Concannon belonged more to the early tradition of writing women-centered history with an emphasis on women's domestic virtues, but this could be mobilized for political ends in Ireland during the revolutionary period.

A review of *Women of '98* in the *Irish Citizen*, a feminist journal, demonstrates that newer, feminist-oriented conceptual frameworks about how to write women's history could coexist alongside older traditions of women's history in early twentieth-century Ireland. The reviewer, a feminist as well as a nationalist, welcomed a women-focused study of the 1798 Rebellion. She praised Concannon's research and contribution to social history, but objected to the emotional, sentimental style and to some of the conventions, particularly the emphasis on the subjects' conventional femininity and attractiveness. "The words 'sweet,' 'tender,' and 'lovely,' are a trifle overworked, and we hear too much about feminine beauty and charm ... [readers may doubt] whether they can all have been such charming and exceptional women," the reviewer wrote. She singled out a description of two of the heroines "shedding the bright influence of their beauty over the circle of patriotic and romantic young Irishmen" planning the rebellion, and asked readers to consider how ludicrous it would sound if a historian wrote of male beauty influencing patriotic Irishwomen. The reviewer concluded by asserting that "we can make allowance for some excess of enthusiasm about feminine sex-charm in the writings of male authors," but that this was less justifiable coming from women.[25]

Daughters of Banba was also heavily prescriptive and shot through with melodrama. It described various groups of women throughout Irish history, including women in Irish legends; female saints; early modern women of the aristocracy, bourgeoisie, and peasantry; and women exiled from Ireland. Here she was innovative, as it was less common to write about more ordinary groups of women as opposed to "women worthies."[26] Concannon stated that she wanted to write a women-centered history of Ireland; national histories, she maintained, tend to leave out the female population, and are therefore incomplete.[27] *Daughters of Banba* reinforced the presence of women in Irish history while promoting Concannon's ideal of the role of women in the Free State. Concannon asked the reader to reflect upon what Irish women suffered during "the tremendous struggle, and then let us resolve to make them the only return they desire – to be faithful, even as they were faithful."[28] If contemporary Irish women were to reject ideals such as piety, nationalism, and self-sacrifice, they would, it seemed, blaspheme the memory of their foremothers. Concannon believed women should help create an Ireland devoted to "Faith and Fatherland," and that the lives of historic Irish women could serve as exemplary motivational tools. She described an idealized family life in the past to provide historical models for an influential role for modern women in the domestic sphere, where their influence as republican and Catholic mothers had important implications for the future of the Irish nation.[29]

Helena Concannon's books on nuns, such as *The Poor Clares in Ireland* (1929) and *Irish Nuns in Penal Days* (1931), were also significant contributions to women's history in the Free State era. As noted, her works on religious women, though based on substantial research, were hagiographical rather than critical, and can be located in the tradition of Catholic confessional historiography. Other Irish female writers in the nineteenth and early twentieth centuries had written biographies of nuns, such as Catherine McCauley, the founder of the Sisters of Mercy, for hagiographical and didactic purposes as well.[30] Concannon, then, sought to glorify the Catholic Church, which grew in institutional strength during the Free State years, in addition to highlighting the contributions of nuns to Irish and Catholic history. Besides Catholic devotional writers, there were also university-educated, secular, feminist British women historians who wrote on female religious orders in this period. Concannon's works on nuns differed greatly from her British contemporary Eileen Power's *Medieval English Nunneries* (1921), which critically analyzed convents from the perspective of social and institutional history.[31] Concannon's books highlighted the spiritual resistance, tenacity, and courage of the Irish nuns in the face of religious persecution spearheaded by English Protestant authorities. These books also sold well, as religious history and devotional works were popular in the Free State era.[32]

Concannon's emotional writing style can be located within a wider literary context. Literary scholars, examining the device of sentimentality in relation to women poets and novelists, have offered insights that could be applied to Concannon. Jane Tompkins observes that charges of sentimentality have helped exclude popular women writers from the canon of "serious" literature, (or, in Concannon's case, "serious" historical scholarship). She proposes an alternative reading of sentimental literary works; rather than failed attempts to meet the requirements of the canon, they could be viewed as "political enterprise[s], halfway between sermon and social theory, that both codif[y] and attempt to mold the values of their time."[33] Sentimental literature may serve to humanize, speak for, and affirm the lived experience of those who have been oppressed and marginalized. The device of sentimentality "enabled [Irish writer Katherine] Tynan to express her indignation over Ireland's plight."[34] The same could be said of Concannon, whose writing style contrasted dramatically with the tone of other, professional Irish historians, facetiously described by one critic as "suavely hard-boiled and emotionally anesthetized."[35] One of her major concerns in her books was to portray the Irish Catholic women as righteous, worthy, completely innocent victims of oppression who in no way deserved their fate. This stands in contrast to unionist historians of her generation, who identified more with the early modern English ruling elite than with their historic subordinates. She resembled Mary Agnes Hickson and Margaret Cusack in terms of her emphasis on the moral superiority of the victims from the confessional community with which she empathized.

Concannon's books tended not to be reviewed in mainstream, serious historical journals, such as the *English Historical Review, History*, and later *Irish Historical Studies*, but rather in scholarly religious journals and popular devotional periodicals. Her engagement with the new, Moody–Edwards school of history was limited, although she did have friends teaching in Irish universities. Concannon's books on Irish women's history received some glowing reviews in religious journals. A reviewer of *Women of '98* wrote that "there was need of a woman's pen to do justice to many forgotten women ... Mrs. Concannon has done a great work in rescuing their memory from oblivion, and passing it on to other men and women as a torch pointing the way to noble deeds."[36] The reviewer, G. Pierse, hoped that Concannon or another author would write a similar book on "the noble women of the present eventful period of our history."[37] Pierse particularly liked the book's "lovely, fascinating, and pathetic" descriptions of the domestic lives of famous figures of 1798.[38]

Concannon wrote a great deal of journalism. Her articles on women, history, religion, social issues, and charity appeared in many popular magazines. Her journalism, like her books, often revealed a conservative religious outlook that paradoxically argued for enhancing the status of women. This was not for feminist or emancipationist reasons, but to promote republican motherhood and her ideal of a Catholic Ireland with "pure" family life, religious devotion, and austerity – a vision she shared with Eamon de Valera and many social commentators of the era. By using the vocabulary of conservative Catholicism, she urged a wider social and political role for women while avoiding the enmity that secular, liberal feminists aroused when they advocated similar projects.[39] Her articles on women and charity indicated an understanding and approval of the relationship between charity and social control.[40]

Concannon was in dialogue with the major trends in European women's politics during the 1920s and 1930s, particularly the ideology of "maternalism." Historians have identified maternalist politics, which helped lay the groundwork for the welfare state, as a central concern of European women activists in the 1920s and 1930s. Proponents of maternalist politics, not all of whom were feminists, promoted social welfare measures for women and children, such as mother's allowances and health benefits. Notable maternalist movements developed in Western Europe, the United States and Australia.[41] The ideology of maternalism, Koven and Michel contend, focused on the domestic role of women "while simultaneously legitimating women's public relationships to politics and the state ... maternalist ideologies, while evoking traditional images of womanliness, implicitly challenged the boundaries between public and private, women and men, state and civil society."[42] Concannon promoted the ideal of female domesticity while supporting the extension of social welfare measures in Ireland, and therefore helped facilitate the emergence of the welfare state in Ireland. The political and social priorities of maternalism also related to Concannon's engagement with the currents of interwar-era Catholic social thought.

Concannon's political career

Helena Concannon, encouraged by Eamon de Valera, successfully campaigned for a seat in the Dail as a Fianna Fail candidate for the National University of Ireland in 1933. Concannon served in the Dail from 1933 to 1937, and in the Senate from 1938 until her death in 1952. She was the second Irish female historian to become a Senator, after Alice Stopford Green.[43] Concannon was one of three female Dail Deputies (TDs) in the 153-seat Dail between 1933 and 1937, and one of the few female elected representatives in a European Parliament during the interwar period. The other female TDs were Bridget Redmond of Fine Gael and Margaret Mary Pearse of Fianna Fail, both of whom credited their elections to their membership in famous political families. Concannon, in contrast, facilitated her political career through her own activism and by writing histories that supported Irish nationalism, like her predecessor Alice Stopford Green.

Concannon countered criticisms of Fianna Fail and justified the party's policies by frequent appeals to religion and Irish history. Her role as a politician is significant because it played off her role as a historian; in her books and in political discourse, she promoted the same constructs of womanhood, nationalism, religion, and Irish identity. She brought her specific understanding of women's history to policymaking, demonstrating an interplay between women's history and women and legislation. Her political choices, like her historical writings, were influenced by her specifically Catholic Irish nationalism.

The major Dail debates in which Concannon participated dealt with the universities, women's issues, social welfare, and the Constitution. She often began speeches by announcing, "I speak as a woman," thereby fashioning herself as a spokesperson for other women.[44] She resembled politically active feminists in that she was middle class, educated, and had a housekeeper, which enabled her to pursue a career outside the home.[45] Feminists, however, were vilified as self-appointed and unrepresentative by political and clerical power brokers when they spoke on behalf of women, and she was not.[46]

Concannon's views on women were outlined in a lengthy speech urging more funding for rural domestic economy schools. There was considerable overlap between her advocacy of domestic womanhood in her books and in her political speeches. Concannon idealized rural life and farming families, and believed that farmers' wives had an important role to play in building up the self-sufficient, pastoral Ireland that she and others, such as Eamon de Valera, promoted. She maintained that the solution to Ireland's problems was to "make a course of six months [in a domestic economy school] compulsory on all Irish girls before they would be allowed to marry. Then we could look forward cheerfully to the future of the country."[47] She added that the schools would teach girls cooking, dairying, and poultry-rearing, and train them as nurses and maids.

Concannon's recommendations, like her books, reflected a limited view of the majority of Irish women, as she elevated domestic training schemes over other educational schemes that could lead to alternative forms of employment. She may not have believed female domesticity was natural and instinctive, since women apparently needed experts to teach them the domestic role. In common with other elite commentators, both feminist and non-feminist, she believed that lower class women were incompetent homemakers who needed to be taught the right methods.[48] Concannon found that her ideas were sometimes disregarded; her belief in mandatory domestic training for young women was not taken seriously by the government.[49]

One of the last debates Concannon intervened in during her term as a TD concerned the 1937 Constitution, the brainchild of Eamon de Valera. This was a more republican and Catholic-oriented document than the 1922 Free State Constitution, and was part of the process of moving Ireland towards full national sovereignty through political means.[50] The Constitution also reflected contemporary Catholic social teaching on women and the family. Article 41.2.1–2 declared that "... the State recognizes that by her life within the home, woman gives to the State a support without which the common good cannot be achieved ... the State shall, therefore, endeavour to ensure that mothers shall not be obliged by economic necessity to engage in labour to the neglect of their duties in the home."[51] This article reflected the ideal of republican motherhood, since it discursively limited female citizenship in the public sphere, and defined a woman's primary civic responsibility as service to her family (i.e. raising future citizens), which benefited the State.[52]

Feminists, including Concannon's constituents and fellow members of the Women Graduates' Association, led by Mary Hayden, protested the clauses on women, and urged voters to reject the Constitution. Concannon, however, wholeheartedly embraced the Constitution. Women activists argued that Articles 40 and 41 could be used to legitimize further discrimination against working women, and that the Constitution did not spell out social welfare benefits, such as family allowances or universal health insurance that would make outside work unnecessary for poor mothers. (Article 40 gave the state the power to enact legislation with "due regard to the differences of capacity, physical and moral, and of social function").[53] Concannon supported the Constitution because of its republican and Catholic ethos. She also wanted to promote social legislation, such as public assistance and children's allowances,[54] which would enable poor mothers to avoid having to seek outside employment "to the neglect of their duties in the home." She denied that the Constitution intended to restrict women's rights, and maintained that she would protest if she thought it did.[55] The Constitution was ratified, although feminists successfully managed to have certain controversial articles omitted from the document.[56]

Concannon gave a number of Senate speeches that illuminated her intellectual and religious priorities, as well as her views on women and nationalism. She played a notable role during the 1945 Senate debates on censorship. Maintaining that suggestive literature was unhealthy and led to chaos, which could overwhelm and destroy a well-regulated state, she supported draconian censorship legislation. Most of the other Irish women historians at the time, in contrast, were critical of censorship, especially Dorothy Macardle and Rosamond Jacob. Concannon enthusiastically praised the men on the Censorship Board who read and banned questionable books, adding, "of course no woman would undertake that revolting task."[57] Modern intellectuals, in her view, defined classic literary works as those calculated to offend morality; she was pleased, therefore, that Ireland banned many "classics". She denounced Senator Kingsmill Moore for criticizing censorship when the Board "performed the thankless task, the revolting task, of reading the sordid stuff that some people tell us is classical."[58] Her intervention in this debate underscored that she was an anti-libertarian republican who believed that individual rights could be sharply curtailed if they appeared to threaten the community.[59]

The final years of Concannon's political career were marked by disappointments as well as triumphs, particularly in relation to women and nationalism. She had forcefully advocated social welfare legislation to help women and families, arguably her most important political contribution. Such legislation was enacted by the 1940s, but Concannon still had reservations about the domestic abilities of Irish women. In a speech on the Social Welfare Bill, 1948, she declared, "Above all, we must train our women to run their homes properly, to rear their children properly, and to cook their food properly. These are the things we must aim at."[60] This suggests that she was disappointed with the women of Ireland, as well as with her colleagues in the government. After all her years of advocacy on behalf of domestic training, it seems they still had not embraced the message. Later that year, she expressed mixed feelings about the Republic of Ireland Bill. Appealing to history, she wondered aloud what "the men of '98, the men of '48, or the men of '16 would have given to be assured that this day would come" and added that it proved they had not suffered and died in vain.[61] She welcomed ending the External Relations Act. However, she added that Ireland should not "rejoice prematurely ... we have not got independence, as long as six of our counties are under the British crown ... our prayer ... must be for an Ireland free, Gaelic, and undivided."[62]

Helena Concannon died on February 27, 1952, leaving a mixed legacy. Having started out as a cultural and political outsider, she gained access to power through her work as a popular nationalist historian and activist, and became part of the Free State establishment. She sometimes played an "enforcer" role, supporting anti-libertarian measures, such as censorship. She had a mixed record on women; while she helped the material condition of some by promoting social legislation, she alienated others by idealizing traditionalist models of womanhood that many could not live up to (and that she, as a childless married woman with a career, did not live up to). Despite the limitations inherent in her work, Helena Concannon should be recognized for her crucial contributions to Irish women's history in the first half of the twentieth century.

Dorothy Macardle (1889–1958)

Dorothy Macardle was one of the most famous and successful Irish historians of her generation. Her monumental work of contemporary history, *The Irish Republic*, narrated the memory and meaning of the Irish revolution from a republican perspective. In addition to history, she wrote short stories, plays, novels, and drama criticism. Macardle was also well known in Ireland as a feminist and as a political and social activist. A republican activist during the War of Independence and the Civil War, she supported the Fianna Fail party from the 1920s onwards, sharing her friend Eamon de Valera's goal of using the political process to achieve an independent Irish republic. Her political vision extended far beyond Ireland, as she supported the goals of the League of Nations and later the United Nations. Her political and social engagement, liberal Irish nationalism, and internationalism shaped her writing and linked her with women historians in Ireland and in Europe. Her work can therefore be viewed in both an Irish and an interwar-era European context.

Dorothy Macardle was born in Dundalk, Co. Louth on March 7, 1889. Her father, Sir Thomas Callan Macardle, was a wealthy businessman and the chairman of the Dundalk brewery, Macardle, Moore & Co. Ltd. Minnie Lucy (Ross) Macardle, Dorothy's mother, was the daughter of a British army officer and had grown up in England. Dorothy's father was Catholic, and a Home Ruler rather than a republican, while her mother appears to have converted from Anglicanism to Catholicism when she married. Dorothy, the eldest of five children, had three brothers and one sister.[63] She was educated at Alexandra College, a predominantly Protestant girls' school in Dublin. Macardle earned an Honors BA in English at UCD in 1912, and a teaching diploma in 1914.[64] Between 1918 and 1922, she wrote plays, articles, stories, and poetry in addition to teaching English at Alexandra College, living near the College in her friend Maud Gonne MacBride's house on St. Stephen's Green.[65] One of the few Irish women historians to reject her family's political affiliation, she was drawn to republicanism in this period through friendships with political radicals in Dublin.[66]

During the War of Independence (1919–21), Macardle supported the republican cause as a publicist associated with the Sinn Fein Department of Publicity.[67] In the course of publicizing the Black and Tans' treatment of Irish civilians, Macardle met the prominent republican journalists Frank Gallagher, later editor of the *Irish Press* and a life-long friend, and Erskine Childers, who would be executed by Free State soldiers during the Civil War. The Sinn Fein publicists managed to convey their alternative accounts of the war to the European and American media, thereby discomfiting the British government.[68] Macardle also worked on the Management Committee of the Irish White Cross, a republican-oriented human rights and relief organization. She went on fact-finding tours with other women involved in the organization, such as Maud Gonne MacBride and Charlotte Despard.[69]

Macardle supported Eamon de Valera and the IRA rather than the Free State during the Civil War of 1922–23. She continued her work as a propagandist, writing for the republican journal *Eire*, and worked with Maud Gonne MacBride in the Women Prisoners' Defence League, which protested the treatment of IRA prisoners by the Free State forces. Macardle herself was arrested in a raid on Sinn Fein headquarters in November 1922, and was imprisoned in Mountjoy and later in Kilmainham.[70] She shared a prison cell in Mountjoy with Rosamond Jacob, a writer who later became her flatmate. She taught history for the first time at Kilmainham, where fellow prisoner Lily

O'Brennan found her class on "Revolutionary Irish History" illuminating.[71] After her release in May 1923, she turned to full-time writing and journalism, having lost her teaching position at Alexandra College. She enthusiastically supported de Valera's decision to enter constitutional politics in 1926, and became a member of the Fianna Fail party executive. She also served as Fianna Fail Director of Publicity for several months.[72] During the late 1920s and early 1930s, Macardle wrote plays and worked as a journalist for the *Nation* and the *Irish Press*, in addition to researching and writing *The Irish Republic*.

Macardle, like many progressive European women historians during the 1920s and 1930s, was an internationalist as well as a nationalist. Like the British historian Eileen Power, she strongly supported the League of Nations during the 1930s, hoping it could promote women's rights and solve international disputes peacefully. Macardle had the opportunity to cover sessions of the League of Nations in Geneva in 1935, when Eamon de Valera was presiding.[73] She wrote about the Abyssinian crisis[74] as well as women's issues in her reports on the League of Nations for the *Irish Press*.[75] Her articles demonstrate her belief in a liberal internationalism, and her hope that conflicts could be resolved through diplomatic means. An international body like the League of Nations, she believed, could also redress injustices such as unequal nationality laws for women, a contentious issue for feminists at the time.

The Irish Republic (1937)

The Irish Republic, one of the most popular Irish histories ever written, made Dorothy Macardle one of the most famous and influential Irish historians of her generation. Her monumental political history of Ireland from 1916 to 1923 constructed and transmitted a coherent and influential republican interpretation of the Irish revolution to a wide audience, and was mobilized for its political usefulness by Eamon de Valera and his republican-oriented Fianna Fail party from the 1930s to the 1960s. Macardle's book was significant as a work of contemporary political history written by a woman historian in the 1930s, as well as for the political uses for which it was pressed into service.

The Irish Republic needs to be located within the "history wars" that raged in Ireland in the 1920s and 1930s. During the 1920s, the Free State, pro-Treaty partisans then in power clearly had the upper hand in these propaganda battles. With skilled polemicists and a sympathetic media, they were in a prime position to put forth their view of the Treaty and the Civil War, to the detriment of the republican faction. This began to change in the 1930s when Fianna Fail was in power. Frank Pakenham's *Peace By Ordeal*, published in 1935, interpreted the 1921 Anglo-Irish Treaty negotiations in a manner more favorable to de Valera and the opponents of the Treaty.[76]

Eamon de Valera was the prime mover in the making of *The Irish Republic*. He longed for a documents-based history of revolutionary Ireland that situated him at the center of the narrative, validated the republican perspective, and effectively counteracted the opposition.[77] He turned to Macardle, who as a republican journalist had much experience in refuting hostile anti-republican polemics and propaganda. While *The Irish Republic* was politically motivated, Eunan O'Halpin contends that "the shrouding of essentially political works with the coverings of scholarship was then the fashion among de Valera's and republicanism's critics ... her compendious work can hardly be judged any more partisan or loosely argued than, for example, the Trinity historian [W.A.] Phillips's *The Revolution in Ireland*, a southern unionist lament on the passing of the old Dublin Castle order."[78]

Macardle agreed with de Valera that it was critical to promote the republican understanding of contemporary Irish history to the wider public to counteract the British and pro-Treaty historical narratives in which they were vilified. Republicans, she believed, were not only the underdogs in the revolution, but in historiography and in the media as well. "Journalists and fiction writers and ... historians more or less hostile to Ireland," she wrote, had "present[ed] a ... somewhat incredible picture in which a small band of terrorists domineers over the Irish populace and holds the British Empire at bay." The time had come for "an account of the Irish Republican struggle from the viewpoint of an Irish Republican."[79] Despite Macardle's insistence that de Valera left her alone to write her history as she saw fit, the evidence points to a considerable amount of intervention on de Valera's part.[80]

The Irish Republic began with a traditional republican overview of history, and went on to examine the 1916 Rising, the War of Independence (1919–21), and the Civil War (1922–23) from a republican perspective. Macardle established the republican tradition with the 1798 Rising, and traced this tradition through to the early twentieth century. The Irish Republican Brotherhood inherited the revolutionary tradition, which coexisted with constitutional politics during the nineteenth and twentieth centuries. Macardle emphasized the democratic and nonsectarian dimension of Irish republicanism, as well as the role of Protestants in the nationalist movement.[81] She received help with this chapter from Rosamond Jacob.[82] Macardle's treatment of Irish participation in the First World War is interesting in light of later perceptions that Irish republicans sought to minimize and silence the history of the Great War while inflating the popularity of the 1916 Rising. She noted that Irishmen joined up for different reasons,[83] and stressed that revolutionary republicans were a minority at the time of the Rising. The executions of the leaders of the Rising, however, changed public opinion and generated greater sympathy for the insurgents and hostility towards the British authorities.[84]

Macardle emphasized the republicans' democratic credentials. She stressed that Sinn Fein had won the 1918 elections, and therefore had a popular mandate for its actions. Republican candidates for the Dail had also been successful in the May 1921 elections, again confirming widespread republican and anti-Partition sentiment among the Irish electorate.[85] Irish representatives had tried to gain admittance to the Paris Peace Conference in 1919, demonstrating their commitment to conflict resolution through diplomacy, but did not gain a hearing, underscoring the limitations of Woodrow Wilson's rhetoric about freedom for small nations.[86] The British government, the unionists, and the Free Staters were undemocratic, Macardle argued, in contrast to the Irish republicans. While the republicans addressed British security concerns and suggested guarantees by the British Commonwealth of Nations, Britain threatened to renew the war if the 1921 Treaty, which allowed for dominion status rather than independence, was not accepted.[87] The Republicans upheld the elected Dail, which the Free Staters destroyed.[88] Overall, then, Macardle did her utmost to marshal arguments emphasizing the democratic credentials of the republicans and the antidemocratic nature of their opponents.

Other themes touched on by Macardle include the roles of women, labor, sectarianism, and the Catholic Church. She mentioned the role of women in the 1916 Rising, the War of Independence, the White Cross, and the Civil War, during which she and other republican women were imprisoned.[89] The Irish labor movement met with Macardle's approval when it helped advance nationalist goals. Although she was not a socialist, she admired James Connolly and Constance Markiewicz, who were key figures in the creation of the

Irish Citizen Army, which fought in 1916. She highlighted Irish republican opposition to sectarian divisions from the 1790s onwards.[90] While Macardle emphasized the suffering of ordinary Irish people at the hands of the Black and Tans, as well as the sectarian violence and expulsion suffered by Belfast Catholics at the hands of their Protestant neighbors,[91] she also denounced the sectarian killings of ten Protestant men in Cork in April 1922, arguing that they violated republican principles.[92] The Catholic Church as an institution was not presented in an especially favorable light. As a republican, Macardle resented the Church hierarchy for favoring the Treaty and the Free State side in the Civil War. In December 1921, she wrote, "Christmas sermons became pro-Treaty sermons in more places than one."[93]

The account of the Civil War in *The Irish Republic* was more controversial in Ireland than the account of the War of Independence, as it was the Civil War rather than the earlier conflict that shaped Irish party politics from the 1920s onwards. The Fine Gael party traced its origins back to the Free State supporters who accepted the 1921 Anglo-Irish Treaty, while Fianna Fail originated with the anti-Treaty republicans who formed a new party in 1926 to advance their republican agenda in the Dail. In Macardle's narrative, instances of Free State violence, such as the executions of republican prisoners and the Ballyseedy Cross incident,[94] received much attention, while republican violence was downplayed. The republicans, particularly de Valera, were presented as deeply principled, doing their utmost to prevent conflict until driven to fight by the provocations of the Free Staters, and, subsequently, trying to find a peaceful resolution to the Civil War.[95] The book ended with a discussion of the steps made towards the creation of a sovereign republic since Eamon de Valera and Fianna Fail came to power.[96]

The Irish Republic was widely reviewed in Irish newspapers and journals at the time, and was also noticed in Britain, where it was originally published by Victor Gollancz.[97] The lengthiest review appeared in the Fianna Fail newspaper, the *Irish Press*, in March 1937. The reviewer complimented Macardle's narrative style and ability to tell a captivating story, while simultaneously presenting a detailed analysis in a rigorous fashion. She was commended for her strategy of citing British and other non-republican sources, which supported her case far more convincingly than a complete reliance on partisan republican sources.[98] While the reviewer held republican sympathies and admired de Valera, "E.A." also pointed out omissions and elisions reflective of Macardle's own partisanship. Macardle discussed the Civil War "without mentioning some of the worst acts of Republicans ... [she] is overkind in dealing with republican excesses."[99] To support this contention, "E.A." posited that if Free State troops rather than republicans had been responsible for the death of Free State Deputy Sean McGarry's child, Macardle would have treated the matter differently.[100] On the whole, however, "E.A." believed *The Irish Republic* to be an admirably well-researched, engaging, accurate, and thorough account of contemporary Irish history.

A sarcastic review appeared at the same time in the *Irish Independent*, a paper favored by Fine Gael supporters. During the Civil War, their sympathies had been with the Free Staters, collectively presented in a negative light in *The Irish Republic*. While writers who shared Macardle's politics had argued that historical works could be written from a republican perspective and still be taken seriously as history, the *Irish Independent* reviewer, who was anti-republican and hostile to de Valera, doubted that *The Irish Republic* was truly a work of history. "If only," the reviewer lamented, "Miss Macardle's view-point was not so constantly forced upon with Mr. de Valera's infallibility ... not even proclaimed but taken for granted ... in the background." The reviewer referred to various transgressions by the IRA before and after the outbreak of the Civil War in June 1922, and implied that Macardle was a hero-worshipper, noting that "the book closes fittingly with a gushing tribute to 'the quiet tenacity of de Valera's leadership.' "[101]

Macardle as a historian occupied an ambiguous space in the realm of Irish historiography at a time when major innovations were taking place in the discipline. She could be located in the Irish tradition of the journalist-historian involved in politics, as well as in the tradition of politically active nationalist women historians. She had much in common with Alice Stopford Green, who like Macardle struggled to overturn orthodox contentions about Irish history, and her contemporaries Helena Concannon, a Fianna Fail senator and historian, and Rosamond Jacob, who combined writing with social and political engagement. She also resembled an earlier academic historian, W.A. Phillips of Trinity College, who wrote a partisan work on the Irish revolution from a unionist perspective.[102] Macardle was helped by other women historians, such as Mary Hayden, who did not share

Macardle's republican outlook, and Rosamond Jacob, who did. Her attainment of state recognition for her work, and her close ties to the government, contradict the truism that historians who gained access to state power from the nineteenth through mid-twentieth centuries tended to be *male* writers of elite political histories that bolstered state power.[103] In a wider European perspective, there were other politically committed women historians in countries with independence movements, and in ones with radical nationalist regimes, who also wrote contemporary history. It was an especially popular choice for nationalist women historians in Italy. Women may have been drawn to contemporary history because it was a new subfield, lacking in academic prestige and less likely to be guarded by intellectual gatekeepers in the academy.[104]

Irish Historical Studies, the journal of the new academic Irish historians, was founded in 1938. It disallowed articles on contemporary history, which it defined as events that had taken place within the preceding fifty years.[105] Thus, journalists, non-academic historians, and university historians of an older school, rather than the new professionals, tended to write contemporary history. Many academic historians were interested in recent Irish history, though, and Macardle's work did reach them. R.D. Edwards wrote a positive assessment of *The Irish Republic* in a discussion of several recent works, contending that "Miss Macardle has performed a very great service for her subject."[106]

Macardle continued her social and political engagement and her writing in the two decades following the publication of her major work. She was an outspoken opponent of the 1937 Constitution due to its clauses on women. She wholeheartedly supported the Allies during the Second World War because of her strong opposition to fascism. During the 1940s and early 1950s, she wrote four novels and another non-fiction work. After the Second World War, she transferred her former support for the League of Nations to the United Nations and its humanitarian, social, and cultural sections. She acted on her humanitarian, internationalist ideals by writing her second work of contemporary history, *Children of Europe* (1949), an account of the plight of children during and after the war based on her own investigative journalism. An early and significant contribution to the social history of the Second World War and the Holocaust, the book augmented standard military histories of the war, and had much in common with *The Children's Century* (1948), a book by the feminist and internationalist Norwegian historian, Mimi Sverdrup Lunden, which also dealt with the plight of children traumatized by their wartime experiences.[107] During the 1950s, Macardle was active in the Irish Association of Civil Liberties, which fought censorship.

Dorothy Macardle died on December 23, 1958. References to Macardle appeared from time to time in historical works in the decades after her death. As the political implications of Irish historiography increasingly attracted the attention of historians during the crisis years in Northern Ireland, Macardle's well-known republican history was sometimes singled out for negative scrutiny. She was famously assessed as the "hagiographer royal to the Republic."[108] However, ten years later, historian Eunan O'Halpin contextualized *The Irish Republic* by noting that its political partisanship was no more egregious than works on contemporary Irish history written by non-republican writers in the 1920s and 1930s. He maintained that Macardle was a highly competent researcher who was careful about documentation. Moreover, the book represented the constitutional republicanism of the Fianna Fail government, not the dissident republicanism of those who refused to recognize the Irish Free State.[109]

Macardle's work is of lasting historical significance. *The Irish Republic* represents the political stance and understanding of history prevailing among Irish republicans who had joined Fianna Fail and who had consolidated their hold on state power by the late 1930s.[110] Emerging at a time when Eamon de Valera was consolidating his vision of an independent Ireland, it became a foundational text of the republic, transforming a marginal, alternative republican history into an orthodox, state-sanctioned national narrative. Overall, Macardle, who resembled other interwar-era women historians in Europe in her political and social engagement in a national and international context, substantially contributed to the field of contemporary history, a research area then sidelined by the new professional historians in Ireland.

Rosamond Jacob (1888–1960)

Rosamond Jacob's interest in Irish history began when she was very young. In early 1903, the fourteen-year-old committed nationalist wore a button bearing the likenesses of Irish nationalist leaders Wolfe Tone, Robert Emmet, and Charles Stewart Parnell to school.

This did not go over well with the more unionist-minded students at the Protestant girls' school she attended. When one girl grabbed Rosamond's button, Rosamond chased her and got it back. This led to a political debate about Irish nationalism with other unionist classmates, whom Rosamond, a future historian, considered somewhat lacking in historical knowledge. "We had a good deal of argument," Rosamond recorded in her diary. "They said that rebels never succeeded, and they actually denied that the Americans were rebels in 1776!"[111]

Rosamond Jacob was significant as a historian of eighteenth-century Ireland during the Free State period. Her major work, *The Rise of the United Irishmen, 1791–4* (1937), departed from older conventions of writing about the United Irishmen and Ireland in the 1790s, and reflected her secular, leftist republican politics. Like Dorothy Macardle, she also worked as a novelist and journalist, and was involved in the nationalist movement and in feminist politics. Her politics had an international dimension, as she played a leading role in the Irish branch of the Women's International League for Peace and Freedom (WILPF) in the Free State period, and networked with like-minded women when she attended women's conferences throughout Europe.

Rosamond Jacob was born in Waterford on October 13, 1888. She came from a middle-class and nationalist Quaker family long established in Ireland. An ancestor, Richard Jacob, had moved to Cork from southern England in the late 1600s after joining the Society of Friends. Many of his descendants became prominent in business, especially William Beale Jacob, who in the 1850s established W. & R. Jacob and Company, which produced biscuits.[112] Rosamond's father, Louis Jacob (originally from Clonmel, Co. Tipperary) worked at a family-owned estate agency, and her mother, Waterford native Henrietta Harvey Jacob, was actively involved in various political and social causes. Rosamond's older brother, Thomas Harvey Jacob, became a nationalist activist and head of the agency. Rosamond was educated at home by governesses, except for one year at Newtown, a Quaker school, prior to attending a Protestant girls' secondary school in Waterford.[113] She did not attend university, but furthered her education at the School of Art in Dublin.[114]

Rosamond Jacob, like Helena Concannon, was immersed in Irish nationalism from an early age, though their backgrounds were very different. The progressive, social justice-oriented Jacobs were not formally religious, but they had a strong Quaker social identity. They were pacifists and republicans, believing in the ideal of a democratic Irish republic achieved through peaceful means. Jacob's father was highly critical of British imperialism.[115] These characteristics set them apart from many other Irish Protestants, including Quakers, though there was also a republican tradition within the Society of Friends in Ireland.[116] Jacob's political and intellectual formation owed much to her family and to her own reading. As a child, she read pamphlets on Irish leaders and episodes in history, such as *Robert Emmet: the Story of His Life and Death*, *Rescue of the Military Fenians*, and the *Life of John Mitchel*.[117] As an adolescent, she read standard Irish histories and memoirs, such as Wolfe Tone's *Autobiography*.[118] She demonstrated an interest in international politics at a young age when she followed the Boer War and came out in favor of the Boers, like other Irish nationalists at the time.[119]

Jacob began her lifelong association with Irish nationalism and feminism as a young woman in Waterford, joining the Gaelic League and Sinn Fein with her brother Tom in 1906 and the Irish Women's Franchise League (IWFL) several years later. Sinn Fein appealed to Jacob because it was more radical than John Redmond's Irish Parliamentary Party. The IWFL, founded by Hanna Sheehy Skeffington and Margaret Cousins in 1908, sought to emulate Emmeline Pankhurst's militant Women's Social and Political Union (WSPU) in England, and reflected frustration with the limitations of the constitutional feminist groups.[120] As a republican, Jacob disliked the fact that mainstream Irish feminists petitioned Parliament for the vote, rather than contest the legitimacy of British rule in Ireland. Jacob was a pacifist opponent of the First World War and disrupted Redmond's war recruitment efforts.[121] A major feminist victory for Jacob occurred in 1917, when, as a Waterford delegate to the Sinn Fein Convention, she pressured other delegates to agree that women in an independent Ireland would be enfranchised; Arthur Griffith, Sinn Fein's founder, gave her his personal assurance.[122]

Jacob, like Concannon and Macardle, sympathized with the republican cause in the War of Independence and the Civil War, and opposed the Treaty. However, she did not glorify violence and wished that an Irish republic could be achieved through nonviolent mass noncooperation, much like Gandhi's movement in India.[123] Jacob joined a group of other women who tried to prevent the Civil War in

June 1922 by negotiating with the Free State forces and the IRA, but to no avail.[124] She was arrested in a raid on her friend Hanna Sheehy Skeffington's house, and spent a month in Mountjoy Prison, sharing a cell with Dorothy Macardle. Jacob resigned from Sinn Fein in 1926, since by then she supported Eamon de Valera's plan to enter constitutional politics in order to reform the government and undo the Oath of Allegiance to the Crown.[125] She had a problematic relationship with Fianna Fail in the 1930s, and became associated with a left-wing republican circle centered on the journal *An Phoblacht*, edited first by Peader O'Donnell and then by Frank Ryan.[126]

During the 1920s and early 1930s, Jacob was the secretary of the Irish section of the WILPF. The WILPF, founded in 1919, had evolved from a women's peace conference at the Hague during the First World War, and during the interwar era focused on disarmament and international cooperation.[127] Jacob was an internationalist as well as a nationalist, and emphasized the importance of feminist solidarity around the globe. She attended WILPF congresses in Vienna in 1921, Dublin in 1926, and Prague in 1929.[128] Other European feminist historians besides Jacob were involved in international women's organizations between the 1920s and the 1940s, such as the Norwegian historians Anna Caspari Agerholt and Mimi Sverdrup Lunden, who were affiliated with the International Council of Women and the leftist Democratic Women's World Organization respectively.[129]

Jacob was active in leftist politics as well as feminism in the 1930s. She became interested in Soviet Communism because she had always admired leftist figures in Irish nationalism, such as Michael Davitt, James Larkin, and especially James Connolly, whose politics had all incorporated a social and economic critique.[130] As a secular feminist who believed in social and economic justice, Jacob had become disillusioned with aspects of the Free State, such as the political power of the Catholic Church, gender inequality, and continuing unemployment and poverty. To discover if the USSR had a different record on these issues, she visited the country in the spring of 1931 as a journalist under the auspices of the Friends of the Soviet Union (FOSU). While she was taken in by some aspects of the Soviet Union, she also commented critically on the scarcity of women in the highest echelons of government.[131] Her receptiveness to Soviet propaganda in the 1930s seemed to stem from wishful thinking-she hoped that somewhere there existed a country characterized by secularism, gender equality, and an equitable distribution of wealth. However, she remained an independent leftist, rather than joining the Irish Communist Party.[132] She supported numerous campaigns between the 1930s and the 1950s, including Indian independence, international disarmament, opposition to capital punishment, and the feminist campaign against the 1937 Constitution.[133] During the 1940s, she continued her feminist activism through the WILPF and the Women's Social and Progressive League,[134] and in the 1950s joined CND (the Campaign for Nuclear Disarmament) and the Irish Association of Civil Liberties, headed by her friend Dorothy Macardle. She was also a member of the Irish Women Writers' Club, of which Macardle was also the founder and president.[135]

The Rise of the United Irishmen, 1791–4

Jacob's major historical work was *The Rise of the United Irishmen* (1937). It was a significant contribution to the historiography of the United Irishmen and eighteenth-century Irish political history, as it represented a departure from the leading interpretations of eighteenth-century Ireland current in the Free State period. Some Anglo-Irish Protestants, such as W.E.H. Lecky, idealized the aristocratic late eighteenth-century Irish Parliament, and valorized the Parliamentary leader Henry Grattan, rather than the more democratic United Irishmen. Catholic nationalist historians found the secular republicanism of the United Irishmen problematic, and downplayed the United Irishmen while promoting a narrative of the 1798 Rebellion featuring "heroic priest leaders and a goaded but morally pure peasantry ... under attack solely because of their religious persuasion."[136]

In the 1930s, the Catholic nationalist narrative of the United Irishmen and the 1798 Rebellion, a narrative which originated in the nineteenth century, was widely promoted in Ireland. Some of Wolfe Tone's nationalist biographers in the 1920s and 1930s were unable to fully accept the non-Catholic Tone as an Irish hero, while an exceptionally hostile Catholic nationalist biographer, Leo McCabe, vilified Tone as an "infidel."[137] The liberal republican writer, Sean O'Faolain, was more sympathetic to Tone, and edited *The Autobiography of Wolfe Tone* in 1937, the same year in which McCabe's and Jacob's books were published.

Jacob wrote her book from a leftist, secular republican perspective. She described the reformist phase of the Society of the United

Irishmen, from their formation in 1791 until their suppression by the British government in 1794. They consequently reorganized as a secret society and planned the 1798 Rebellion. Jacob focused on the society's republican political thought, constitutional agitation for the reform of Parliament, nonsectarianism, and solidarity with republican groups in other countries in the late eighteenth century. Jacob's heroes are the United Irishmen, especially Wolfe Tone and Thomas Russell, rather than Henry Grattan or heroic priests. The United Irishmen were mainly middle-class Irish Protestants and liberal Catholics who attacked aristocratic privilege and favored the emancipation and enfranchisement of Catholics. Jacob wrote that they were originally peaceful reformers, rather than advocates of an armed uprising against Britain to secure an independent, democratic, secular Irish republic. The significance of this book's appearance in Ireland in 1937 was that it seemed designed to show Irish people the roots of their nation's republican tradition. As Damian Doyle notes, Jacob's "focus on the past was an attempt to illuminate the faults and misdeeds of the present."[138] Liberals and leftists like Jacob were dismayed by the power of the Catholic Church and restrictions on civil liberties in the Free State. Thus, Jacob sought to show that the original Irish republicans were secular, liberal, democratic, and nonsectarian.

Though Jacob's book is more of a conventional history than the works of Concannon and Macardle, it did not entirely conform to academic conventions. *The Rise of the United Irishmen* was intended for the general reader, and Jacob acknowledged her lack of experience in researching and writing history. She relied heavily on older secondary sources, such as R.R. Madden's *The United Irishmen: Their Lives and Times*, John Mitchel's *History of Ireland*, and W.E.H. Lecky's *A History of Ireland in the Eighteenth Century*. She also examined published works such as Wolfe Tone's autobiography, letters and memoirs, and the *Northern Star*, a radical Belfast newspaper begun in 1792 by the United Irishmen, and suppressed in 1797. Her book, then, is both a synthesis and a work of interpretation. Jacob was also explicit in her admiration for the United Irishmen and their ideals and objectives. Like Concannon and Macardle, she was highly critical of the British government and of loyalists. Jacob did not glorify the violence of either side, but thought disparities in power should be taken into account when discussing the atrocities committed by the Irish rebels and the militia and yeomanry. While loyalist writers tended to focus on rebel atrocities and downplay the treatment of Irish civilians in 1798, Jacob discussed the violence against civilians committed by General Lake's forces. Many civilians were tortured, for instance, in an effort to extract information about the United Irishmen. Jacob attributed outrages by the rebels to a breakdown in discipline,[139] anticipating an assessment reached by late twentieth-century historians.[140]

Jacob's leftist and feminist stances permeated *The Rise of the United Irishmen*. She cited James Connolly's *Labour in Ireland* when explaining class issues in eighteenth-century Ireland, and condemned the Anglo-Irish aristocracy for their treatment of the peasantry.[141] In her discussion of the 1791 *Declaration and Resolutions of the Society of the United Irishmen*, she contended that while this document is admirable, it "takes it for granted, in perfect good faith, that there is but one sex in humanity, and that male. The idea that women were human beings, with human rights, had then occurred to scarcely anyone except Mary Wollstonecraft and Thomas Paine."[142] Her emphasis on the "international brotherhood" of eighteenth-century republicans is comparable to her own internationalism and solidarity with progressives around the world.

While Jacob related to Constantia Maxwell, Sile ni Chinneide, and Helena Concannon as a historian of eighteenth-century Ireland, comparisons could also be drawn with American female historians who wrote on colonial America and the Revolutionary War. Jacob met Maxwell in 1937, and they discussed eighteenth-century history and publishing houses. Jacob was not entirely sympathetic to Maxwell's approach to eighteenth-century Irish history, as Maxwell admired the Anglo-Irish aristocracy and placed them at the center of the narrative. She wrote in her diary that Maxwell was working on a "new book on garrison 'country houses.' "[143] Sile ni Chinneide, as a liberal republican interested in eighteenth-century history, had more in common with Jacob, but did not publish monographs on eighteenth-century Ireland. Jacob was aware of Concannon, but was critical of her sentimental approach to women's history. In a wider context, Jacob shared an interest in eighteenth-century history with some American women historians, such as Alice Morse Earle, who wrote on the colonial and revolutionary periods. These historians, who wrote between the 1890s and 1930s, tended to be far more conservative than Jacob, and did not invoke the eighteenth century to legitimize present-day progressive aspirations. Many of them had strong anti-immigrant views and idealized preindustrial, eighteenth-century America as a simple, virtuous society "devoid of non-whites, non-Protestants, and the social tensions they were thought to have brought to modern American life."[144]

Jacob's book was reviewed in popular journals as well as academic ones. A nationalist reviewer in the *Irish Book Lover* lauded *The Rise of the United Irishmen* and its author. While some academic historians were disdainful of popular women historians who were openly sympathetic to non-elite groups, "R.H." called Jacob's book "a welcome corrective to Lecky's classic." Lecky was an admirer of Henry Grattan and the elite Irish Parliament. The reviewer added that "while she writes with a wide sympathy and understanding that are lacking in Lecky's pages, she shows throughout at the same time the balance and impartial outlook of the true historian."[145]

The Rise of the United Irishmen was also reviewed by Robert Dudley Edwards. He was teaching at Carysfort Training College in 1937, but would begin his long career at UCD the following year. Edwards found some aspects of the book praiseworthy, such as Jacob's willingness to question Lecky's assessment of Ireland in the 1790s. In other respects Edwards was more ambivalent. He maintained that a critical analysis of archival manuscripts would be too challenging for a non-professional historian who had not received "scientific training."[146] He believed that by criticizing the shortcomings of 1790s Ireland, Jacob demonstrated her inability to view historical actors and events in their "proper historical perspective."[147]

After completing *The Rise of the United Irishmen*, Jacob worked on a serious biography of Matilda Tone, Wolfe Tone's wife whom she believed should be recovered and inserted into the historical record. She could not find a publisher, and transformed the work into a novel, which was finally published in 1957.[148] Jacob brought a feminist sensibility towards women's history to her biography, presenting Matilda Tone as a strong, courageous, independent woman, and an equal partner in her marriage. Her work anticipated late-twentieth century approaches to eighteenth-century Irish women's history, which recovered the lives and contributions of women using a range of sources.[149]

Rosamond Jacob died on October 11, 1960. Of the three historians, her work was closest to academic history. She was important as a historian of the eighteenth century whose interpretation of the revolutionary period diverged from the more widespred Catholic nationalist interpretation, and as an innovative writer of Irish women's history who challenged earlier conventions of writing about famous Irish women of the past. She also was notable for her feminist activism and political and social engagement in Ireland and in an international context. Like Macardle, she was empowered by feminism, internationalism and her involvement in the Irish nationalist movement, although she was critical of aspects of the intellectual and political culture of the Irish Free State.

Conclusion

Helena Concannon, Dorothy Macardle, and Rosamond Jacob combined social and political engagement with writing significant works of religious, women's, eighteenth-century, and contemporary history. The three non-academic historians embraced different nationalist narratives. Concannon was a conservative Catholic, Macardle was a liberal republican from a mixed religious background, and Jacob, who came from a Waterford Quaker family, was a leftist republican and an agnostic. They were important as popular non-academic historians who reached a wide readership in an era when the Irish historical profession was undergoing modernization.

Their careers are important because they shed light on the interplay between gender, politics, and historiography in Ireland during this period of post-revolutionary consolidation. Moreover, the careers of these three women complicate aspects of the paradigm of Western women historians because of the relationship between their historical writing and their engagement with national politics.[150] Concannon became a Fianna Fail TD and later a Senator largely *because* she wrote popular, politicized women's and religious history. Macardle and Jacob, who helped found the Fianna Fail party, wrote on Irish political history. Thus, in the early years of Irish independence and state consolidation, a few politically active women wrote histories supportive of Irish nationalism, thereby assuming a greater public and political role. However, Macardle and Jacob were not uncritical supporters of the nationalist establishment; in the 1930s they resumed the critical role they had played as suffragists and republicans prior to Irish independence. Even Concannon, a conservative Catholic nationalist who appeared to be a pillar of the Free State establishment, experienced some disillusionment and disappointments.

Other non-academic women historians

Isabel Grubb, Grace Lawless Lee, and Ada Longfield were university-trained Irish historians who worked in libraries, historical societies, and museums, rather than in universities. They were less public and politically engaged than the other non-academic women historians in the Free State period, but wrote significant works on religious and early modern history, demonstrating that professional history was produced by Irish historians operating in intellectual contexts outside of Irish universities during the late 1920s and 1930s. Similarly, there were professionally trained women historians elsewhere in Europe, including in France and the Scandinavian countries, who worked outside of universities. Amateur women historians in the nineteenth century had played important roles as editors of archival documents and as research assistants to scholars; in the twentieth century, the management of archives and material culture became increasingly professionalized, and Grubb, Lee, and Longfield were part of that process.

These three historians had much in common. They came from affluent Protestant families in the southern part of Ireland; Grubb was a Quaker from Tipperary, while Lee and Longfield were members of the Church of Ireland from Cork. Grubb and Lee were both drawn to historical research through their fathers, who were interested in Irish antiquities. Lee and Longfield studied history at Trinity College as undergraduates, while Grubb earned a BA and MA in history at the University of London. Longfield received an MA in history at the London School of Economics; like Grubb, she had a female professor who mentored her. The three historians were interested in new approaches to social and economic history, though their topics were different. Grubb wrote on Quaker history, Lee specialized in Huguenot history, and Longfield focused on early modern trade between Ireland and England.

Isabel Grubb (1881–1972)

Isabel Grubb was important for her research on Quaker history, for her work as an archivist in the Society of Friends Historical Library, and for the role she played in the Irish and international Quaker community. As a university-trained historian, she bridged the divide between confessional Quaker history and new approaches to documents-based social and economic history. Her work can be located within the context of the growth of Quaker history since the late nineteenth century,[151] as well as in the context of interwar-era social and economic history. She related to Quaker women historians from Ireland and Britain, such as Rosamond Jacob and Alice Clark, who also combined historical scholarship with social engagement, and to the network of female historians and their students at the University of London. Lastly, her work as an archivist links her with women archivists in Europe and the United States, some of whom created women's archives in the 1930s.

Isabel Grubb was born in Carrick-on-Suir, Co. Tipperary in October 1881. Her father, J. Ernest Grubb, was a businessman and local politician, and her mother, Rebecca Jacob Grubb, was active in charity work. The Grubbs had lived in Tipperary for several generations, and Isabel's grandparents had been involved in Quaker relief efforts in Carrick-on-Suir during the Famine. J. Ernest Grubb was a moderate nationalist who supported Home Rule and belonged to the Land League. He was also interested in local history and antiquities.[152] Isabel, the youngest of five children, attended Mountmellick School, a Quaker girls' school in County Laois. She received a BA in history from the University of London in 1906, and taught at Mountmellick from 1909 to 1915.

Grubb returned to the University of London for graduate work, and earned an MA in history in 1916. Her thesis, "Social Conditions in Ireland in the Seventeenth and Eighteenth Centuries, as Illustrated By Early Quaker Records," was supervised by Dr Caroline Skeel of Westfield College. Grubb was therefore part of the network of female social and economic historians connected with the University of London in the early decades of the twentieth century. Many of them were, like Grubb, politically progressive and socially engaged. She shared similarities with a British Quaker female historian, Alice Clark, who received a PhD in history from the LSE, wrote *The Working Life of Women in the Seventeenth Century*, and was involved in the Quaker War Relief Campaign during the First World War and the international peace movement after the war.[153] Grubb's graduate training in London linked her with another Irish woman historian, Ada Longfield, and with R.D. Edwards and T.W. Moody, who earned PhDs at the University of London's Institute of Historical Research two decades after Grubb. Moody, like Grubb, was a Quaker, and also had a female mentor in London, Dr Eliza Jeffries Davies. Thus, although Grubb worked outside academia, she had the credentials to teach history at an Irish university, and had received graduate training similar to that of the new academic historians. After receiving her MA, Grubb resumed her teaching career in England. In 1925, she continued her historical research at Woodbrooke, a Quaker institution in Birmingham.[154]

Grubb was a Quaker activist with an international outlook, as well as a historian. She was deeply involved in intervisitation during the 1920s and 1930s, and traveled throughout Europe and the United States. In 1929, she attended a conference in Iowa organized by the American Friends Service Committee. Grubb returned to the United States in 1937 to attend the Second World Conference of Quakers, held at Swarthmore College in Pennsylvania. This conference was significant, because those attending decided to promote international cooperation on Quaker projects through the establishment of the Friends World Committee for Consultation, or FWCC. Grubb became one of the Irish representatives of the FWCC and a vice-chair of its European section.[155] During the 1930s she was also the assistant clerk to Ireland Yearly Meeting.[156]

Grubb's two major historical works, and a biography of her father, were written during the Free State period. She also wrote historical articles for Quaker journals. Her first book, *Quakers in Ireland, 1654–1900* (1927),[157] was based largely on primary sources in the Friends Historical Society in Dublin. The Society had been founded in 1903, and Grubb's father, as a member of the executive committee, had been instrumental in collecting Quaker records, manuscripts, and books. Grubb's book addressed the early history of the Quakers in Ireland, including their persecution at the hands of the authorities because of their refusal to swear oaths and pay tithes to the Church of Ireland, and the role played by Quaker businessmen, such as Anthony Sharp of Dublin. Grubb then discussed the experiences of Quakers during the conflicts of 1689–91 and 1798. Other chapters cover Quaker preaching and religious practices, social activism in nineteenth-century Ireland, particularly Quaker relief work during the Famine, and Quakers and education.

The following year she published a biography of her father, J. Ernest Grubb,[158] the most influential person in her life. This hagiographical work is useful for its information on Quaker involvement in relief work, business, and Irish politics. J. Ernest Grubb, in addition to being a businessman, was also a supporter of Home Rule and a member of the Land League. Isabel Grubb noted how her family's nationalism attracted the attention of British soldiers in 1920, during the War of Independence. The soldiers searched the Grubb home for Sinn Fein literature, and asked if they had an Irish flag. The Grubbs supported the Free State during the Civil War, as they were moderate nationalists rather than republicans.[159]

Quakerism and Industry Before 1800 (1930)[160] was written in the context of interwar-era British economic history. Grubb used new works by leading British economic historians, such as R.H. Tawney, the Hammonds, and T.S. Ashton, in addition to primary sources. She discussed Quaker ethics and social teachings, and their implications for business and philanthropy, as well as highlighting Quaker achievements in British industries. Grubb's work was influenced by the approach of the economic historian and Christian socialist R.H. Tawney of the LSE, who brought his religious commitment to his examination of capitalist development in the early modern period and its relationship to religion.[161] A reviewer commented that *Quakerism and Industry Before 1900* was an interesting study of "the relation between religious belief and economic history [which] has been much discussed in recent years."[162]

Grubb worked for many years as an archivist at the Friends' Historical Library in Dublin. She was atypical in terms of the value she placed on Quaker records, as many academic historians focused on State Papers for their research on political and administrative history. The important documents Grubb donated to the Friends Historical Library included the journal of Mary Shackleton Leadbeater, described as possibly "the most complete record of the private life of any individual who has lived in Ireland" and "one of the very few surviving European diaries that details the adolescent years of a young woman living in a rural community."[163] Grubb's belief in the value of a Quaker woman's diary, and in the documents of women's lives in the past, links her with European and American women historians and archivists who founded women's archives in the interwar years. The International Archives for the Women's Movement, for example, was founded in Amsterdam in 1935, while American historian Mary Beard tried to establish a World Center for Women's Archives in the 1930s.[164] Grubb, then, was innovative as an archivist and played an instrumental role in promoting the Friends' Historical Library as a resource for scholars.

Isabel Grubb died in 1972. She was unique as a professionally trained woman historian in Ireland who wrote Quaker history in the 1920s and 1930s, bridging confessional history with the newer approaches of social and economic history. She resembled other Quaker women historians such as Rosamond Jacob in Ireland and Alice Clark in Britain. They fused historical scholarship with political and social engagement, had an international outlook, and brought an interest in social justice to their work. Grubb, like Ada Longfield, R.D. Edwards, and T.W. Moody, had attended graduate school at the University of London, so like many of the historians her intellectual formation was partly shaped in a context outside of Ireland. Grubb also shared similarities with women archivists who valued documents on women's lives and who founded new archives.

Grace Lawless Lee (1906–64)

Grace Lawless Lee was significant in that she, like Isabel Grubb, researched the history of a minority Protestant community in Ireland. She differed from Grubb in that she studied history at Trinity College as an undergraduate, rather than at the University of London. The only Irish woman historian who combined marriage and children with historical scholarship, she worked for many years as a researcher in London.

Grace Lawless Lee, who came from a middle-class Protestant family, was the daughter of a Cork doctor, Philip George Lee. She became interested in history through her father, a member of the Cork Historical and Archaeological Society.[165] Lee entered Trinity College in 1924, and graduated with a BA in 1928. Trinity College awarded her the Blake National History Scholarship in 1933 for her thesis on Huguenots in Ireland, which was supervised by Professor Edmund Curtis. She published her thesis three years later as *The Huguenot Settlements in Ireland*.[166]

Like Isabel Grubb, Lee wrote one of the few histories of a small, minority Protestant community in Ireland.[167] While both wrote in a laudatory fashion about Quakers and Huguenots, or French Calvinists, respectively, they had been trained in modern methods of historical research at the university level, and produced histories based on archival sources. Lee examined the collections of the Huguenot Society of London, which held documents on Huguenots in Ireland as well as in England, and records in private collections in

Ireland. Her book, which combined social and economic history with religious history, first explained the historical context, discussing the Huguenot flight from France to Ireland in the aftermath of the Revocation of the Edict of Nantes in 1685, which ended religious tolerance for Calvinists in France. She then discussed Huguenot settlers and their experiences in different parts of Ireland. Lee assessed the Huguenot contribution to Irish trade, industries, education, and society in the eighteenth century, noting, for example, their prominence in the textiles industry. She concluded on an approving note: "The Huguenots in Ireland need no panegyrist to justify their citizenship ... their sober industry and worth paid, many times over, the debt they owed to the country which had afforded them protection."[168] *The Huguenot Settlements in Ireland* was reviewed by Constantia Maxwell, who praised it as a "scientific monograph" based on careful research.[169]

Grace Lawless Lee married John David Gwynn, the eldest son of the provost of Trinity College, in 1934. The couple, who had a son and a daughter, made their home in London for many years. Thus, Grace Gwynn was the only Irish female historian under consideration who combined historical scholarship with marriage and children. She was elected to membership in the Huguenot Society of London, a historical and genealogical society, following the publication of her book in 1936. Her involvement with the Society deepened in the 1950s; she became a Council member in 1953, and the Society's Research Assistant in 1958. As a Research Assistant, she helped scholars and edited and catalogued archival documents. Like many of the other women historians, Gwynn sought to communicate her knowledge to a wide audience. She wrote on Huguenot history for local newspapers, and lectured on Huguenot history on the BBC in 1959. Grace Gwynn died on May 23, 1964, and was primarily remembered for the contributions she made to the Society through her research on "her beloved Huguenots."[170] The Grace Lawless Lee Fund for historical research was established in her memory at Trinity College in 1975.

Ada Longfield (1899–1987)

Ada Longfield was significant in the Free State years as a woman historian with an advanced degree who contributed to the study of early modern Irish economic history, and who worked in a museum rather than in academia. Her research interests were shaped in both an Irish and a British context, and resembled those of her Irish predecessor Alice Stopford Green as well as academic women historians in Britain and France. A prolific writer, she was less politically engaged than many of the other women historians of the Free State period.

Ada Longfield, like Grace Lawless Lee, came from a Cork Protestant background and attended Trinity College. She was born in India in 1899, the daughter of a major in the British army. Her formative years were spent in West Cork. As an undergraduate at Trinity College, she studied history with Edmund Curtis, and graduated in 1921 with a senior moderatorship. She then entered the London School of Economics for graduate work, where her thesis supervisor and mentor was the well-known economic historian, Eileen Power. Like Isabel Grubb, Longfield found a network of women historians and students in London who shared her interest in social and economic history. Longfield was awarded an MA in 1926 for her thesis on "Anglo-Irish Trade in the Sixteenth Century."[171] The LSE was known for its institutional support for the study and teaching of social and economic history, and a number of British female historians researched topics in these subfields at the LSE during the interwar period. Eileen Power, Longfield's supervisor, was particularly interested in merchants and trade in the medieval period, and Power's colleague R.H. Tawney lectured on early modern international trade at the LSE during the 1920s.[172] Longfield's research interests also resemble those of French women historians associated with the *Annales* School during the interwar period, such as Therese Sclafert, who researched trade routes in the Middle Ages.[173]

Longfield's *Anglo-Irish Trade in the Sixteenth Century* was published in 1929 as part of a series entitled "Studies in Economic and Social History," edited by R.H. Tawney and Eileen Power. Her book shared similarities with Alice Stopford Green's *The Making of Ireland and its Undoing*, which had addressed Anglo-Irish trade in the Tudor period two decades earlier. Longfield, however, wrote primarily for an academic audience, and had been professionally trained in the research methods of interwar-era social and economic history, formerly marginal subfields that now had institutional support. Longfield, like Green, analyzed Anglo-Irish trade relations by placing them in the context of England's policy of mercantilism. She wrote that Irish industries had declined dramatically due to English colonial policymakers mandating that Irish raw materials, such as linen yarn, be exported to England, rather than be kept for home industries. England had cut off Irish trade with the Continent, particularly Spain, to capture an Irish market for English imports. She devoted chapters to the trade in fish, hides, wool, cattle, timber, and other Irish exports and imports, using sixteenth-century English customs accounts and Port Books as her sources.

Longfield, who appeared to hold moderate nationalist sympathies, maintained that "no really representative native administration" would have allowed Ireland's economic needs to be subordinated to those of England,[174] echoing Green's views. She concurred with Green that Ireland had enjoyed an extensive foreign trade in the late medieval period, which had been devastated by English statecraft. She highlighted economic motivations for the Tudor wars and the enactments against Irish trade with the Continent, rather than presenting and justifying them as having been motivated solely by England's national security needs. While religious and political conflict influenced economic relations, "probably the most powerful factor was that of exploitation. Indeed the desire to exploit Ireland, as Spain exploited the New World for trade, industry, and settlement, was behind most of the commercial policy advocated for Ireland in the sixteenth century."[175]

Reviews of *Anglo-Irish Trade in the Sixteenth Century* appeared in English journals such as *History* and the *English Historical Review*, and in the *Nation*, the Fianna Fail paper. Philip Wilson, a specialist on early modern Ireland, commented that few histories had addressed late medieval and early modern Irish economic history, with the exception of "the brilliant but sometimes misleading work of the late Mrs. Green ... it is with sincere pleasure, therefore, that we welcome the appearance of Miss Longfield's work." He praised her painstaking work in the archives. However, he was resistant to economic interest as an explanatory factor in the Tudor interference with Irish foreign trade, agriculture, and industry, and emphasized England's national security needs instead.[176] A writer in the *English Historical Review* also rejected her main line of argument, without specifying an alternative framework of understanding, but conceded that Ireland had significant agricultural and industrial sectors in the late medieval period.[177]

A positive assessment of Longfield's book was offered by "Glensman," an Irish nationalist reviewer in the *Nation*, who read a contemporary meaning in her study. "Glensman," invoking Empire

Free Trade, felt that *Anglo-Irish Trade in the Sixteenth Century* "showed the parallels and the similarities of British trade policy in Ireland. In these respects British trade policy in the twentieth century differs not at all from that of the sixteenth."[178] He believed that Longfield's book disproved British stereotypes about the inferiority of the Irish by demonstrating the extent of Irish trade prior to its devastation by the Tudors, reinforcing one of the main arguments of Alice Stopford Green's *The Making of Ireland and its Undoing*. "Glensman" believed that *Anglo-Irish Trade in the Sixteenth Century* was particularly valuable because Longfield, on the basis of thorough research in documentary evidence, affirmed a nationalist interpretation of early modern Irish economic history, although she was not an extreme nationalist herself. "Without showing evidence of any decidedly pro-Irish tendency," "Glensman" wrote, "the author analyses coldly and scientifically and the work is perhaps the more valuable on that account ... [she is] a historian gifted with discernment and the proper historian temperament."[179] Longfield lent credibility to the nationalist interpretation not only as an Irish Protestant with moderate political views, but also as an LSE-trained historian who had rigorously analyzed the primary sources.

Longfield received further training at the Victoria and Albert Museum, and worked as a curator in the National Museum of Ireland's Art and Industrial Division. Her curatorial work reinforced her interest in material culture. She also became involved in the Irish Historical Society in the late 1930s, demonstrating her interest in the new, Moody–Edwards school of academic history. She married Harold Leask, the Inspector of Monuments, in 1940, and because of the marriage bar was compelled to resign from her curatorial position.[180] Ada Longfield Leask did, however, remain involved in the Royal Society of Antiquaries of Ireland. She worked as an independent historian, and researched Irish material culture, such as eighteenth-century textiles. She wrote articles for the Royal Society of Antiquaries of Ireland's (RSAI) *Journal*, as well as for more popular magazines covering art, antiques, and design. Ada Longfield Leask died in 1987, and left a bequest to the RSAI, which testified to its importance in her intellectual life.[181]

In conclusion, while Grubb, Lee, and Longfield were not as public and politically active as Concannon, Macardle, and Jacob, they nevertheless played significant roles as historians of Ireland. All three were university-trained historians, and two had been educated at the University of London, the academic home of some of the leading British economic and social historians, as well as the institution where the founders of the Moody–Edwards school received their graduate training. Lee and Longfield found an early mentor in Edmund Curtis during their undergraduate years at Trinity.

The works of these historians were significant at the time, and demonstrated that historical works of professional quality were being written by scholars who did not hold teaching positions in the history departments of Irish universities during the Free State period. Grubb and Lee wrote on the under-researched topic of small Protestant communities in Ireland, while Longfield wrote on sixteenth-century Irish trade. In addition to researching their own works, they helped other scholars and the general public through their auxiliary roles as archivists, research assistants, and curators. Longfield's professional opportunities were cut off by gender-based discrimination. Despite having to leave the National Museum upon marriage, she continued to work as a historian outside the institution. The scholarly circles connected with the Society of Friends Historical Library, the Huguenot Society, and the Royal Society of Antiquaries of Ireland were important networks for Grubb, Lee, and Longfield. The research interests of these three historians related to those of academic women historians during the interwar period, particularly women historians in Britain associated with the University of London. Additionally, their careers resembled those of other European women who earned graduate degrees in history, including doctorates, and worked in schools, libraries, archives, and at home rather than in universities.[182]

6 Conclusion

Irish women historians were represented in popular fiction by the 1980s. Clare O'Brien, the protagonist of Maeve Binchy's novel *Echoes*, attends University College Dublin (UCD) on a scholarship in the late 1950s, and studies history. She plans to attend graduate school, and maps out her imagined future to her friends:

> She had it all planned out. She would get her B.A. in August 1960, then she would study for two years for her M.A. That would bring her up to 1962. Yes, fine. Then she would go to Oxford or Cambridge to do a doctorate, her Ph.D. She would tutor, of course, while she was there. That would get her to 1964. Then she would go to America, to Vassar or Bryn Mawr, for three years as a visiting fellow. In 1967, she would return and she would take a position as Professor of Modern History in either Trinity College or UCD – wherever the History professor died first. To make her mark on the place she should serve a seven-year term, writing, of course, all the time. Then, at the age of thirty-four, she would marry. It would be just in time for her to have two children, and no more. She would marry a don in some other field and they would have a small unpretentious house covered with ivy, and lined with books. They would live near a café and they would eat out most evenings, all of them, including the babies as soon as they were old enough to get their hands around chips.[1]

What was it like in reality to be a female history student or academic historian in Ireland in the 1950s? The situation was decidedly mixed. Following a high point in the 1940s, the number of female historians pursuing graduate work in history in Irish universities dropped during the following two decades.[2] University history departments came to be widely perceived as male preserves by the 1950s, despite earlier gains made by women.[3] However, several women academics who had been hired earlier were still teaching in the 1950s and 1960s, such as Jocelyn Otway-Ruthven of Trinity College and Mary Donovan O'Sullivan and Sile Ni Chinneide of University College, Galway (UCG), and a few newcomers were hired, such as Maureen Wall at UCD.[4]

Three major changes occurred in the late 1960s that affected both the writing of Irish history and women historians in academia. These included the emergence of the crisis in Northern Ireland in 1969, the growth of higher education, and the second wave of the feminist movement. Irish historians began to reconsider the ways in which political history was written, out of concern that polemical nationalist presentations of history might reinforce preexisting attitudes and exacerbate the conflict. Many male historians became more public, as they were invited to explain the roots of the Northern Irish conflict on television and in the newspapers. The increase in the number of university students from the late 1960s onwards is attributable to government legislation raising the school leaving age, as well as to greater affluence. More students, including women, pursued graduate degrees, and this helped lead to a greater number of women academics in history and other departments since the 1970s. Lastly, feminists raised questions about job discrimination and successfully pushed for greater access and equitability in academia; at Trinity College, for instance, partly due to Jocelyn Otway-Ruthven's efforts, women were admitted to Fellowship in 1968. Feminist historians also turned to the writing of Irish women's history, which they conceptualized in far different terms than those envisioned by Helena Concannon in the 1920s and 1930s.

Conclusion: Irish women historians, 1868–1949

This study has placed women at the center of the social history of Irish historiography, and contextualized them within larger paradigms of female historians in the West in the nineteenth and twentieth centuries. Irish women historians were not marginal figures in the development of the profession. While some wrote innovative and influential works that helped shape scholarly debates in their subfield, others wrote popular, politicized histories that were problematic to professional historians, but reached a wide audience and helped shape notions of a national past, national identity, and communal historical memories. Some popular women historians also functioned as the "others" against whom academic historians could define themselves as they created their own identities as professionals. Irish women historians were often involved in politics, and several gained access to power precisely because of the way they wrote history. The fact that two female historians, Alice Stopford Green and Helena Concannon, became senators in the 1920s and 1930s was highly unusual by European and American standards.

Political affiliation and political and social engagement were central to the identity and intellectual formation of many Irish women historians between the 1860s and the 1940s. Their writings gave direct or indirect support to nationalist or unionist interpretations of history and political aspirations. They produced history in a period of intense politicization in Ireland, spanning the era of nationalist advocacy of Home Rule and its contestation by unionists, to the emergence and consolidation of the new Irish state. Irish women historians such as Mary Agnes Hickson, Margaret Cusack, Alice Stopford Green, Helena Concannon, and Dorothy Macardle were all notable for their intervention in political debates and in historiographical disputes with political dimensions.

Women historians in Ireland wrote on a range of topics. These included general histories of Ireland and Irish history textbooks for students of all levels, works on medieval and early modern Ireland, histories of eighteenth-century Ireland that focused on a range of protagonists, and works of social, economic, religious, women's, and contemporary history. The different approaches to their topics reflected the writer's political and social priorities, as well as academic training. For example, Margaret Cusack's general Irish histories and textbooks reflected her Catholic nationalism, while her contemporary Emily Lawless wrote a history of Ireland from a moderate unionist perspective. Constantia Maxwell and Rosamond Jacob specialized in eighteenth-century Ireland; while Maxwell favored the Anglo-Irish upper classes, Jacob, a left-wing republican, identified with the United Irishmen and their republican aspirations. Helena Concannon and Isabel Grubb both wrote on Irish religious history; Concannon wrote within a confessional Catholic framework, while Grubb wrote about Quakers and incorporated the newer approaches to social and economic history she had been exposed to as a graduate student at the University of London. Many of the historians sought to write in a more popular style for a mass readership, and some tried to reach wider audiences by writing for newspapers and journals, and, later, by broadcasting on the radio. Macardle and Jacob were particularly noteworthy for their interdisciplinarity; in addition to their work as historians and journalists, they also wrote plays and novels.

The careers of these historians are linked with transformations in the status of women in Ireland between the 1860s and the 1940s. In the 1860s, women in Ireland and elsewhere in Europe could not vote or enter universities; by the 1940s, Irish women were voting and serving in the government, and studying and teaching in universities. These changes in opportunities for women occurred simultaneously with the emergence of a new state. The career opportunities of Irish women historians were facilitated, in some cases, by the specific political configurations of the new Ireland. Alice Stopford Green and Helena Concannon forged political careers through their nationalist activism and writing of nationalist histories, Dorothy Macardle was commissioned by Eamon de Valera to write a contemporary political history of Ireland because of her role in the nationalist movement and skill as a writer, and the nationalist and Irish-language movement supporter Sile Ni Chinneide was appointed to a lectureship at UCG as part of the new state's language policy. Several of the historians were actively involved in the feminist movement, especially Mary Hayden, Mary Donovan O'Sullivan, Dorothy Macardle, and Rosamond Jacob; Macardle and Jacob combined feminism with Irish republican activism and internationalism.

Some of the Irish women teaching history in universities were ambivalent about the new developments in academic history by the late 1930s. While the National University of Ireland (NUI) appointed women, most of whom had not been trained in history, to history positions beginning in 1909, by the late 1930s academic history would be shaped largely by men who had earned doctorates in British universities. Some of the academic women had a problematic relationship with professionalism and "scientific" history, such as Mary Hayden, while Sile Ni Chinneide did not publish monographs. By the late 1940s, following the death of Mary Hayden and the retirement of

Pauline Henley, there were no senior women historians teaching in UCD and UCC. Academic women historians had not disappeared entirely, however; Constantia Maxwell, Olive Armstrong, and Jocelyn Otway-Ruthven were still teaching at Trinity, and Mary Donovan O'Sullivan and Sile ni Chinneide were teaching and supervising graduate students at UCG. The UCG historians were involved in outside activities as well, such as the Galway Historical and Archaeological Society, and, in Ni Chinneide's case, involvement with government boards and commissions. Thus, they received recognition as professional historians outside of academia as well. Other women, both "amateur" and professionally trained historians, wrote history outside of academia, working as teachers, journalists, librarians, archivists, and museum professionals.

Comparisons can be drawn between Irish women historians and their counterparts in other European countries and in the United States. Mary O'Dowd argues that they were similar to their European counterparts in their research interests, particularly in social and economic history, and in their ambivalence towards scientific history and the professionalization process.[5] While there were shared interests and points of convergence, topics and approaches framed in an Irish political and intellectual context could differ considerably from historical scholarship produced elsewhere. Thus, historians as diverse as Helena Concannon and her British contemporary Eileen Power wrote on women's history in the 1920s, with a focus on nuns; Concannon was a conservative Catholic, while Power was a secular, progressive feminist, and thus their works on nuns took very different forms. The leftist republican Rosamond Jacob mobilized eighteenth-century history for progressive political purposes in Ireland in the 1930s, while non-professional American women historians who wrote on the eighteenth century were often more conservative. The Irish women historians diverged from their female counterparts elsewhere in their early entry into university careers and their relative lateness in earning PhDs. However, the women's attainment of teaching positions in the early years of the NUI mirrors developments in other new institutions in Europe, such as the London School of Economics, which were relatively open to women when they were first established.

The political and social engagement of Irish women historians also has many parallels with female historians outside of Ireland who were involved in feminism, nationalism, and internationalist movements. A specifically feminist internationalism, for instance, linked Rosamond Jacob with Norwegian women historians involved in international women's organizations, while nationalist women historians throughout Europe inflected their writing with their political aspirations. Overall, parallels can be drawn between the careers of Irish women historians and those in other small, peripheral European countries with successful independence and women's suffrage movements, as well as with those in neighboring Britain, where a substantial number of Irish historians, both women and men, studied history as graduate students.

Historian Anthony Brundage, the biographer of Alice Stopford Green's husband, J.R. Green, wrote, "None of this should be taken as a lament for the disappearance of a supposed golden age of vigor, clarity, and readability in historical writing, with Green as its most gifted exponent ... it would be absurd to wish that historical writing had not moved beyond the level of [J.R. Green's work]."[6] Similarly, this study has not posited a golden age for women historians in the era prior to the modernization of the profession. Rather, it has argued for a social history of historiography that recovers Irish women historians, places them in historical context, and fully analyzes their careers in order to expand our knowledge of women historians, women's history, and Irish historiography. Ultimately, history is not only a "manly study".

Notes

Introduction

1. See, for example, Bonnie Smith, *The Gender of History: Men, Women, and Historical Practice* (Cambridge, MA.: Harvard University Press, 1998); Mary O'Dowd, "From Morgan to MacCurtain: Women Historians in Ireland From the 1790s to the 1990s," in Maryann Gialanella Valiulis and Mary O'Dowd, eds, *Women & Irish History: Essays in Honour of Margaret MacCurtain* (Dublin: Wolfhound Press, 1997), 35–58; Ilaria Porciani and Mary O'Dowd, "History Women," *Storia della Storiografia* 46 (2004), 3–34; Rosemary Ann Mitchell, " 'The Busy Daughters of Clio': Women Writers of History From 1820 to 1880," *Women's History Review*, 7, 1 (1998), 107–34; Joan Thirsk, "The History Women," in Mary O'Dowd and Sabine Wichert, eds, *Chattel, Servant, or Citizen: Women's Status in Church, State, and Society* (Belfast, 1995), 1–11; Julie Des Jardins, *Women and the Historical Enterprise in America: Gender, Race, and the Politics of Memory, 1880–1945* (Chapel Hill, NC: University of North Carolina Press, 2003); Maxine Berg, "The First Economic Women Historians," *Economic History Review*, 45 (1992); Berg, *A Woman in History: Eileen Power, 1889–1940* (Cambridge: Cambridge University Press, 1996); Mary Spongberg, *Writing Women's History Since the Renaissance* (Basingstoke: Palgrave Macmillan, 2002). For the recovery of women in disciplines related to history, see, for example, Margarita Diaz-Andreu and Marie Louise Stig Sorenson, eds, *Excavating Women: A History of Women in Archaeology* (London and New York: Routledge, 1998).
2. Smith, *The Gender of History*, 1, 3, 7–8, 11.
3. O'Dowd, "From Morgan to MacCurtain," 56; Anne Colman, "Far From Silent: Nineteeth-Century Irish Women Writers," in Margaret Kelleher and James H. Murphy, eds, *Gender Perspectives in Nineteenth-Century Ireland* (Dublin: Irish Academic Press, 1997), 203–11.
4. Mitchell, "The Busy Daughters of Clio," 108.
5. Thirsk, "The History Women," 1–11.
6. See articles in *Storia della Storiagrafia/History of Historiography*, vol. 46 (2004).
7. See Ciaran Brady, " 'Constructive and Instrumental': The Dilemma of Ireland's First 'New Historians,' " in Ciaran Brady, ed, *Interpreting Irish History: The Debate on Historical Revisionism* (Dublin: Irish Academic Press, 1994), 3–31; and, most recently, Evi Gzotzaridis, *Trials of Irish History: Genesis and Evolution of a Reappraisal, 1938–2000* (London and New York: Routledge, 2006). See also Brendan Bradshaw, "Nationalism and Historical Scholarship in Modern Ireland," *IHS*, 26 (November 1989), 329–51.

8. This section is informed by the analysis of gender, emotion, and history in Bonnie Smith's *The Gender of History*.
9. Of the twenty Irish women historians whose careers I consider, 13, or 65 percent, were single. They included Mary Agnes Hickson, Emily Lawless, Eleanor Hull, Margaret Cusack, Mary Hayden, Constantia Maxwell, Jocelyn Otway-Ruthven, Olive Armstrong, Sile Ni Chinneide, Pauline Henley, Rosamond Jacob, Dorothy Macardle, and Isabel Grubb. Mary Ferguson, Alice Stopford Green, Mary Donovan O'Sullivan, Helena Concannon, Ada Longfield Leask, and Maureen Wall married but had no children. Grace Lawless Lee was the only one who married and had children.
10. Lecky advised and gave books to Mary Agnes Hickson, Emily Lawless, Margaret Cusack, and Alice Stopford Green. Bigger corresponded with Alice Stopford Green, Eleanor Hull, and Helena Concannon, and helped them with their books.
11. Only seven, or 35 percent, were raised as Catholics. They included Mary Hayden, Mary Donovan O'Sullivan, Sile ni Chinneide, Pauline Henley, Helena Concannon, Dorothy Macardle, and Maureen Wall. The agnostic Macardle left the Catholic Church as a young adult. Cusack wrote history as a nun and as a Catholic nationalist, but had been raised as a Protestant and returned to Protestantism after leaving the convent. Most of the Protestant women belonged to the Church of Ireland, though Jacob and Grubb were Quakers.

1 Unionist Women Historians, 1868–1922

1. Cited in Philippa Levine, *The Amateur and the Professional: Antiquarians, Historians, and Archaeologists in Victorian England, 1838–1886* (Cambridge: Cambridge University Press, 1986), 37. Gladstone served as Prime Minister from 1868 to 1874, 1880–85, 1886, and 1892–94.
2. Ilaria Porciani and Mary O'Dowd, "History Women," *Storia della Storiografia*, 46 (2004), 5–28.
3. K. Theodore Hoppen, *Ireland Since 1800: Conflict and Conformity* (London: Longman, 1989), 117–25.
4. Alan O'Day, *Irish Home Rule, 1867–1921* (Manchester: Manchester University Press, 1998), 111–17.
5. O'Day, *Irish Home Rule*, 166–73.
6. Hoppen, *Ireland Since 1800*, 133; O'Day, *Irish Home Rule*, 258–62.
7. W.E.H. Lecky (1838–1903): *The Leaders of Public Opinion in Ireland* (London: Longman's Green, 1861; reprinted 1871, 1903); *A History of England in the Eighteenth Century*, 8 vols. (London: Longman's Green, 1878–90); *A History of Ireland in the Eighteenth Century*, 5 vols. (London: Longman's Green, 1892). Lecky's *A History of England* contained sections on Ireland, which comprised the five volumes of the 1892 cabinet edition of *A History of Ireland*. The 1892 cabinet edition of *A History of England* contained seven volumes. See Donal McCartney, *W.E.H. Lecky, Historian and Politician, 1838–1903* (Dublin: Lilliput Press, 1994), 92–3.

8. J.A. Froude (1818–94): *The English in Ireland in the Eighteenth Century*, 3 vols. (London: Longman's Green, 1872–4).
9. Thomas Dunbar Ingram (1826–1901): *A History of the Legislative Union of Great Britain and Ireland* (London: Macmillan, 1887); *Two Chapters of Irish History* (London: Macmillan, 1888). See McCartney, *W.E.H. Lecky, Historian and Politician*, 148–50, 245.
10. Richard Bagwell (1840–1918): *Ireland Under the Tudors*, 3 vols. (London: Holland Press, 1885); *Ireland Under the Stuarts and During the Interregnum*, 3 vols. (London: Holland Press, 1909–16).
11. Goddard Orpen (1852–1932), *Ireland Under the Normans, 1169–1333*, 4 vols. (Oxford: Clarendon Press, 1911–20). See also Sean Duffy, "Historical Revisit: Goddard Henry Orpen, *Ireland Under the Normans, 1169–1333* (1911–20)," *Irish Historical Studies*, 32, 126 (November 2000), 246–59.
12. For other unionist historians of Ireland who wrote during this period, such as C.L. Falkiner and F.E. Ball, see Alvin Jackson, "Unionist History," in Ciaran Brady, ed., *Interpreting Irish History: the Debate on Historical Revisionism* (Dublin: Irish Academic Press, 1994), 256–7. Falkiner and Ball were active in unionist politics and stood as candidates in elections. See also McCartney, *W.E.H. Lecky*, 149–50, 245.
13. McCartney, *W.E.H. Lecky*, 65.
14. Ibid., 96–7.
15. Ibid., 77–9, 137–43, 187–93; R.F. Foster, "History and the Irish Question," in Brady, ed., *Interpreting Irish History*, 131–3.
16. McCartney, *W.E.H. Lecky*, 148–9, 245. A reviewer in the *English Historical Review* commented on Ingram's partisanship, asserting that his book represented "a contribution to the history of Ireland as trustworthy and instructive as would be ... a speech on the blessings of slavery by a Virginia planter." Airy, 377–8. Osmund Airy, review of *Two Chapters of Irish History* by T. Dunbar Ingram, *E.H.R.*, vol. 4 (April 1889), 377–8.
17. McCartney, *W.E.H. Lecky*, 122.
18. Duffy, "Historical Revisit," 246–54. While the preconceptions typical of elite Irish unionists partially informed Orpen's disenchanted view of Gaelic Ireland, Duffy notes that Orpen was sometimes critical of English interference in Norman Ireland. Duffy, "Historical Revisit," 258.
19. See Orpen's reviews in the *EHR* during these years, such as those of William O'Connor Morris's *Ireland 1494–1868*, vol. 12 (1897), 162–3; Lecky's *Leaders of Public Opinion in Ireland* (3rd edn),vol. 18 (1903), 590; and James Hogan's *Ireland in the European System*, vol. 37 (1922), 142. For more on Orpen's political outlook, see his correspondence with Patrick Lyons and R.K. Wilson, Goddard Orpen Papers, N.L.I. MS 17,785; and with Edmund Curtis, Edmund Curtis Papers, TCD MS 2452(10).
20. The surveys of Irish history by Sullivan, Mitchel, and McCarthy were singled out by J.Pope-Hennessy as especially popular with readers in a Cork parish in the 1880s. See Pope-Hennessy, "What Do the Irish Read?" *Nineteenth Century*, 15 (January–June 1885), 920. Cited in R.F. Foster, "History and the Irish Question," in Brady, ed., *Interpreting Irish History*, 135.

21. A.M. Sullivan (1830–84), *The Story of Ireland, a Narrative of Irish History from the Earliest Ages to the Present Time* (Dublin: T.D. Sullivan, 1867); Patrick Callan, "Irish History in Irish National Schools, 1900–1908" (UCD, MA Thesis, 1975), 70.
22. A.S. Mac Shamhrain, "Ideological Conflict and Historical Interpretation: the Problem of History in Primary Education c. 1900–1930," *Irish Educational Studies*, 10, 1 (1991), 236–7. See also R.F. Foster, *The Irish Story: Telling Tales and Making It Up in Ireland* (Oxford: Oxford University Press, 2002), 6–10, for a more recent critical view of Sullivan's contribution to Irish historiography.
23. Luke Gibbons, *Transformations in Irish Culture* (Cork: Cork University Press, 1996), 15.
24. John Mitchel (1815–75): *The History of Ireland: From the Treaty of Limerick to the Present Time* (New York: Sadleir, 1868). This book, which went through several reprints, was a continuation of the Abbe MacGeoghegan's *History of Ireland from the Earliest Times to the Treaty of Limerick*. Mitchel's other popular nationalist works include his *Jail Journal* (New York, 1854) and *The Last Conquest of Ireland (Perhaps)* (Dublin, 1861).
25. James S. Donnelly, Jr., "Mass Eviction and the Great Famine: the Clearances Revisited," in Cathal Porteir, ed., *The Great Irish Famine* (Dublin: RTE/Mercier Press, 1995), 173.
26. Patrick Kavanagh, *A Popular History of the Insurrection of 1798* (Dublin, 1870). The book was reprinted nine times, attesting to its wide appeal. See Kevin Whelan, " '98 After '98: The Politics of Memory," in Whelan, *The Tree of Liberty: Radicalism, Catholicism and the Construction of Irish Identity, 1760–1830* (Notre Dame and Cork: University of Notre Dame Press and Cork University Press, 1996), 170.
27. Eugene J. Doyle, *Justin McCarthy* (Dundalk: Dundalgan Press, 1996), 28. Justin Huntly McCarthy (1856–1936): *An Outline of Irish History, from the Earliest Times to the Present Day* (London: Chatto and Windus, 1883); *Ireland Since the Union* (London: Chatto and Windus, 1887). John Pope-Hennessy, in his *Nineteenth Century* article, stated that *An Outline of Irish History* was particularly popular with the Irish reading public in the 1880s. Cited in Foster, "History and the Irish Question," 135.
28. J.G. Swift MacNeill (1849–1926): *The Irish Parliament: What it Was and What it Did* (London and New York: Cassell, 1885, 2nd edn, 1912); *How the Union was Carried* (London: K. Paul, Trench, 1887); *The Constitutional and Parliamentary History of Ireland Till the Union* (Dublin: Talbot Press, 1917). See McCartney, *W.E.H. Lecky*, 140–1, 243.
29. Patrick Joyce (1827–1914): *A Short History of Ireland, From the Earliest Times to 1608* (London; Longmans, Green, 1893); *A Social History of Ancient Ireland* (London: Longmans, 1903). See also Gabriel Doherty, "The Irish History Textbook, 1900–1960: Problems and Development," *Oideas*, 42 (1994), 15.
30. Eoin MacNeill (1867–1945): *Phases of Irish History* (Dublin: M.H. Gill, 1919); *Celtic Ireland* (Dublin: M. Lesters, 1921). *Phases of Irish History* is noteworthy for MacNeill's critique of the orthodox unionist historiography of early and medieval Ireland; see especially the eighth through

twelfth chapters. See also Duffy, "Historical Revisit," 248–50, for the conflicting perspectives of MacNeill and Orpen regarding Celtic Ireland. See also Michael Tierney, *Eoin MacNeill, Scholar and Man of Action 1867–1945* (Oxford: Clarendon, 1980).

31. The phrase is Toby Barnard's. See Barnard, "1641: a Bibliographical Essay," in Brian Mac Cuarta, SJ, ed., *Ulster 1641: Aspects of the Rising* (Belfast, 1993), 183.
32. Anon., "In Memoriam M.C. Ferguson," *Alexandra College Dublin Magazine*, 2, 26 (June 1905), 3–4.
33. Ibid., 3; M.C. Ferguson, *Sir Samuel Ferguson in the Ireland of His Day*, vol. 1 (Edinburgh: William Blackwood and Sons, 1896), 180.
34. O'Dowd, "From Morgan to MacCurtain," 45.
35. M.C. Ferguson, *Sir Samuel Ferguson*, vol. 1, 6–7, 134–6, 246–55. See also Mark Doyle, "Bridging Identities: Protestants as Nationalists in the Repeal Era," unpublished paper, presented at the 13th Annual Irish Studies Graduate Conference, Boston College, October 13, 2001.
36. Elizabeth Crooke, *Politics, Archaeology, and the Creation of a National Museum in Ireland: An Expression of National Life* (Dublin: Irish Academic Press, 2000), 30, 98–9.
37. M.C. Ferguson, *Sir Samuel Ferguson in the Ireland of His Day*, vol. 2 (Edinburgh: William Blackwood and Sons, 1896), 16–43, 167–9. See also Sara Champion, "Women in British Archaelogy: Visible and Invisible," in Margarita Diaz-Andreu and Marie Louise Stig Sorenson, eds, *Excavating Women: A History of Women in European Archaeology* (London and New York: Routledge, 1998), 175–9.
38. Ibid., 205–13.
39. "The extension of the franchise [in 1884] shifted the balance of power from the trained, educated, and propertied classes to the inexperienced and ignorant masses, who contribute little or nothing towards the burdens of the State, although their votes – numerically greater – have made them its masters." Ibid., 232.
40. M.C. Ferguson, *The Story of the Irish Before the Conquest: From the Mythical Period to the Invasion Under Strongbow* (London: Bell and Daldy, 1868). The book was reprinted in 1890 and 1903.
41. R.F. Foster, "The Story of Ireland," in *The Irish Story: Telling Tales and Making It Up in Ireland* (Oxford: Oxford University Press, 2002), 10.
42. Foster, "The Story of Ireland," 10.
43. Ferguson, *The Story of the Irish*, iii.
44. Crooke, *Politics, Archaeology, and the Creation of a National Museum in Ireland*, 91.
45. Ferguson, *The Story of the Irish*, iv.
46. Ibid., 158–60, 223–6.
47. Ibid., 230–3.
48. Ibid., 267–8, 273–81.
49. Ibid., 293.
50. Russell McMorran, "Mary Hickson: Forgotten Kerry Historian," *Kerry Magazine* (2000), 34–5.
51. McMorran, "Mary Hickson," 35–6.

52. McMorran, "Mary Hickson," 36–7; Mary Agnes Hickson to W.E.H. Lecky, Lecky Papers, TCD MS 1827–8/472, October 10, 1887.
53. Mary Agnes Hickson, ed., *Selections From Old Kerry Records* (London: Watson and Hazell, 1872–4).
54. Maxine Berg, *A Woman in History: Eileen Power, 1889–1940* (Cambridge: Cambridge University Press, 1996), 6; Julie Des Jardins, *Women and the Historical Enterprise in America: Gender, Race, and the Politics of Memory, 1880–1945* (Chapel Hill, NC: University of North Carolina Press, 2003), 335–6.
55. Christine L. Krueger, "Why She Lived at the PRO: Mary Anne Everett Green and the Profession of History," *Journal of British Studies*, 42 (January 2003), 68.
56. She was living in a home for elderly Protestants in Mitchelstown, Co. Cork in the 1880s. In 1889, a baronet, Sir Robert Arthur Denny, left her an annuity of forty pounds per annum. See Barnard, "1641: a Bibliographical Essay" in Mac Cuarta, SJ, ed., *Ulster 1641*, 185; and Hickson to Lecky, Lecky Papers, TCD MS 1827–8/549, July 4, 1889.
57. Hickson to Lecky, Lecky Papers, TCD MS 1827–8/237, September 17, 1881. Hickson asked Lecky to provide her with an introduction to the London Library, and promised to send him samples of the depositions. See also TCD MS 1827–8/255a, June 6, 1882; TCD MS 1827–8/308, November 29, 1884; and TCD MS 1827–8/474, October 15, 1887.
58. Hickson, *Ireland in the Seventeenth Century: or the Irish Massacres of 1641–2*, 2 vols. (London: Longmans, 1884). Edited and with an introduction by M.A. Hickson, with a preface by J.A. Froude. Discussions of the scholarly conflict are provided in O'Dowd, "From Morgan to MacCurtain," 44; Barnard, "1641: A Bibliographical Essay," 182–6; and McCartney, *W.E.H. Lecky*, 71–8.
59. McCartney, *W.E.H. Lecky*, 71; Barnard, "1641: A Bibliographical Essay," 182–3.
60. McCartney, *W.E.H. Lecky*, 140.
61. Ibid., 71–8.
62. O'Dowd, "From Morgan to MacCurtain," 44.
63. McCartney, *W.E.H. Lecky*, 72.
64. Hickson to Lecky, TCD MS 1827–8/263, July 10, 1882. She sounded a similar note in the introduction to her book, where she insisted that "the truthfulness of the Protestant witnesses, who are so careful to record the good as well as the bad treatment they met with, cannot be doubted." Hickson, *Ireland in the Seventeenth Century*, 122. See also Hilary Simms, "Violence in County Armagh, 1641," in Brian Mac Cuarta, SJ, ed., *Ulster 1641*, 130, for deposition evidence on Phelim O'Neill.
65. Hickson, *Ireland in the Seventeenth Century*, 163.
66. The British settler population in Ulster in 1640 was 34,000. See Simms, "Violence in County Armagh, 1641," 123–38. Simms adds that "large numbers of British settlers were murdered and massacred at that time but it was not [a conspiracy to exterminate all Ulster Protestants]... but a series of uncontrolled massacres and murders carried out by local Irish

leaders and their men." Simms, "Violence in County Armagh, 1641," 137–8.

67. In 1767, an English Protestant minister, Ferdinando Warner, analyzed the depositions and posited an "impressively precise" Ulster Protestant death toll of 4028. See Barnard, "1641: A Bibliographical Essay," 182. McCartney notes that "the fact that Protestant writers like Warner [and others] distrusted the evidence of these depositions carried much weight with [Lecky]." McCartney, *W.E.H. Lecky*, 229. Lecky called Warner "the most trustworthy and moderate Protestant historian" and found his estimated death toll credible. Lecky to Alice Stopford Green, Alice Stopford Green Papers, NLI MS 15, 085, February 4, 1887.
68. Hickson, *Ireland in the Seventeenth Century*, 164–5.
69. McCartney, *W.E.H. Lecky*, 229.
70. *Edinburgh Review*, 160, 328 (October 1884), 490–521; S.R. Gardiner, *Academy*, 26 138 (July 26, 1884), 53.
71. Robert Dunlop, "The Depositions Relating to the Irish Massacres of 1641," *EHR*, 1, 4 (October 1886), 740–4. Cited in McCartney, *W.E.H. Lecky*, 75.
72. Mary Agnes Hickson, *EHR.*, 2 (January 1887), 133–7; *EHR*, 2 (July 1887), 527.
73. For the "politics of imaginative solidarity" see Elizabeth Butler Cullingford, *Ireland's Others: Gender and Ethnicity in Irish Literature and Popular Culture* (Cork: Cork University Press, 2001). Hickson contradicted the view of archivist John Gilbert that "because witnesses gave evidence of their losses in cattle, money, and clothes ... their testimony [in the depositions] ought to be received with suspicion." She responded with an analogy linking 1641 with the 1880s, a time of Land League and Home Rule agitation, arguing that "because the poor wife of a boycotted husband, killed by a party of 'Moonlighters,' claims compensation for the loss of her cows and her corn, her evidence as to his murder must not be rejected as worthless." Hickson, *Ireland in the Seventeenth Century*. This was singled out by the *Edinburgh Review* writer as an especially compelling argument. See *Edinburgh Review*, 160, 328 (October 1884), 501.
74. Hickson, *Ireland in the Seventeenth Century*, 51, 101, 111.
75. Hickson to Lecky, TCD MS 1827–8/472, October 10, 1887. In regard to the Mitchelstown incidents "a coroner's jury returned a verdict of willful murder against the district inspector of the R.I.C. and five named policemen." Conor Cruise O'Brien, *Parnell and His Party* (Oxford: Clarendon, 1957), 212.
76. Toby Barnard, "Sir John Gilbert and Irish Historiography," in Mary Clarke, Yvonne Desmond, and Nodlaig P. Hardiman, eds, *Sir John T. Gilbert, 1829–1899: Historian, Archivist, and Librarian* (Dublin: Four Courts Press, 1999), 95–8.
77. Barnard, "1641: A Bibliographical Essay," 185.
78. Emily Lawless, *The Story of Ireland* (New York: G.P. Putnam's Sons, 1887). Her other major works include *Hurrish: a Study* (Edinburgh: William Blackwood, 1886); *With Essex in Ireland* (London: Ibister, 1890); *Grania (The Story of an Island)* (New York: Macmillan, 1892); *Maelcho: A Sixteenth-Century Narrative* (London: Smith and Elder, 1894); and *Maria Edgeworth*

(London: Macmillan, 1904). For an assessment of Lawless as a novelist, see James M. Cahalan, "Forging a Tradition: Emily Lawless and the Irish Literary Canon," in Kathryn Kirkpatrick, ed., *Border Crossings: Irish Women Writers and National Identity* (Dublin: Wolfhound Press, 2000), 38–57. See also Lia Mills, "Forging History: Emily Lawless's *With Essex in Ireland*," *Colby Quarterly* (June 2000). Lawless's career as a poet and historian linked her to the less well-known Jane Emily Herbert, who was primarily a poet but who also wrote a survey of Irish history.

79. Kit O'Ceirin, *Women of Ireland: A Bibliographical Dictionary* (Kinvara: Tir Eolas, 1996), 123; "Obituary: The Hon. Emily Lawless," *Times*, October 23, 1913.
80. Cahalan, "Forging a Tradition," 41–2, 54.
81. Cahalan, "Forging a Tradition," 42.
82. W.E. Gladstone, *Special Aspects of the Irish Question: A Series of Reflections In and Since 1886* (London: John Murray, 1892), 87. Cited in Betty Webb Brewer, " 'She Was a Part of It': Emily Lawless (1845–1913)," *Eire-Ireland*, 18, 4 (Winter 1983), 122. See also Cahalan, "Forging a Tradition," 40.
83. "Obituary: The Hon. Emily Lawless," *Times*, October 23, 1913.
84. Cahalan, "Forging a Tradition," 41.
85. Emily Lawless, *Maria Edgeworth* (London: Macmillan, 1904).
86. Lawless to Lecky, Lecky Papers, TCD MS 1827–36/550, July 5, 1889.
87. Lawless to Lecky, Lecky Papers, TCD MS 1827–36/639, December 30, 1890. Brewer maintains that "dramatic presentation, an emphasis on personalities and relationships, and a wealth of sensory detail breathe life into Lawless's history and produce the finest scenes in her historical novels." Brewer, " 'She Was a Part of It,' " 126. Lawless also discussed *Grania*, *Essex*, and *Maelcho* with Lecky. See TCD MS 1827–36/2480, 2482, undated.
88. Lawless to Lecky, Lecky Papers, TCD MS 1827–36/639, December 30, 1890.
89. Emily Lawless, *The Story of Ireland* (New York: G.P. Putnam's Sons, 1887), 24. Mary O'Dowd notes that a number of women Celtic scholars and historians involved with the Irish literary revival believed in the high status of women in early Ireland. O'Dowd, "From Morgan to MacCurtain," 49. However, this idealized view was challenged by later historians.
90. Lawless, *The Story of Ireland*, 47–59.
91. Ibid., 262–9.
92. Ibid., 328.
93. Ibid., 404–19.
94. "Obituary: Miss Eleanor Hull," *Times*, January14, 1935; Robin Flower, "Miss Eleanor Hull," *Times*, January 16, 1935.
95. Eleanor Hull to Patrick Pearse, Pearse Papers, NLI MS 21,054 (5), undated.
96. Eleanor Hull, *Pagan Ireland* (Dublin: M.H. Gill, 1904); Hull, *Early Christian Ireland* (Dublin: M.H.Gill, 1905).
97. O'Dowd, "From Morgan to MacCurtain," 48–9, 297.
98. J.J. Lee, *Ireland 1912–1985: Politics and Society* (Cambridge: Cambridge University Press, 1989), 28–31.
99. R.D. Edwards and Mary O'Dowd, *Sources for Early Modern Irish History 1534–1641* (Cambridge: Cambridge University Press, 1985), 199, 204.

100. Eleanor Hull to Shane Leslie, Leslie Papers, NLI MS 22,852, June 15, 1916.
101. Eleanor Hull, "Ireland's Allegiance to the Crown," *Nineteenth Century and After* (December 1921), 1081.
102. Ibid., 1084–6.
103. Ibid., 1086.
104. Eleanor Hull, *A History of Ireland and Her People to the Close of the Tudor Period* (London: Harrap, 1926); Hull, *A History of Ireland and Her People From the Stuart Period to Modern Times* (London: Harrap, 1931). See *Alexandra College Dublin Magazine*, 5, 43 (December 1913), 54–5, for a notice of alumna Eleanor Hull preparing a history of Ireland. For the delays in publication, see Eleanor Hull to F.J. Bigger, Bigger Papers, Belfast Central Library, May 11, 1925. While Hull's career straddled the periods before and after independence, her *History of Ireland* is discussed here because most of it was prepared in the years prior to 1922.
105. TCD School of History, Minutes of Committee, 1912–1973, TCD MUN/History/V/8/1, May 31, 1929; O'Dowd, "From Morgan to MacCurtain," 54.
106. Hull, *A History of Ireland* , 8.
107. Hull, *A History of Ireland*, 8.
108. Ibid., 25–9. Hull sometimes addressed the role of women in Irish history, and discussed the achievements of notable women such as Grania O'Malley, a sixteenth-century sea captain. Hull commended O'Malley's courage and independence, asserting that "Grania ruled her husband and her district with equal vigour." Hull, *A History of Ireland*, 323. Hull was a proponent of the influential view, derived from her study of the textual evidence, that women in Celtic Ireland enjoyed extensive legal, political, and social rights, a view echoed by other women scholars with feminist sensibilities. O'Dowd, "From Morgan to MacCurtain," 49.
109. Hull, *A History of Ireland*, 53–4.
110. Ibid., 161.
111. Ibid., 233–7.
112. Ibid., 359.
113. Ibid., 480.
114. Ibid., 481.
115. Goddard Orpen, review of Eleanor Hull, *A History of Ireland and Her People to the Close of the Tudor Period, EHR*, 42 (July 1927), 617.
116. Alice Stopford Green, review of Eleanor Hull, *A History of Ireland and Her People to the Close of the Tudor Period, Manchester Guardian*, undated [1926]. See Alice Stopford Green Papers, NLI MS 9932, for the newspaper clipping.

2 Nationalist Women Historians, 1868–1922

1. Irene Ffrench Eagar, *Margaret Anna Cusack, a Biography* (Dublin: Arlen House, 1979), 18–19, 34–7; Kit O'Ceirin, *Women of Ireland: a Biographical Dictionary* (Kinvara: Tir Eolas, 1996), 54; Mary O'Dowd, "From Morgan

to MacCurtain: Women Historians in Ireland From the 1790s to the 1990s," in Maryann Gialanella Valiulis and Mary O'Dowd, eds, *Women & Irish History: Essays in Honour of Margaret MacCurtain* (Dublin: Wolfhound Press, 1997), 43–4, 46, 294.

2. Eagar, *Margaret Anna Cusack*, 49–72, 77. Cusack wrote different versions of a history of Ireland: *An Illustrated History of Ireland* (London: Longman's Green, 1868); *A Patriot's History of Ireland* (London: Burns and Oates, 1871); *The Student's Manual of Irish History* (London: Longman's, 1870); *A Compendium of Irish History* (Boston: Patrick Donahue, 1871); and *History of the Irish Nation: Social, Ecclesiastical, Biographical, Industrial, and Antiquarian* (Kenmare: Kenmare Publications, 1876). *A History of the Kingdom of Kerry* (London: Longman's Green, 1871) and *A History of the City and County of Cork* (Dublin: McGlashan and Gill, 1875) covered local history. Her biographies include *Life of St. Patrick* (London: Longman's Green, 1871), *Life of Father Matthew* (Dublin: James Duffy, 1874), and a biography of Daniel O'Connell entitled *The Liberator: His Life and Times, Political, Social, and Religious* (Kenmare: Kenmare Publications, 1872). *The Present Case of Ireland, Plainly Stated* (New York: P.J. Kenedy, 1881), dealt with contemporary political and social issues.
3. O'Ceirin, *Women of Ireland*, 55; Eagar, *Margaret Anna Cusack*, 147–50. See also John White, "The Cusack Papers: New Evidence on the Knock Apparitions," *History Ireland*, 4, 4 (Winter 1996), 39–43.
4. Cusack to W.E.H. Lecky, Lecky Papers, TCD MS 1827–36/705, May 19, 1892. Cusack wrote to Lecky that she was struggling to survive after leaving the convent: "while so called Christian people are very ready to shout No Popery, they are slow indeed to help anyone who leaves Rome." She asked Lecky if he or any "liberal-minded men" could help her now. She had written to Lecky earlier to ask for a copy of *The Leaders of Public Opinion in Ireland*, and to request a donation for poor relief in Kerry. He complied with both requests. See TCD MS 1827–36/66, January 5, 1871; TCD MS 1827–36/131, January 11, 1878; TCD MS 1827–36/132, May 20, 1878.
5. Her reputation was posthumously rehabilitated, and in 1970 she was acknowledged as the founder of the order now called the Sisters of St. Joseph of Peace. O'Ceirin, *Women of Ireland*, 55–6.
6. O'Dowd, "From Morgan to MacCurtain," 43. Cusack, *A Compendium of Irish History* (Boston: Patrick Donohoe, 1871), iii–v; Anne Colman, "Introduction," in Colman, *A Dictionary of Irish Women Poets* (Galway: Kenny's, 1996), 18; Cusack, *The Illustrated History of Ireland*, (1868; reprint, New York: Gramercy Books, 2001), 3–14. All references are to the 2001 addition. See also Cusack, *A History of the Kingdom of Kerry* (1871; reprint, Dublin, Edmund Burke Publisher, 1995), v–viii.
7. Cusack, *Illustrated History of Ireland*, 188–90, 220–1, 257–64.
8. Ibid., 392–418, 408–4, 500–14.
9. Ibid., 574–80, 620–8. See also Kevin Whelan, " '98 After '98: The Politics of Memory," in Whelan, *The Tree of Liberty: Radicalism, Catholicism and the Construction of Irish Identity 1760–1830* (Cork: Cork University Press, 1996), 170.

10. O'Dowd, "From Morgan to MacCurtain," Cusack, *Illustrated History of Ireland*, 641–57.
11. Cusack, *Illustrated History of Ireland*, 275; Cusack, *A Compendium of Irish History*, 255–64.
12. For the "devotional revolution," see K. Theodore Hoppen, *Ireland Since the Famine: Conflict and Conformity* (London and New York: Longman, 1989), 143–8, 151–2.
13. Elizabeth Smyth, " 'Writing Teaches Us Our Mysteries': Women Religious Recording and Writing History," in Beverly Boutilier and Alison Prentice, eds, *Creating Historical Memory: English Canadian Women and the Work of History* (Vancouver: UBC Press, 1997), 102.
14. Russell McMorran, "Mary Hickson: Forgotten Kerry Historian," *Kerry Magazine* 2000), 36; O'Dowd, 43.
15. Cusack, *The Present Case of Ireland, Plainly Stated* (New York: P.J. Kenedy, 1881), 5,19, 358.
16. O'Dowd, "From Morgan to MacCurtain," 44.
17. In 1913, she became the first woman to be awarded an honorary doctorate from the University of Liverpool. Alice Stopford Green Papers, NLI MS 15,127. A decade later, she was awarded an honorary doctorate from the National University of Ireland. Alice Stopford Green to Mrs. DeVilliers, Alice Stopford Green Papers, NLI MS 8714 (1), undated.
18. R.B. McDowell, *Alice Stopford Green: A Passionate Historian* (Dublin: Allen Figgis, 1967), 5–17. See also Alice Stopford Green Papers, NLI MS 15,125, for her reminiscences of her childhood.
19. Anthony Brundage, *The People's Historian: John Richard Green and the Writing of History in Victorian England* (Westport, CT.: Greenwood Press, 1994), 1–6, 74–96.
20. Brundage, *The People's Historian*, 5.
21. See Joan Thirsk, "The History Women," in Mary O'Dowd and Sabine Wichert, eds, *Chattel, Servant or Citizen: Women's Status in Church, State, and Society* (Belfast: Institute of Irish studies, 1995), 1–11; Rosemary Ann Mitchell.
22. *The Constitutional History of England* (Oxford: Clarendon, 1887–1891); E.A. Freeman, *The History of the Norman conquest of England* (Oxford: Clarendon, 1873–9).
23. Brundage, *The People's Historian*, 138–48.
24. Ibid., 133–5, 143; Louise Creighton, *A Social History of England* (London: Rivington's, 1887).
25. Brundage, *The People's Historian*, 154–6; O'Dowd, "From Morgan to MacCurtain," 46–7.
26. McDowell, *Alice Stopford Green*, 46; Thirsk," The History Women," 2.
27. Lecky wrote, for example, "John Mitchel's (the rebel's) history of Ireland in the eighteenth century is a very able, though of course a very one-sided book." W.E.H. Lecky to Alice Stopford Green, Alice Stopford Green Papers, NLI MS 15,085, February 4, 1887. In the 1890s, she became interested in Irish history for the American textbook market, as the publisher

Alexander Macmillan asked her to write a British history textbook that fully addressed Ireland and Scotland. She soon came to see the framing of Irish history within a master narrative of English history as problematic, and felt Ireland should have its history written separately. See Sandra Holton, "Gender Difference, National Identity, and Professing History: the Case of Alice Stopford Green," *History Workshop Journal*, 53 (2002), 121–2.
28. Alice Stopford Green, *Henry II* (London: Macmillan, 1888); Alice Stopford Green, *Town Life in the Fifteenth Century* (London: Macmillan, 1894).
29. McDowell, *Alice Stopford Green*, 47.
30. James Tait, review of Mrs. J.R. Green, *Town Life in the Fifteenth Century, English Historical Review*, 10 (January 1895), 157–9.
31. Alice S. Green, review of Francis Hibbert, *The Influence and Development of English Gilds as Illustrated by the History of the Craft Gilds of Shrewsbury, E.H.R.*, vol. 7 (October 1892); Alice S. Green, review of Rev. J. Malet Lambert, *Two Thousand Years of Gild Life, EHR* 8 (April 1893), 338–44.
32. Alice Stopford Green Papers, NLI MS 15, 125.
33. McDowell, *Alice Stopford Green*, 51–5; Sandra Holton, "Gender Difference, National Identity, and Professing History," 121–2, 126.
34. McDowell, *Alice Stopford Green*, 62–5.
35. H.W. Nevinson, *Manchester Guardian*, May 30, 1929.
36. Maire Comerford Papers, UCDA LA18.
37. Stephen A. Royle, "St. Helena as a Boer Prisoner of War Camp: Information From the Alice Stopford Green Papers," *Journal of Historical Geography*, 24, 1 (1998), 60. Those in the pro-Boer camp included Irish nationalists, the children of Anglican clergymen, and feminists. Green belonged to the first two categories, but was not a feminist campaigner. See also Kenneth O. Morgan, "The Boer War and the Media," *Twentieth Century British History*, 13, 1 (2002), 3, 11, 15. Margaret Ward discusses the role of another prominent Irish woman, Maud Gonne, in organizing opposition to the Boer War in Ireland. See Margaret Ward, *Maud Gonne: Ireland's Joan of Arc* (London: Pandora Press, 1990), 57–60.
38. McDowell, *Alice Stopford Green*, 65; Alice Stopford Green, "Mary Kingsley," *Journal of the African Society*, 1 (October 1901), 1–16. I am indebted to Angus Mitchell for bringing this article to my attention.
39. See, for an encapsulation of her findings and recommendations, Alice Stopford Green, "The Boers and the War," [letter to the editor], *Times*, November 13 , 1900, 8. She criticized the methods used by the British army in the Boer War, and argued that the British government should show magnanimity and begin talks with Boer leaders.
40. Royle, "St. Helena as a Boer Prisoner of War Camp," 65.
41. For Green's views on South Africa, see Alice Stopford Green's to Mrs. De Villiers, Alice Stopford Green Papers, NLI MS 8714 (3), February 5, 1914.
42. McDowell, *Alice Stopford Green*, 68–74.
43. Angus Mitchell, ed, *The Amazon Journal of Roger Casement* (Dublin: Lilliput Press, 1997), 61, 280.

44. McDowell, *Alice Stopford Green*, 74.
45. She described the challenges of writing documents-based history to a friend, concluding, "it's not exactly like the novels all my friends polish off by the score." Alice Stopford Green to Oliver Wendell Holmes, Alice Stopford Green Papers, NLI MS 11,487, June 29, 1905.
46. See, for example, the editorials in the *Chicago Evening American*, October 29, 1904, October 31, 1904. Newspaper clippings in the Alice Stopford Green Papers, NLI MS 9932.
47. McDowell, *Alice Stopford Green*, 79; O'Dowd, "From Morgan to MacCurtain," 48.
48. See, for example, Green's letter to the *Church of Ireland Gazette*, September 29, 1905. An opponent of Home Rule, writing in the *Gazette*, had proclaimed that Irishmen should "see in [Irish history], as in a mirror, the faults of their character and the results of those faults [unfitness for Home Rule]." To support his point, the writer, who like many at the time believed in innate and unchanging national characteristics, had invoked a sixteenth-century Papal Nuncio who had criticized the Irish, adding that the same criticisms were true today. A Papal Nuncio was an ideologically useful choice to support unionist contentions about Irish Catholic inferiority, as Irish nationalists could not retort that he was an English anti-Catholic bigot of dubious credibility. While the writer explicitly mobilized a partisan understanding of history to oppose Home Rule, Green responded without mentioning Home Rule. She noted that "the writer charges the Irish people and their ancestors with crimes and errors so grave as to rightly shut them out from any claim to self-esteem or dignity, as well as to the management of their own affairs." She then placed the Papal Nuncio in historical context. Green noted that while unionists often stated that the Irish should forget history, their party had "an unlucky habit of betraying its own principles ... it cannot refrain from loudly appealing to 'history' the moment it happens on any old sentence that may serve to defame the Irish character." While the *Gazette*'s writers had recommended self-criticism as a healthy exercise for Irish nationalists, Green suggested that self-criticism should "enter ... the borders of the *Church of Ireland Gazette*, and make war on the puerilities that have too long done ignoble service among us." The previous year, she had challenged points raised by Horace Plunkett in her review of his book *Ireland in the New Century* in the *Westminster Gazette*, March 11, 1904. Newspaper clippings in the Alice Stopford Green Papers, NLI MS 9932.
49. See Maxine Berg, "The First Women Economic Historians," *Economic History Review*, xlv, 2 (1992), 308–14.
50. Mervi Kaarninen and Tiina Kinnunen, "Hardly Any Women at All: Finnish Historiography Revisited," *Storia della Storiografia*, 46 (2004), 157.
51. Julie des Jardins, *Women and the Historical Enterprise in America: Gender, Race, and the Politics of Memory, 1880–1945* (Chapel Hill, NC: University of North Carolina Press, 2003), 105–13.
52. Alice Stopford Green, *The Making of Ireland and its Undoing, 1200–1600* (1908; London: Macmillan, 1913). All references are to the 1913 reprint edition.

53. Green, *The Making of Ireland*, ix–xii.
54. Ibid., 494.
55. Ibid., 13–14, 52–5.
56. Ibid., 81–8.
57. Ibid., 250–9.
58. Ibid., 89–113.
59. Ibid., 113–17.
60. Ibid., 179–93. See also Sean Duffy, "The Problem of Degeneracy," and Katharine Simms, "Relations With the Irish," in James Lydon, ed., *Law and Disorder in Thirteenth-Century Ireland: the Dublin Parliament of 1297* (Dublin: Four Courts Press, 1997).
61. Ibid., 124.
62. Ibid., 124–9.
63. For colonial archaeology in an Irish context, see Elizabeth Crooke, *Politics, Archaeology, and the Creation of a National Museum of Ireland* (Dublin: Irish Academic Press, 2000), 59.
64. For hostile reviews of *The Making of Ireland and its Undoing*, see Goddard Orpen, *English Historical Review*, 24 (January 1909), 129–35; Robert Dunlop, "Truth and Fiction in Irish History," *Quarterly Review*, vol. 210, no. 418 (January 1909), 259–75; and H.J. Lawlor, *Scottish Historical Review*, 6 (January 1909), 194–8. Green claimed that she had never "met a single educated man in London, historian or otherwise, who does not *know* that Ireland was savage till the good Elizabeth at the least possible cost of men and blood, gently lifted it into the ranks of civilized people." Green to Holmes, Alice Stopford Green Papers, NLI MS 11,487, June 6, 1908.
65. See especially Dunlop, "Truth and Fiction in Irish History." For more recent scholarship on the relations between the Normans and the Irish see Katharine Simms, "Relations With the Irish," and Sean Duffy, "The Problem of Degeneracy," 67–86, 87–106.
66. Roger Casement noted that the Anglo-Irish were vindicated in *The Making of Ireland*, as Green wrote that the late medieval Irish civilization was destroyed by the outside interference of the English, rather than by internal conflict in which the Anglo-Irish were implicated. He thought the book may have "exaggerated the evidence of a growing fusion of interests between the old English in Ireland and the Irish people." While he thought the book could potentially promote reconciliation between different traditions in Ireland, it would not work in cases where "Anglo-Irish critics [were] apparently angry at being deprived of any share of the glory of the destruction wrought by the Tudor Wars." Roger Casement, "Mrs. Green's History," *Freeman's Journal*, December 19, 1908.
67. In the context of the time, unionist historians might have been more inclined to think of themselves as unbiased because they were upholding contemporary political and historical orthodoxies embraced by those who held power in the British political and intellectual establishments, including the world of academic history. See, for instance, the reviews of Irish histories in the prestigious *English Historical Review* from the 1880s

through the 1920s, in which reviewers were often more aware, and critical of, Irish nationalist partisanship than unionist partisanship.

68. The eminent British historian of early modern Ireland, Robert Dunlop, serves as a good example of how a reviewer's scholarly criticisms could be influenced by presentist thinking. See Dunlop, "Truth and Fiction in Irish History," 261–5, 272. In a presentist analogy, he compared the Normans in fifteenth-century Ireland to the Germans in early twentieth century Poland and Bohemia, maintaining that the "superior" Normans and Germans constantly fought to keep themselves separate from the "inferior" Irish and Slavs respectively. "To everyone except to the Czechs and Poles themselves German culture represents a higher form of civilization than the native. So it was in Ireland in the fifteenth century; and, just as the Germans in Bohemia and Poland dread being absorbed in the surrounding native element, so did the English in Ireland." Dunlop, "Truth and Fiction in Irish History," 262. He also proclaimed that despite Irish opposition, the Union had to be upheld, because England's national security needs overrode all other considerations. "We hope that, when their legitimate demands are conceded ... Irishmen will recognize that there are some concessions which no English statesman, having a regard to the safety of his own country, can consent to grant. Ireland has always been the back-door to England ... It must be admitted that, though we have succeeded in keeping the door closed by main force, we have made Ireland unhappy in the process ... we are now trying, to the best of our ability, to make Ireland a happy and prosperous country. But, whether we succeed or not, we are bound to keep the key of the back door in our possession." Dunlop, 258. For more on Dunlop, see C.H. Firth, "Robert Dunlop," *History*, 15 (January 1931), 322. Steven Ellis cites Dunlop's unionist perspectives on Ireland in his "Nationalist Historiography and the English and Gaelic Worlds in the Late Middle Ages," in Ciaran Brady, ed., *Interpreting Irish History: the Debate on Historical Revisionism* (Dublin: Irish Academic Press, 1994), 162.
69. Green to Holmes, Alice Stopford Green Papers, NLI MS 11,487, August 8, 1908.
70. Green to Holmes, Alice Stopford Green Papers, NLI MS 11,487, April 7, 1909. Joseph Lee wrote that Green's work was instrumental "in shifting the [politicized] debate about the hidden medieval Ireland onto a sources basis." J.J. Lee, "Some Aspects of Modern Irish Historiography," in Ernst Schulin, ed., *Gedenkschrift zur Martin Gohring. Studien zur Europaischen geschicte* (Wiesbaden, 1969), 435.
71. Green to Holmes, Alice Stopford Green Papers, NLI MS 11,487, December 22, 1908.
72. McCartney, 65–85.
73. Green to Holmes, Alice Stopford Green Papers, NLI MS 11,487, December 22, 1908. See also, "A Literary Boycott," in the *Evening Telegraph*, December 10, 1908; *Freeman's Journal*, December 14, 1908. Newspaper clippings in the Alice Stopford Green Papers, NLI MS 9932.

74. "Mr. Roger Casement and the Rejection of Mrs. Green's Book," *Freeman's Journal*, December 11,1908. Casement also wrote a positive review of *The Making of Ireland and Its Undoing* in the *Freeman's Journal*; see "Mrs. Green's History," *Freeman's Journal*, December 19, 1908. I am indebted to Angus Mitchell for bringing the letter and review to my attention.
75. Mrs. Sean T. O"Kelly, the *Nation*, June 8,1929.
76. Lucy McDiarmid, *The Irish Art of Controversy* (Dublin: Lilliput Press, 2005), 5, 7.
77. "When the little book appeared it thrilled every patriot heart in Ireland, and no doubt caused not a few new ones to beat for the first time with love and pride. Of those engaged in the movement, for all time to be known as Sinn Fein, whether young men dreaming of the day when they could strike a blow for Irish freedom; whether language revivalists; whether politicians or journalists with new Irish economic policies – none failed to read *Irish Nationality*. Its publication was an event, and that generation of men and women never forgot it." Mrs. Sean T. O'Kelly, review of *Irish Nationality* [revised edition] by Alice Stopford Green, the *Nation*, October 26, 1929. The Home University Library published books on literature, religion, political and social science, and science as well as history, and classified *Irish Nationality* under Political and Social Science.
78. Green to Holmes, Alice Stopford Green Papers, NLI MS 11,487, December 23, 1910.
79. Alice Stopford Green, *Irish Nationality* (1911; London, 1929), 198–203, 247. All references are to the 1929 revised edition.
80. Ibid., 240.
81. Ibid., 251.
82. Alice Stopford Green, *The Old Irish World* (London: Macmillan, 1912), 11.
83. Alice Stopford Green Papers, May 3, 1910, NLI MS 9932 (52).
84. Green, *The Old Irish World*, 12–31.
85. Ibid., 30–1.
86. Ibid., 53.
87. Terry Eagleton, "Revisionism Revisited," in *Crazy John and the Bishop and Other Essays on Irish Culture* (Cork: Cork University Press, 1998), 320.
88. Green, *The Old Irish World*, 168–97.
89. *Freeman's Journal*, December 14, 1908. Newspaper clipping in the Alice Stopford Green Papers, NLI MS 9932.
90. Alice Stopford Green Papers, NLI MS 9932, May 3, 1910.
91. Mary Cullen, "History Women and History Men: the Politics of Women's History," *History Ireland*, Summer 1994, 32–3.
92. A.K. Longfield, *Anglo-Irish Trade in the Sixteenth Century* (London: Routledge, 1929); M.D. O'Sullivan, *Old Galway, History of a Norman Colony in Ireland* (Cambridge: W. Heffer and Sons, 1942).
93. Kenneth Nicholls, "Gaelic Society and Economy in the High Middle Ages," in *A New History of Ireland*, II (Oxford: Clarendon, 1976), 397–438; Wendy Childs, "Ireland's Trade with England in the Later Middle Ages," *Irish Economic and Social History*, 9 (1982), 5–33; Timothy O'Neill, *Merchants and Mariners in Medieval Ireland* (Dublin: Irish Academic Press, 1987).

94. By the late twentieth century, some historians of medieval Ireland came to view Green as a very underrated historian. The economic sections of *The Making of Ireland and its Undoing* were acknowledged as the strongest parts of her book, and represented her best work. Sean Duffy to author, November 20, 2001. See also O'Dowd, "From Morgan to MacCurtain," 47.
95. Alice Stopford Green, "For Order, Law, Brotherhood, and Peace," *Irish Volunteer*, July 18, 1914; "Cumman Na mBan, Meeting in Dublin," *Irish Volunteer*, May 9, 1914. Green became the president of the London branch of Cumann na mBan. Maire Comerford Papers, UCDA LA18.
96. McDowell, *Alice Stopford Green*, 96–7. For Green's letters to Molly Childers regarding the gun-running, see the Childers Papers, TCD MS 7848/429–442, July–August 1914.
97. Alice Stopford Green to Shane Leslie, Shane Leslie Papers, NLI MS 22, 852, November 10, 1916.
98. Angus Mitchell, *Casement* (London: Haus, 2003), 121, 130; McDowell, *Alice Stopford Green*, 103–5. For letters from friends praising her efforts to save Casement's life, see the Alice Stopford Green Papers, NLI MS 15, 121, August 1916.
99. O'Ceirin, *Women of Ireland*, 93; Alice Stopford Green, unpublished essay, Alice Stopford Green Papers, NLI MS 9932. For more on the conscription crisis, see Adrian Gregory, " 'You Might as Well Recruit Germans: British Public Opinion and the Decision to Conscript the Irish," in Adrian Gregory and Senia Peseta, eds, *Ireland and the Great War: 'A War to Unite Us All'?* (Manchester: Manchester University Press, 2002); Patrick Maume, *The Long Gestation: Irish Nationalist Life, 1891–1918* (New York: St. Martin's Press, 1999), 206–7.
100. J.J. Lee, *Ireland 1912–1985: Politics and Society* (Cambridge: Cambridge University Press, 1989), 28–31.
101. Alice Stopford Green to Oliver Wendell Holmes, Alice Stopford Green Papers, NLI MS 11,487, September 8, 1921; Maire Comerford Papers, UCDA LA18; Alice Stopford Green Papers, NLI MS 15,073 (1); *Irish Statesman*, August 16, 1919; *Report of the Irish White Cross to 31 August 1922* (Dublin: Martin Lester, 1922); Leon O Broin, *Protestant Nationalists in Revolutionary Ireland: the Stopford Connection* (Dublin: Gill and Macmillan, 1985), 167–8.
102. Lee, *Ireland 1912–1985*, 172–4.
103. Alice Stopford Green to Molly Childers, Childers Papers, TCD MS 7848/455, December 30, 1921.
104. Maire Comerford Papers, UCDA LA18.
105. Alice Stopford Green to Mrs. De Villiers, Alice Stopford Green Papers, NLI MS 8714 (7), April 26, 1924, August 14, 1924.
106. Green to de Villiers, Alice Stopford Green Papers, NLI MS 8714 (8), September 30, 1927.
107. Sandra Holton, "Gender Difference, National Identity, and Professing History: the Case of Alice Stopford Green," *History Workshop Journal*, no. 53 (2002), 124.
108. Green to de Villiers, Alice Stopford Green Papers, NLI MS 8714 (7), September 16, 1925. Referring to the divorce debates in the government,

she wrote that the Catholic hierarchy aimed to show "that they are the only force that counts in Ireland – and that [non-Catholics] must ... remember that no conscience counts unless it is a Catholic one." See also Leon O Broin, *Protestant Nationalists in Revolutionary Ireland* 202–3, 211–12.

109. See Seanad Debates, vol. 1, cols. 1437–40, 1660–2, 1709–10; vol. 2, col. 583; vol. 3, cols. 171–5. For the Dominion group, see Green to de Villiers, Alice Stopford Green Papers, NLI MS 8714 (7), May 13, 1925.
110. Alice Stopford Green Papers, NLI MS 15,126. *The Making of Ireland and its Undoing* and *History of the Irish State to 1014* were used as textbooks by Mary Hayden and Eoin MacNeill at UCD in the 1920s.
111. O'Dowd, "From Morgan to MacCurtain," 43.
112. Green to de Villiers, Alice Stopford Green Papers, NLI MS8714 (7), May 13, 1925.
113. See F.M. Powicke, review of *History of the Irish State to 1014* by Alice Stopford Green, *History* (April 1926), 56–9; Goddard Orpen, review of *History of the Irish State to 1014* by Alice Stopford Green, *E.H.R.*, 4 (July 1926), 427–9.
114. G.P. Gooch, "Notes and News," *History* (July 1929), 118.
115. R.F. Foster, "History and the Irish Question," in Brady, ed., *Interpreting Irish History*, 138.
116. See Alice Stopford Green, *History of the Irish State to 1014* (London: Macmillan, 1925).
117. A.S. Mac Shamhrain, "Ideological Conflict and Historical Interpretation: the Problem of History in Irish Primary Education c. 1900–1930," *Irish Educational Studies*, 10, 1 (1991), 232–4.
118. Foster, "History and the Irish Question," in Brady, ed., 122, 137–9.
119. In 1967, R.B. McDowell wrote *Alice Stopford Green, A Passionate Historian* (Dublin: Allen Figgis, 1967). A generally positive biography of Alice Stopford Green, it provided a helpful account of her political activities, but engaged less with Green as a historian. Leon O Broin's *Protestant Nationalists in Revolutionary Ireland: The Stopford Connection* was useful in setting Green's outlook and political engagement in a familial context.
120. Sean Duffy to author, November 20, 2001; O'Dowd, "From Morgan to MacCurtain," 47.
121. See Sandra Holton, "Gender Difference, National Identity, and Professing History: the Case of Alice Stopford Green," for an insightful discussion of the relation between Green's identity as an Irishwoman and her historical scholarship. Articles and books on women historians by, among others, Mary O'Dowd, Maxine Berg, and Bonnie Smith have all included mentions of Green, who, as noted, can be located both in Irish and international historiographical contexts. For a recent study of Roger Casement that discusses his friendship with Green, see Angus Mitchell, *Casement* (London: Haus, 2003).
122. Lucy McDiarmid, *The Irish Art of Controversy* (Dublin: Lilliput Press, 2005).

3 Women Historians in the NUI, 1922–1949

1. Their careers mainly coincided with the Free State period. After the Civil War, William Cosgrave's Cumann na nGaedhal government was in power until 1932, when the more republican Fianna Fail party, led by Eamon de Valera, came to power. Fianna Fail was in power until 1948. De Valera's tenure as Taoiseach (prime minister) of the Free State government was characterized by the gradual erosion of political ties with Britain and moves towards complete independence, culminating in the creation of the 1937 Constitution and the policy of neutrality during the Second World War. De Valera's successor, John Costello of the Fine Gael (formerly Cumann na nGaedhal) party proclaimed Ireland a republic in 1949.
2. The NUI historians owed their status as university-based professional historians to the Irish Universities Act of 1908, which mandated equal access for men and women in the three constituent colleges of the National University of Ireland.
3. Julie Des Jardins, *Women and the Historical Enterprise in America: Gender, Race, and the Politics of Memory* (Chapel Hill: University of North Carolina Press, 2003). Maxine Berg, "The First Women Economic Historians," *Economic History Review*, 45(1992), 308–29; Mervi Kaarninen and Tiina Kinnunen, " 'Hardly Any Women at All': Finnish Historiography Revisited," *Storia della Storiografia*, 46, (2004), 152–70; Ida Blom, "Women in Norwegian and Danish Historiography," *Storia della Storiografia*, 46 (2004), 130–51.
4. Mary O'Dowd, "From Morgan to MacCurtain: Women Historians in Ireland From the 1790s to the 1990s," in Maryann Gialanella Valiulis and Mary O'Dowd, eds, *Women & Irish History: Essays in Honour of Margaret MacCurtain* (Dublin: Wolfhound Press, 1997)," 50, and communication to author, October 2004. Fernanda Perrone, "Women Academics in England, 1870–1930," *History of Universities*, xii (1993), 362–3.
5. Eoin MacNeill (1867–1945) wrote numerous articles based on his innovative research, as well as *Phases of Irish History* (Dublin: M.H. Gill, 1919) and *Celtic Ireland* (Dublin: M. Lester, 1921). John M. O'Sullivan (1881–1948) did not produce a major historical monograph, but frequently contributed articles on early modern European history to scholarly journals such as *Studies*. The works of George O'Brien (1892–1960) include *The Economic History of Ireland in the Eighteenth Century* (Dublin: Maunsel, 1918), *The Economic History of Ireland in the Seventeenth Century* (Dublin: Maunsel, 1919), and *The Economic History of Ireland From the Union to the Famine* (London: Longmans, Green, 1921). McCartney, 67–79.
6. Edmund Curtis (1881–1943) wrote *Roger of Sicily and the Normans in Lower Italy, 1016–1154* (New York and London: G.P. Putnam's Sons, 1912), *History of Medieval Ireland* (Dublin: Maunsel & Roberts, 1923), *Richard II in Ireland (1394–5) and the Submission of the Irish Chiefs* (Oxford: Clarendon Press, 1927), and *A History of Ireland* (London: Methuen, 1936). See James Lydon, "Historical Revisit: Edmund Curtis, *A History of*

Medieval Ireland (1923, 1938)," *IHS*, 31, 124 (November 1999), 535–48. The works of W.A. Phillips (1864–1950) include *Modern Europe, 1815–1899* (London: Rivingtons, 1903); *The Confederation of Europe* (London: Longmans, Green, 1914); and *The Revolution in Ireland, 1906–1923* (London: Longmans, Green, 1923).

7. James Hogan wrote *Ireland in the European System, 1500–1557* (London: Longmans, 1920), as well as works of political science. See Donncadh O Corrain, ed., *James Hogan, Revolutionary, Historian, and Political Scientist* (Dublin: Four Courts Press, 2001).
8. McCartney, 70.
9. Finin O'Driscoll, "Social Catholicism and the Social Question in Independent Ireland: the Challenge to the Fiscal System," in Mike Cronin and John M. Regan, eds, *Ireland: the Politics of Independence, 1922–49* (New York: St. Martin's, 2000), 133.
10. Eunan O'Halpin describes Phillips's *The Revolution in Ireland* (1923) as "a southern unionist lament on the passing of the old Dublin Castle order" and Hogan's *Could Ireland Become Communist? The Facts of the Case* (1935) as "a far-fetched polemic." See Eunan O'Halpin, "Historical Revisit: Dorothy Macardle, *The Irish Republic* (1937)," *IHS*, 31, 123 (May 1999), 390. O'Halpin notes that politicized historians could be found both inside and outside of academia in Free State Ireland.
11. E.M. Hogan, "James Hogan, a Biographical Sketch," in O Corrain, ed., *James Hogan*, 8–20.
12. Edwards' major publication in this period was *Church and State in Tudor Ireland* (Dublin: Talbot Press, 1935). For discussions of Edwards and his work, see Aidan Clarke, "Robert Dudley Edwards (1909–1988)," *IHS*, 26, 102 (November 1988), 121–7; James Murray, "Historical Revisit: R. Dudley Edwards, *Church and State in Tudor Ireland* (1935)," *IHS*, 30, 118 (November 1996), 233–41.
13. Moody's major publication in the 1930s was *The Londonderry Plantation, 1609–41* (Belfast: William Mullan, 1939). Moody's career is discussed in Helen F. Mulvey, "Theodore William Moody (1907–1984): an Appreciation," *IHS*, 24, 94 (November 1984), 121–30. His first book is analyzed in Raymond Gillespie, "Historical Revisit: T.W. Moody, *The Londonderry Plantation, 1609–41* (1939)," *IHS*, 29, 113 (May 1994), 109–13.
14. Articles on medieval and early modern Irish political and constitutional history predominated in the early volumes of *IHS*, reflecting the interests of the new establishment. There were also articles on early Irish religious history, and, by 1950, on nineteenth-century political and economic history. See *IHS*, vols 1–7, 1938–50.
15. This professionalization occurred half a century later than similar processes in the United States and Britain. The American Historical Association was founded in 1884, and the *English Historical Review* was established in 1886.
16. Ciaran Brady, " 'Constructive and Instrumental:' The Dilemma of Ireland's First 'New Historians'," in Ciaran Brady, ed., *Interpreting Irish History: the*

Debate on Historical Revisionism (Dublin: Irish Academic Press, 1994), 6. See also Evi Gkotzaridis, *Trials of Irish History: Genesis and Evolution of a Reappraisal, 1938–2000* (London and New York: Routledge, 2006).

17. For another discussion of the relationship between the new historical establishment and the state, see Conor McCarthy, *Modernisation, Crisis, and Culture in Ireland, 1969–92* (Dublin: Four Courts, 2000), 84–92, 99–101, 107–8.
18. Brady, " 'Constructive and Instrumental,' " 17–20. See also Peter Burke, *The French Historical Revolution: The Annales School, 1929–1989* (Stanford: Stanford University Press, 1990), 21–2; Maxine Berg, *A Woman in History: Eileen Power, 1889–1940* (Cambridge: Cambridge University Press, 1996), 166–70.
19. O'Dowd, "From Morgan to MacCurtain," 52–7. Natalie Zemon Davis, "Women in the World Of the *Annales*," *History Workshop Journal*, 33 (1992), 121–30.
20. Susan Parkes, *A Danger to the Men? The History of Women at Trinity College, 1904–2004* (Dublin: Lilliput Press, 2004), 84.
21. Porciani and O'Dowd, "History Women", 31; Des Jardins, *Women and the Historical Enterprise in America*, 219–25.
22. Medb Ruane, "Mary Hayden," in *Ten Dublin Women* (Dublin: Women's Commemoration and Celebration Committee, 1991), 47–50. See also Joyce Padbury, "Mary Hayden: First President of the Women Graduates' Association," in Anne Macdona, ed., *From Newman to New Woman: UCD Women Remember* (Dublin: New Island, 2001), xii–xvii; Mary Horkan, "The Women Graduates' Association: Beginnings," in Macdona, xviii–xxiv.
23. Donal McCartney, *UCD, A National Idea: The History of University College Dublin* (Dublin: Gill & Macmillan, 1999), 73–9.
24. McCartney, *UCD, A National Idea*, 79–80.
25. Ibid., 67–79.
26. Ibid., 83–4. In 1980, in contrast, there were no female professors, though there were six female senior lecturers.
27. O'Dowd, "From Morgan to MacCurtain," 50.
28. Calendar of University College Dublin, 1922–3 (Dublin, 1922); Calendar of University College Dublin, 1929–30 (Dublin, 1929); Calendar of University College Dublin, 1933–4 (Dublin, 1933).
29. Mary Hayden Papers, NLI MS 24,007 (9).
30. Mary Hayden Papers, NLI MS 24,007 (3)–(4).
31. Mary Hayden Papers, NLI MS 24,007 (8).
32. McCartney, *UCD, A National Idea*, 69–70.
33. She may also have supervised UCC professor James Hogan's MA thesis. E.M. Hogan, "James Hogan: a Biographical Sketch," in O Corrain, ed., *James Hogan*, 7.
34. Dora Casserley, *History of Ireland* (Dublin: Educational Company of Ireland, 1941).
35. B.L.W., "Obituaries: Anne T. Casserley," *Alexandra College Dublin Magazine*, 12 (June 1964), 38. Anne Casserley was Dora's sister and a fellow teacher at Alexandra. For Casserley's textbook, see David Fitzpatrick, "The

Futility of History: a Failed Experiment in Irish Education," in Ciaran Brady, ed., *Ideology and the Historians* (Dublin: Lilliput Press, 1991), 181–2.
36. Aidan Clarke, "Robert Dudley Edwards (1909–1988)," *Irish Historical Studies*, xxiv (1988–89), 121–7.
37. *Bulletin of the Institute of Historical Research* 11, 33 (February 1934), 185–9.
38. Hayden to Edwards, August 1936–June 1937, Robert Dudley Edwards Papers, UCDA LA 129/4–8.
39. Ruane, "Mary Hayden", 50–3.
40. Senia Paseta, "Ireland's Last Home Rule Generation: The Decline of Constitutional Nationalism in Ireland, 1916–30," in Cronin and Regan, eds, *Ireland: the Politics of Independence*, 22.
41. Ruane, "Mary Hayden", 51; Caitriona Beaumont, "Women and the Politics of Equality: the Irish Women's Movement, 1930–1943," in Gialanella Valiulis and O'Dowd, eds, *Women and Irish History*, 173–88. Feminists expressed concern about the part of Article 41 of the 1937 Constitution which stated, "In particular, the State recognizes that by her life within the home, woman gives to the state a support without which the common good cannot be achieved ... the State shall, therefore, endeavour to ensure that mothers shall not be obliged by economic necessity to engage in labour to the neglect of their duties in the home."
42. Hunter Guthrie, S.J., "Woman's Role in the Modern World," *Irish Monthly* (May 1941), 248–50.
43. Mary Hayden, "Woman's Role in the Modern World," *Irish Monthly* (July 1941), 397.
44. Ibid., 400–1.
45. Mary Hayden and George A. Moonan, *A Short History of the Irish People* (1921; London: Longmans Green and Co. Ltd.,1927), iii. All references are to the 1927 edition.
46. Mary O'Dowd, "From Morgan to MacCurtain," 52.
47. Hayden and Moonan, *A Short History of the Irish People*, 38–60.
48. Ibid., 65–9.
49. Ibid., 107–67.
50. See, for example, Steven Ellis, "Nationalist Historiography and the English and Gaelic Worlds in the Late Middle Ages," in Brady, ed., *Interpreting Irish History* 162–3.
51. Hayden and Moonan, *A Short History of the Irish People*, 199.
52. Ibid., 238–9, 297.
53. Ibid., 362.
54. Ibid., 363–7; Maureen Wall, "The Penal Laws, 1691–1760" in Gerard O'Brien, ed., *Catholic Ireland in the Eighteenth Century: Collected Essays of Maureen Wall* (Dublin: Geography Publications, 1989), 5–6, 21–4.
55. Hayden and Moonan, *A Short History of the Irish People*, 367–79.
56. Ibid., 426–39.
57. Ibid., 490–4.
58. See R. Dudley Edwards and T. Desmond Williams, eds, *The Great Famine: Studies in Irish History* (Dublin: Browne and Nolan, 1956). For comments, see Cormac O'Grada, "Making History in Ireland in the 1940s and 1950s: The

Saga of *The Great Famine*," in Brady, ed., *Interpreting Irish History*, 269–87.

59. Hayden and Moonan, *A Short History of the Irish People*, 496–8. However, while keeping the food in Ireland and distributing it to the destitute would have alleviated the crisis somewhat, Irish merchants and "large" farmers would have adamantly opposed that course of action. In addition, the British government was too committed to free trade to impose the retention of grain and cattle exports. See Mary E. Daly, "The Operations of Famine Relief, 1845–47," in Cathal Poirteir, ed., *The Great Irish Famine* (Cork: Mercier Press, 1995), 130.
60. Hayden and Moonan, 532.
61. Ibid., 541.
62. Ibid., 551–2.
63. Ibid., 561.
64. Ibid., 560–1.
65. Ibid., 559–61.
66. Ibid, 567–74.
67. This may account for the book's defensive tone, as she was aware that Irish nationalist historians were not always taken seriously as historians by those who did not share their political views.
68. I am indebted to Kevin O'Neill for discussing these ideas with me. Edwards and O'Dowd note when Mary Hayden published her textbook, her nationalist viewpoint "was conservative and in no way revolutionary." R.W. Dudley Edwards and Mary O'Dowd, *Sources for Early Modern Irish History, 1534–1641* (Cambridge: Cambridge University Press, 1985), 203.
69. Brian o hUiginn, "A History Text-book," *Irish Press*, May 28, 1935, 6.
70. In the 1980s, Hayden's former student Dudley Edwards maintained that "Mary Hayden's approach to the Tudor and early Stuart period was dispassionate and not uncritical. Indeed, it would be highly unrealistic to imagine that Mary Hayden's nationalism lacked objectivity." Edwards and O'Dowd, *Sources for Early Modern Irish History*, 203.
71. J.J. Lee, "Some Aspects of Modern Irish Historiography," in Ernst Schulin, ed., *Gedenkschrift zur Martin Gohring. Studien zur Europaischen geschicte* (Wiesbaden, 1968), 439.
72. R.F. Foster, "History and the Irish Question," in Brady, ed., *Interpreting Irish History* 144.
73. B.J. Elliott, "The League of Nations Union and History Teaching in England: a Study in Benevolent Bias," *History of Education*, 6, 2 (1977), 138–40.
74. For further discussion of textbooks, see, for example, W.E. Marsden, " 'Poisoned History:' a Comparative Study of Nationalism, Propaganda, and the Treatment of War and Peace in the Late Nineteenth- and Early Twentieth-Century School Curriculum," *History of Education*, 29, 1 (January 2000), 29–48, and, for an American perspective, S.J. Foster, "The Struggle For American Identity: Treatment of Ethnic Groups in United States History Textbooks," *History of Education*, 28, 3 (September 1999), 251–78.
75. Mary Hayden, "Women in the Middle Ages," *The Irish Review*, 3 (August–September 1913), 282–95, 344–58. She gave a talk on this subject

at an Alexandra College Students' Union meeting in 1897. See "The Students' Union," *Alexandra College Dublin Magazine*, 1, 11 (December 1897), 233–6.

76. Lina Eckenstein, Mary Bateson, and Rose Graham all made notable early contributions to the study of medieval religious women. Maxine Berg, *A Woman in History: Eileen Power, 1889–1940* (Cambridge: Cambridge University Press, 1996), 114–21.
77. Hayden, "Women in the Middle Ages," 284–93.
78. Ibid., 288–9.
79. Hayden, "Women in the Middle Ages," 291.
80. Hayden, "Women in the Middle Ages," 358.
81. Berg, *A Woman in History*, 135–9. These historians included Alice Clark, Frances Collier, Dorothy Marshall, Ivy Pinchbeck, and M.G. Jones. See Alice Clark, *The Working Life of Women in the Seventeenth Century* (London: Routledge, 1919); Frances Collier, *The Family Economy of the Working Classes in the Cotton Industry, 1784–1833* (Manchester: Manchester University Press, 1921); Dorothy Marshall, *The English Poor in the Eighteenth Century. A Study in Social and Administrative History* (London Routledge, 1926); Ivy Pinchbeck, *Women Workers in the Industrial Revolution, 1750–1850* (London: Routledge, 1930); M.G. Jones, *The Charity School Movement* (Cambridge; Cambridge University Press, 1938). Ivy Pinchbeck's book was somewhat influential in Ireland, as its account of female industrial workers was invoked by Eamon de Valera to justify restricting women's work in Ireland. Catriona Clear, " 'The Women Can Not be Blamed': The Commission on Vocational Organisation, Feminism, and 'Home-makers' in Independent Ireland in the 1930s and '40s," in Mary O'Dowd and Sabine Wichert, eds., *Chattel, Servant, or Citizen? Women's Status in Church, State and Society* (Belfast, 1995), 180.
82. Mary Macken, "In Memoriam: Mary T. Hayden," *Studies*, 31 (1942), 369–71.
83. Mary Hayden, "Charity Children in 18th-Century Dublin," *Dublin Historical Record*, 5, 3 (March/May 1943), 107.
84. Tadgh Foley and Fiona Bateman, "English, History, and Philosophy," in Tadgh Foley, ed., *From Queen's College to National University: Essays on the Academic History of QCG/UCG/NUI* (Dublin: Four Courts Press, 1999), 409–10; G.A. Hayes-McCoy, "Obituary: Mary J. Donovan O'Sullivan," *Analecta Hibernica*, 26, 12 (1970), xii–xiv.
85. Foley and Bateman, "English, History, and Philosophy," 410.
86. Foley and Bateman, "English, History, and Philosophy," 409–10. See also Mary Clancy, "On the 'Western Outpost': Local Government and Women's Suffrage in County Galway," in Gerard Moran and Raymond Gillespie, eds, *Galway: History and Sociey, Interdisciplinary Essays on the History of an Irish County* (Dublin: Geography Publications, 1996), 573–8.
87. Rosemary Cullen Owens, *Smashing Times: a History of the Irish Women's Suffrage Movement, 1889–1922* (Dublin: Attic Press, 1984), 95–9. See also Eileen Reilly, "Women and Voluntary War Work," in Adrian Gregory and

Senia Peseta, eds, *Ireland and the Great War: 'A War to Unite Us All'?* (Manchester: Manchester University Press, 2002), 49–72.
88. Foley and Bateman, "English, History, and Philosophy," 409–12.
89. Foley and Bateman, "English, History, and Philosophy," 402, 415–16.
90. See sections on "Research," *Irish Historical Studies*, vols 1–10, 1938–57.
91. Sean Duffy, "A Real Irish Historian [interview with James Lydon]," *History Ireland* (Spring 1995), 11. Lydon described O'Sullivan as "a very strong and important influence on my life, and on others."
92. *IHS*, 11 (1959), 343.
93. M.D. O'Sullivan to D'arcy Wentworth Thompson, February 17 and November 14, 1943. Cited in Joe O'Halloran, ed., "The Correspondence of Sir D'Arcy Wentworth Thompson [in St. Andrew's University Library]," *Journal of the Galway Archaeological and Historical Society*, 52 (2000), 90, 92.
94. O'Dowd, "From Morgan to MacCurtain,"51.
95. Michelle O'Brien, "University Treasures: the Visual Art Collection of NUI, Galway," *Cois Coribe* [NUIG Alumni Magazine] (2000). I am indebted to Margaret O hOgartaigh for bringing this article to my attention.
96. See Senia Paseta, *Before the Revolution: Nationalism, Social Change, and Ireland's Catholic Elite, 1879–1922* (Cork: Cork University Press, 1999), for an analysis of this group. See also Paseta, "Ireland's Last Home Rule Generation: the Decline of Constitutional Nationalism in Ireland, 1916–30," in Cronin and Regan, eds, *Ireland: the Politics of Independence*, 13–31. John Redmond led the Irish Parliamentary party, which pushed for Home Rule, until 1918.
97. This section owes much to discussion with Kevin O'Neill.
98. O'Sullivan, "The Centenary of Galway College [the text of a centenary lecture delivered on the 19th November, 1949]." Prepared for publication by Joe O'Halloran. *Journal of the Galway Archaeological and Historical Society*, 51 (1999).
99. M.D. O'Sullivan, "Minorities in the Free State," *Quarterly Review*, 258, no. 512 (1932), 317.
100. Paseta, "Ireland's Last Home Rule Generation," 26.
101. O'Sullivan, "Eight Years of Irish Home Rule," *Quarterly Review*, 254, 504 (April 1930), 230.
102. *Nation*, March 1, 1930, 2. The *Nation*, at this time the Fianna Fail organ, frequently published news about India, criticizing British rule there and presenting Indian nationalism in a favorable light.
103. O'Sullivan, "Eight Years of Irish Home Rule," 231–2.
104. Ibid., 236–7, 240–1.
105. Ibid., 234. It is deeply ironic that she was so hostile to the poor and that she characterized them as republicans. The most impoverished Irishmen had frequently joined the British army, served in the First World War, and were hostile to republicans, like O'Sullivan herself. See Terence Denman, " 'The Red Livery of Shame': The Campaign Against Army Recruitment in Dublin, 1899–1914," *Irish Historical Studies*, xxix, 114 (November 1994).

106. O'Sullivan, "Eight Years of Irish Home Rule," 246. O'Sullivan was not alone in her outlook, as there were other people with similar backgrounds who had favored Irish involvement in the First World War and who had traditionally opposed republicanism. Her views were not, however, widely popular in Ireland in the 1930s. Moreover, her focus on such issues as the right of appeal to the Privy Council would not have resonated with thousands of destitute, anti-republican ex-servicemen, who would have considered other issues more pressing. Thus it was unlikely that a cross-class, anti-republican mass movement could come about to challenge Fianna Fail.
107. Stephen Quinn, "Our Academic Flower Show, 1930," *Catholic Bulletin*, 9, 20 (1930), 857–62. Cited in Foley and Bateman, "English, History, and Philosophy," 411.
108. O'Sullivan, "Minorities in the Free State," 315.
109. O'Sullivan "Minorities in the Free State," 318–19.
110. Ibid., 321–5.
111. Stephen Quinn, "The Western Professor Again," *Catholic Bulletin*, 22, 6 (1932), 437.
112. M.D. O'Sullivan, "Anglo-Irish Relations," *Nineteenth Century and After*, 117 (February 1935), 144.
113. O'Sullivan "Anglo-Irish Relations," 145.
114. Ibid., 148–50.
115. O'Sullivan to Thompson, April 28, 1943, in O'Halloran, 91.
116. Professor Louis Cullen, a UCG undergraduate in the 1950s, remembers O'Sullivan wearing a poppy on Armistice Day. Louis Cullen, conversation with author, November 21, 2001.
117. O'Sullivan to Thompson, December 8,1944, in O'Halloran, 93. O'Sullivan's nephew served in the Navy in the Second World War, just as her father and husband had served in the British military.
118. O'Sullivan to Thompson, February 10, 1947, in O'Halloran, 94.
119. Ibid.
120. M.D. O'Sullivan, "The Centenary of Galway College," 40–1.
121. She admired the work of archaeologist R.A.S. Macalister, whose work on the Celts had antagonized "the saints and the patriots – it doesn't do, as you can imagine, to debunk the Celts. However, Dr. Macalister is one of those all too few scholars in Ireland who prefer fact to fiction!" O'Sullivan to Thompson, January 8, 1936, in O'Halloran, 88.
122. Other histories of Irish cities written in between 1900 and 1940 included P.H. Hore, *History of the Town and County of Wexford*, 5 vols (London E. Stack, 1900–11), and William O'Sullivan, *The Economic History of Cork City From the Earliest Times to the Act of Union* (Cork University Press, 1937).
123. "Whatever our views about the morality of Galway's attitude to the Irish ... we come away from a perusal of these MSS with a profound admiration for the wisdom, constructive insight, and enterprise of these descendants of the original Norman colony." M.D. O'Sullivan, *Old Galway: The History of a Norman Colony in Ireland* (Cambridge: W. Heffer and Sons, 1942), 54.

124. See Sean Duffy, "Historical Revisit: Goddard Orpen, *Ireland Under the Normans*," *IHS*, 32, 126 (November 2000), 258.
125. O'Sullivan, *Old Galway*, 112–13.
126. Ibid., 347–8.
127. O'Dowd, "From Morgan to MacCurtain," 50–1.
128. "These [foreign] students [at UCG]... give us a sense of perspective-badly needed in Irish life ...[they] call us out of our isolationism, our parochialism; they are a gentle reminder that insularity has its intellectual as well as social disadvantages." O'Sullivan, "The Centenary of Galway College," 39.
129. O'Sullivan, *Old Galway*, 385–6.
130. O'Sullivan to Thompson, February 17, 1943. Cited in O'Halloran, 90.
131. P.F., *Dublin Magazine*, 20 (April–June 1943), 71–2.
132. "Colm," *Irish Book Lover*, 29 (May 1943), 23.
133. O'Dowd, "From Morgan to MacCurtain," 53.
134. H.G. Richardson, review of *Old Galway: the History of a Norman Colony in Ireland* by M.D. O'Sullivan, *I.H.S.*, 4 (1944–5), 362. My thanks to Margaret O hOgartaigh for discussing Richardson's review with me.
135. Richardson, 366–7.
136. Richardson, 366–7.
137. O'Sullivan to Thompson, December 8, 1944. Cited in O'Halloran, 92.
138. M.D. O'Sullivan, *Italian Merchant Bankers in Ireland in the Thirteenth Century* (Dublin: Allen Figgis and Co. Ltd., 1962), 1.
139. J. Otway-Ruthven, review of *Italian Merchant Bankers in Ireland in the Thirteenth Century* by M.D. O'Sullivan, *I.H.S.*, 14 (1964–65), 367.
140. G.A. Hayes-McCoy, "Obituary: Mary J. Donovan O'Sullivan," *Analecta Hibernica*, 26, 12 (1970), xii.
141. Nicholas Canny, conversation with author, March 29, 2000, Louis Cullen, conversation with author, November 21, 2001.
142. Foley and Bateman, "English, History, and Philosophy," 412.
143. Dail Debates, vol. 53, June 21, 1934, cols. 992–3.
144. Ibid., col. 993.
145. Foley and Bateman, "English, History, and Philosophy," 412.
146. Louis Cullen, conversation with author, November 21, 2001.
147. *IHS*, 9 (1954–55). Her other MA students in the 1950s included Louis Cullen, Brother S. Mac Gioilla Easpuig, Sean O Broimeil, Brother S.C. O hAmaill, Caitriona Ni Mhuireadhaigh, Fearghal Mac Giolla Dhuinn, Brother S. O Cearbhaill, Bernadette Ni Loinsigh, and Silbhester O Muireadhaigh. See "Research on Irish History" sections in *IHS*, vols 9–12, 1954–60.
148. See "Research on Irish History" sections in *IHS*, vols 9–12, 1954–60.
149. Louis M. Cullen, "The Politics of the Famine and of Famine Historiography," in Breandan O Conaire, ed., *Comhdhail an Chraoibhin 1996 Conference Proceedings: An Gorta Mor (2)* (Roscommon, 1997), 20.
150. Foley and Bateman, "English, History, and Philosophy," 412–13. For her early newspaper articles, see, for example, Sile ni Cinneide, "Taibdearc na Gaillime," *Irish Press*, December 2, 1931, 4. This article dealt with the Irish-language theater in Galway.

151. Other historians who contributed to *Ireland To-day* in the 1930s included R. Dudley Edwards, T. W. Moody, and Rosamond Jacob.
152. Sheila Kennedy [Sile Ni Chinneide], "The Foundations of Modern Ulster," *Ireland To-day*, 1, 2 (1936), 27.
153. Ni Chinneide "The Foundations of Modern Ulster," , 28–9.
154. Sheila Kennedy (Sile Ni Chinneide), "Irish in the Schools [Letter of the Month]," *Ireland To-day*, 2, 3 (1937), 60. See also Adrian Kelly, *Compulsory Irish: Language and Education in Ireland 1870s–1970s* (Dublin: Irish Academic Press, 2002).
155. Sheila Kennedy [Sile Ni Chinneide], "Our Western Seaboard," *Ireland To-day*, 2, 12 (1937), 13–19.
156. Foley and Bateman, "English, History, and Philosophy," 413.
157. Robert J. Savage, Jr., *Irish Television: the Political and Social Origins* (Westport, CT.: Praeger, 1996), 107.
158. Sile Ni Chinneide to R. Dudley Edwards, January 12,1960, Robert Dudley Edwards Papers, UCDA LA22/809 (20). See also Evi Gkotzaridis, *Trials of Irish History*, 80–102.
159. See, for instance, Marianne Elliott, *Partners in Revolution: the United Irishmen and France* (New Haven, CT: Yale University Press, 1982); David Dickson and Hugh Gough, eds, *Ireland and the French Revolution* (Dublin: Irish Academic Press, 1990).
160. For a list of these papers, see *IHS*, (1938–39), 290–1, and 2 (1939–40), 80–1.
161. O'Dowd, "From Morgan to MacCurtain,"56.
162. T.W. Moody, "A New History of Ireland," *IHS*, 16 (1968–69), 254.
163. Sile Ni Chinneide, review of J.G. Simms, *The Williamite Confiscations in Ireland, Journal of the Galway Archaeological and Historical Society*, 26 (1957), 95–6.
164. Ni Chinneide, review of J.G. Simms, 96.
165. Sile Ni Chinneide, "The Gaelic Contribution to Irish Nationalism," *University Review*, 2, 9 (1960), 71, 75.
166. Ni Chinneide, "The Gaelic Contribution to Irish Nationalism," 67.
167. Helen F. Mulvey, "Theodore William Moody (1907–1984): an Appreciation," *IHS*, 24 (1984–85), 121–30.
168. F.X. Martin, "The Thomas Davis Lectures, 1953–1967," *IHS*, 15 (1966–67), 276–302.
169. Patrick Maume, *D.P. Moran* (Dundalk: Dundalgan Press, 1995), 52.
170. Cormac O Grada, "Making History in Ireland the 1940s and 1950s: the Saga of the Great Famine," in Brady, ed., *Interpreting Irish History*, 269–70.
171. Foley and Bateman, "English, History, and Philosophy," 412.
172. Admissions Register, University College Cork, 1912–13. I am grateful to Bernie Deasy, research assistant at the University Archives, UCC, for these references to Henley.
173. Pauline Henley to Etienne Beuque, January 21, 1928, Terence MacSwiney Papers, UCDA P48c/61.
174. Henley to Beuque, March 5, 1928, Terence MacSwiney Papers, UCDA P48c/62.

175. In a letter to Etienne Beuque, a French writer on contemporary Irish history who had asked her about Terence MacSwiney, Henley maintained that Free Staters and republicans were equally patriotic, but advocated different tactics to advance Ireland's interests. She added that "Terence was a common possession and belongs to those glorious days when we were all one." Henley to Beuque, May 14, 1928, Terence MacSwiney Papers, UCDA P48c/63.
176. "Miss Pauline Henley, M.A.," *UCC Record*, 49, 1974.
177. Bernie Deasy, communication to author, 30 January 2001; *UCC College Calendars*, 1930s–1940s.
178. Margaret MacCurtain, conversation with author, November 1999; John A. Murphy, conversation with author, September 24, 2002.
179. Pauline Henley, *Spenser in Ireland* (Cork: Cork University Press, 1928), 168–77.
180. Henley, *Spenser in Ireland*, 7–8.
181. Ibid., 18.
182. G.H.O. [Goddard Henry Orpen], review of Pauline Henley, *Spenser in Ireland*, in *EHR*, 44 (July 1929), 493.
183. Ibid., 494.
184. See Ciaran Brady, "Spenser's Irish Crisis: Humanism and Experience in the 1590s," *Past and Present* vol. 11 (May 1986), 17–49. Patricia Coughlan, ed., *Spenser and Ireland: an Interdisciplinary Perspective* (Cork: Cork University Press, 1989); *Irish University Review*, Special Issue, "Spenser and Ireland," 26, 2 (Autumn/Winter 1996).
185. Patricia Coughlan, "The Local Context of Mutabilitie's Plea," *Irish University Review*, 26, 2 (Autumn/Winter 1996), 328.
186. The 1950s, in particular, were a low point for female graduate students in history in Irish universities. O'Dowd, "From Morgan to MacCurtain," 54. Similarly, a substantial number of women historians worked in British universities in the interwar period, but their numbers dropped off in the middle decades of the twentieth century, and did not increase again until the 1960s. Berg, *A Woman in History*, 12, 247.
187. She began working on her thesis in 1948. See "Research on Irish History," *Irish Historical Studies*, 6 (1948–49), 226. Her background differentiated her from many of the women academics and nonprofessional historians of the Free State years. She came from a nationalist, Catholic, and bilingual family in Donegal; her parents were teachers, and her family was not as affluent as many of the families of the earlier women historians. See Tom Dunne, "Maureen Wall (nee McGeehin) 1918–1972: a Memoir," in Gerard O'Brien, ed., *Catholic Ireland in the Eighteenth Century: Collected Essays of Maureen Wall* (Dublin: Geography Publications, 1989).
188. Maureen Wall "The Penal Laws, 1691–1760," and Maureen Wall, "The Rise of a Catholic Middle Class in Eighteenth-Century Ireland," in Gerard O'Brien, ed., *Catholic Ireland in the Eighteenth Century: Collected Essays of Maureen Wall* (Dublin: Geography Publications, 1989), 1–60, 73–84.

189. Maureen Wall, "The Background to the Rising: From 1914 Until the Issue of the Countermanding Order on Easter Saturday, 1916," and Maureen Wall, "The Plans and the Countermand: the Country and Dublin," in K.B. Nowlan, ed., *The Making of 1916* (Dublin: Stationary Office, 1969), 157–97, 201–51.
190. Dunne, "Maureen Wall."
191. Ibid., O'Dowd, "From Morgan to MacCurtain," 55.

4 Women Historians at Trinity College, 1922–1949

1. Margaret Griffith was only affiliated with the history department for a few years. The daughter of a Galway professor, she completed a master's degree in history at Oxford and was appointed a lecturer in medieval and modern history at Trinity in 1934. She later turned to archival work at the Public Record Office of Ireland, where she introduced major reforms, and wrote two articles for *Irish Historical Studies*. By 1968, Griffith had become the deputy keeper and a member of the advisory board of the New History of Ireland project. R.B. McDowell, interview with author, November 27, 2001; TCD School of History: Minutes of Committee, 1912–1973 [TCD MUN/History/v/8/1]; Susan M. Parkes, ed., *A Danger to the Men? A History of Women at Trinity College Dublin, 1904–2004* (Dublin: Lilliput Press, 2004), 135–6. See also Margaret Griffith, "The Talbot-Ormond Struggle for Control of the Anglo-Irish Government, 1414–47," *IHS*, 2 (September 1941), 376–97; "The Irish Record Commission, 1810–1830," *IHS*, 7 (1950–51), 17–38. For the New History of Ireland project, see T.W. Moody, "A New History of Ireland," *IHS*, 16 (1968–69), 254.
2. I am indebted to Margaret O hOgartaigh for information on Constantia Maxwell's family. See also Census of Ireland, 1911.
3. Obituary in the *Times*, February 7, 1962.
4. Constantia Maxwell, letter to the Provost, May 17, 1945, TCD MUN/P/54/7/187.
5. Obituary in the *Times*, February 7, 1962.
6. Parkes, *A Danger to the Men?*, 108, 135.
7. TCD School of History: Minutes of Committee, 1912–1973, TCD MUN/History/V/8/1.
8. Ibid.
9. Ibid.
10. See R.B. McDowell and D.A. Webb, *Trinity College Dublin 1592–1952* (Cambridge: Cambridge University Press, 1982) 432; Pauric Dempsey, "Trinity College Dublin and the New Political Order," in Mike Cronin and John M. Regan, eds, *Ireland: The Politics of Independence, 1922–1949* (London: Macmillan Press, 2000), 217–31.
11. James Lydon, "Historical Revisit: Edmund Curtis, *History of Medieval Ireland (1923, 1938)*," *Irish Historical Studies*, 31, 124 (November 1999), 541.

12. See "Research on Irish History in Irish and British Universities," *IHS* , 1 (1938–9); "Research on Irish History in Irish and British Universities," *IHS*, 1 (1940–1).
13. TCD School of History: Minutes of Committee, 1912–1973 TCD MUN/History/V/8/1.
14. May L.F. Darlington Papers, Michaelmas Term [1936], TCD MS 10,358.
15. Ibid.
16. May L.F. Darlington Papers, Hilary Term 1937, TCD MS 10,359. See also Maxwell's review of Grace Lawelss Lee's *The Huguenot Settlements in Ireland* (1936), *History*, 21 (September 1936), 163. Maxwell wrote, "The suffering of the Huguenots under persecution, their courage and enterprise, make so strong an appeal to the imagination that it is difficult to think of them without sympathy and admiration."
17. Maxwell to the Provost, September 27,1940, TCD MUN/P/54/7/185.
18. Maxwell to the Provost, May 17, 1945, TCD MUN/P/54/7/187.
19. Ibid.
20. Provost to Maxwell, undated, TCD MUN/P/54/7/188.
21. Mary O'Dowd, "From Morgan to MacCurtain: Irish Women Historians From the 1790s to the 1990s," in Maryann Gialanella Valiulis and Mary O'Dowd, eds, *Women and Irish History: Essays in Honour of Margaret MacCurtain* (Dublin: Wolfhound Press, 1997), 51, 54.
22. David Fitzpatrick, "The Futility of History: A Failed Experiment in Irish Education," in Ciaran Brady, ed., *Ideology and the Historians* (Dublin: The Lilliput Press, 1989), 178–81.
23. Constantia Maxwell, *A Short History of Ireland* (New York: Frederick A. Stokes, 1914), iv.
24. She may have been reinforced in this view due to the fact that the work of mainstream unionist historians tended to be validated as impartial by the British academic historical establishment in authoritative scholarly journals, such as the *English Historical Review*. In contrast, Irish nationalist writers were often denounced for their partisanship when their works received notices in British journals, as reviews of Irish histories in the *English Historical Review*, 1886–1922, demonstrate. This probably had a cumulative effect in shaping readers' views regarding which historians were or were not objective, in addition to contributing to the defensiveness of some Irish nationalist historians like Mary Hayden.
25. Steven Ellis writes that "the Unionist tradition [in historiography] had stressed ... the backwardsness and instability of Gaelic Ireland, and the benefits which the pax Normanica brought to the island." Steven Ellis, "Nationalist Historiography and the English and Gaelic Worlds in the Late Middle Ages," in Ciaran Brady ed., *Interpreting Irish History: The Debate on Historical Revisionism* (Dublin: Irish Academic Press, 1994), 162.
26. Maxwell, *A Short History of Ireland*, 44.
27. Ibid, 53, 69. See also Bernadette Cunningham, "The Culture and Ideology of Irish Franciscan Historians at Louvain 1607–1650," in Brady ed., *Ideology and the Historians*, 11–30 for the significance of the Counter-Reformation in the construction of Irish national identity.

28. Maxwell, *A Short History of Ireland*, 4–9.
29. See James Lydon's discussion of Orpen's views relating to law and society in pre-Norman Ireland, and his conflict with Eoin MacNeill. James Lydon, "Historical Revisit," 543–4.
30. Maxwell, *A Short History of Ireland*, 10–11.
31. Ibid., 17–24.
32. Ibid., 20. See Sean Duffy, "Historical Revisit: Goddard Orpen, *Ireland Under the Normans* (1911, 1920)," *Irish Historical Studies*, 32, 126 (November 2000), on how an Anglo-Irish perspective can be read into Orpen's condemnation of the English monarch's interference in the Normans' affairs.
33. Ibid., 62–5.
34. Ibid., 90.
35. Ibid., 92.
36. Ibid., 100.
37. Ibid., 115.
38. Ibid., 122.
39. Ibid., 122–8.
40. Constantia Maxwell, "The Colonisation of Ulster," *History*, 1 (July–October 1916), 86–90.
41. Ibid., 147–53. See also T.W. Moody, "The Treatment of the Native Population Under the Scheme for the Plantation in Ulster," *Irish Historical Studies*, 1 (March 1938), 59–63.
42. Maxwell, "The Colonisation of Ulster," 157–8.
43. Constantia Maxwell, "The Plantation of Ulster at the Beginning of James I's Reign," *Sewanee Review*, 31 (1923), 169–70.
44. Maxwell's books include: *A School History of Ireland* (Dublin, 1914); *A Short History of Ireland* (New York: Frederick A. Stokes, 1914); a collection of Tudor documents, *Foundations of Modern Ireland: Part I, Civil Policy of Henry VIII and the Reformation* (London: S.P.C.K., 1921); *Irish History From Contemporary Sources, 1509–1610* (London: Allen & Unwin, 1923); edition of Arthur Young's *Tour in Ireland* (London, 1925); edition of Arthur Young's *Travels in France* (London, 1929); *The Political Ideas of Chateaubriand* (London, 1932); *The English Traveller in France* (London, 1932); *Dublin Under the Georges, 1714–1830* (London: George G. Harrap & Co., 1936); *Country and Town in Ireland Under the Georges* (London: George G. Harrap & Co., 1940); *History of Trinity College, Dublin* (London, 1946); *The Stranger in Ireland From the Reign of Elizabeth to the Great Famine* (London, 1954). *Irish History From Contemporary Sources, 1509–1610* (1923) is a source-book of Irish documents that was widely used by university students in Ireland.
45. Obituary in the *Times*, February 7, 1962.
46. Constantia Maxwell, *Dublin Under the Georges, 1714–1830* (1936; revised edition, London: Faber & Faber Ltd., 1956), 16.
47. See A.E. Murray, *A History of the Commercial and Financial Relations Between England and Ireland From the Period of the Restoration* (London: P.S. King

and Son, 1903) and George O'Brien, *The Economic History of Ireland in the Eighteenth Century* (Dublin and London: maunsel, 1918).
48. O'Dowd, "From Morgan to MacCurtain," 51.
49. Maxwell, *Dublin Under the Georges*, 16.
50. For a reconsideration of the position of Irish Protestants in the Free State years, see Pauric Dempsey, "Trinity College Dublin and the New Political Order," in Mike Cronin and John M. Regan, eds., *Ireland: The Politics of Independence, 1922–49* (London: Macmillan Press, 2000), 217–31.
51. M.D.G. [Mary Dorothy George], review of *Dublin Under the Georges* by Constantia Maxwell, *History*, 21 (March 1937), 383.
52. K.J., review of *Dublin Under the Georges* by Constantia Maxwell, *English Historical Review*, 52, (1937), 747.
53. R.W. Dudley Edwards and Mary O'Dowd, *Sources for Early Modern Irish History*, 1534–1641 (Cambridge: Cambridge University Press, 1985), 209.
54. J.G. Simms, review of *Dublin Under the Georges* by Constantia Maxwell, *Irish Historical Studies*, 11 (1959), 248.
55. T.W.M., review of *Country and Town Under the Georges* by Constantia Maxwell, *English Historical Review*, 57 (January 1942), 156–7.
56. M.B., review of *Country and Town Under the Georges* by Constantia Maxwell, *Journal of the Galway Historical and Archaeological Society*, 24 (1951), 73–4.
57. Ibid., 73.
58. Ibid., 74.
59. R.B. McDowell, *Irish Public Opinion, 1750–1800* (London: Faber and Faber, 1944); S.J. Connolly, *Religion, Law, and Power: the Making of Protestant Ireland, 1660–1760* (Oxford: Clarendon, 1992).
60. G.F., "Obituary: Olive Armstrong," *Alexandra College Dublin Magazine*, 11 (June 1959); "Armstrong, Rev. Canon Claude Blakeley, MA, BD, [Olive's brother]" in *Who Was Who*, 1981–90; R.B. McDowell, interview with author, November 27, 2001; Anne V. O'Connor and Susan Parkes, *Gladly Learn and Gladly Teach: Alexandra College and School, 1866–1966* (Dublin: Blackwater Press, 1984), 201–3.
61. Parkes, *A Danger to the Men?*, 109–10.
62. Olive Armstrong, *Edward Bruce's Invasion of Ireland* (London: John Murray, 1923), i.
63. Ibid., 5–10.
64. Ibid., 160–78. Medieval historians still cite Armstrong's work as a source on aspects of the Bruce invasion. See Sean Duffy, *Ireland in the Middle Ages* (New York: St. Martin's Press, 1997), 195.
65. Orpen to Curtis, November 7, 1923, Edmund Curtis Papers, TCD MS 2452.
66. Lydon, "Historical Revisit," 535–48.
67. O'Connor and Parkes, *Gladly Learn and Gladly Teach*, 201; TCD School of History, Minutes of Committee, 1912—1973, TCD MUN/History/V/8/1; G.F., "Obituary: Olive Armstrong."
68. "Prof. J. Otway-Ruthven, Historian of Medieval Ireland," *Times*, March 25, 1989; "Annette Jocelyn Otway-Ruthven," *Girton College Register, 1860–1946*

(Cambridge, 1948), 470; Robin Frame, *Ireland and Britain 1170–1450* (London: Hambledon, 1998), 4–7; Salters Sterling, "Professor Otway-Ruthven, FTCD, Lecky Professor of History, 1951–81," in Parkes, ed., *A Danger to the Men?*, 263–7.

69. Donal McCartney, conversation with author, April 11, 2001; Louis Cullen, interview with author, November 21, 2001.
70. *IHS*, Clara Crawford, "Feudal Tenures in Ireland in the Thirteenth Century," 5 (1946–47), 87. In the 1950s she supervised a PhD thesis by William Nugent, entitled "The Medieval Lordship of Carlow." See *IHS*, 9 (1954–55), 340.
71. *Times*, March 25,1989.
72. R.B. McDowell and D.A. Webb, *Trinity College Dublin 1592–1952* (Cambridge: Cambridge University Press, 1982), 353.
73. R. Dudley Edwards Papers, UCDA LA22/678 (1938, 1945–47) and LA22/689 (1947); Sterling, 264–5.
74. Sterling, 264–5.
75. Jocelyn Otway-Ruthven, "The Native Irish and English Law in Medieval Ireland," *Irish Historical Studies*, 7, 25 (March 1950), 1–16. Her first article for this journal appeared four years earlier. See Jocelyn Otway-Ruthven, "Anglo-Irish Shire Government in the Thirteenth Century," *IHS*, 5 (March 1946), 1–28.
76. Otway-Ruthven, "The Native Irish and English Law," (1950), 1–7.
77. Duffy, *Ireland in the Middle Ages*, 5; Frame, *Ireland and Britain*, 5–7; Steven Ellis, "Nationalist Historiography and the English and Gaelic Worlds in the late Middle Ages," in Brady, ed., *Interpreting Irish History*, 165.
78. See, for instance, Steven Ellis, *Tudor Ireland: Crown, Community and the Conflict of Cultures, 1470–1603* (London: Longman, 1985); Frame, *Ireland and Britain*.
79. Sean Duffy, "A Real Irish Historian [Interview with James Lydon]," *History Ireland* (Spring 1995), 12.
80. Mary O'Dowd, "From Morgan to MacCurtain," 298.

5 Non-Academic Women Historians, 1922–1949

1. Louis J. Walsh was a contemporary of James Joyce at University College, and later appeared as the character MacAlister in Joyce's *A Portrait of the Artist as a Young Man*. I am indebted to Ann Walsh for this information. My analysis in this section owes much to discussion with Sheila, Maria and Ann Walsh. See also Louis J. Walsh, "With Joyce and Kettle at UCD," *Irish Digest*, 12 (1942), 27–9; and Patrick Maume, *D.P. Moran* (Dundalgan: Dundalgan Press, 1995), pp. 17, 37, 39, for more on Louis J. Walsh's career.
2. Obituary, *Irish Times*, February 28, 1952; Mary Macken, "Musings and Memories: Helena Concannon, M.A., D.Litt.," *Studies*, 42 (1953), 90–7.
3. Macken, "Musings and Memories," 91–4, 96.
4. For details, see "The Degani Appointment: Convocation Calls for Explanation," *Report of Convocation of National University*, April 28, 1910, 1–16.

5. A volume of her poetry was published posthumously.
6. Sheila, Maria, and Ann Walsh, conversation with author, November 23, 2001.
7. Helena Concannon, *Makers of Irish History* (Dublin: Talbot Press, 1918).
8. Starkie's diary, May 31, 1918, Starkie Papers, TCD MS 9211, 228–9. Cited in David Fitzpatrick, "The Futility of History: A Failed Experiment in Irish Education," in Ciaran Brady, ed., *Ideology and the Historians* (Dublin: Lilliput Press, 1991), 178.
9. Helena Concannon, *Irish History for Junior Grade Classes, 1460–1660: Defence of Our Gaelic Civilization* (Dublin: Fallon's, 1921), 11.
10. Ibid., 268–70.
11. Ibid., 226.
12. John M. Coolahan, "A Study of Curricular Policy for the Primary and Secondary Schools of Ireland, 1900–1935, with Special Reference to the Irish Language and Irish History" (TCD, PhD Dissertation, 1973), 360.
13. Gabriel Doherty, "National Identity and the Study of Irish History," *English Historical Review* (April 1996), 342.
14. Helena Concannon, *Women of '98* (Dublin: M.H. Gill, 1919); *Daughters of Banba* (Dublin: M.H. Gill, 1922); *The Poor Clares in Ireland* (Dublin: M.H. Gill, 1929); and *Irish Nuns in Penal Days* (London: Sands and Co., 1931).
15. O'Dowd, "From Morgan to MacCurtain," 41–2.
16. Julie des Jardins, *Women and the Historical Enterprise in America: Gender, Race, and the Politics of Memory* (Chapel Hill, NC: University of North Carolina Press, 2003), 16–20; Bonnie Smith, *The Gender of History: Men, Women, and Historical Practice* (Cambridge, MA.: Harvard University Press, 1998); Ida Blom, "Women in Norwegian and Danish Historiography, c.1900–c.1960," *Storia della Storiografia* 46 (2004), 130–51; Maxine Berg, "The First Women Economic Historians," *Economic History Review*, xlv, 2 (1992), 308–21; Maxine Berg, *A Woman in History: Eileen Power, 1889–1940* (Cambridge: Cambridge University Press, 1996); Rosemary Ann Mitchell, "The Busy Daughters of Clio: Women Writers of History From 1820 to 1880," *Women's History Review*, 7, 1 (1998); Rosemary Mitchell, *Picturing the Past: English History in Text and Image, 1830–1870* (Oxford: Clarendon Press, 2000), 140–69; Ilaria Porciani and Mary O'Dowd, "History Women," *Storia della Storiografia* 46 (2004), 3–34.
17. Macken, "Musings and Memories," 96; Thomas Bartlett, "Bearing Witness: Female Evidences in Courts Martial Convened to Suppress the 1798 Rebellion," in Daire Keogh and Nicholas Furlong, eds, *The Women of 1798* (Dublin: Four Courts Press, 1998), 645.
18. Concannon, *Women of '98*, 71.
19. Ibid., 71.
20. Dail Debates, Vol. 67, May 12, 1937, cols. 241–2.
21. Mitchell, *Picturing the Past*, 152.
22. Des Jardins, *Women and the Historical Enterprise in America*, 17.
23. Ibid., 16.
24. O'Dowd, "From Morgan to MacCurtain," 49; Blom, "Women in Norwegian and Danish Historiography," 135; Effi Gazi, "Engendering the

Writing and Teaching of History in Mid-War Greece," *Storia della Storiografia*, 46 (2004), 121–2.

25. Anonymous, review of *Women of '98* by Helena Concannon, *Irish Citizen* (November 1919), 42.
26. See Margaret MacCurtain and Mary O'Dowd, eds, *Women in Early Modern Ireland* (Dublin: Wolfhound Press, 1991), for later scholarly recoveries of early modern Irish women.
27. Concannon, *Daughters of Banba*, ix.
28. Ibid., 260–1.
29. Ibid., 124.
30. O'Dowd, "From Morgan to MacCurtain," 42.
31. Maxine Berg, *A Woman in History: Eileen Power, 1889–1940* (Cambridge: Cambridge University Press, 1996), 116–23.
32. Elizabeth Russell, "Holy Crosses, Guns, and Roses: Themes in Popular Reading Material," in Joost Augusteijn, ed., *Ireland in the 1930s: New Perspectives* (Dublin: Four Courts Press, 1999), 11–28.
33. Jane Tompkins, *Sensational Designs: The Cultural Work of American Fiction 1790–1860* (New York and Oxford: Oxford University Press, 1985), 126. Cited in Donna L. Potts, "Irish Poetry and the Modernist Canon: a Reappraisal of Katherine Tynan," in Kathryn Kirkpatrick, ed., *Border Crossings: Irish Women Writers and National Identity* (Dublin: Wolfhound Press, 2000), 89–90.
34. Potts, "Irish Poetry and the Modernist Canon," 90.
35. Terry Eagleton, "Revisionism Revisited," in *Crazy John and the Bishop and Other Essays on Irish Culture* (Cork: Cork University Press, 1998), 310.
36. G. Pierse, review of *Women of '98, Irish Theological Quarterly*, 14 (1919), 380.
37. Ibid., 380.
38. Ibid., 381.
39. See Clear, "The Women Cannot be Blamed," 179–86.
40. See, for instance, Helena Concannon, "The Caritas Socialis in Austria," *Irish Monthly*, 51 (1923), 157–64. Historians of women have developed a persuasive analysis of middle-class female philanthropy, which holds that charity can be a way of enhancing the giver's authority over those whose lives they wish to reorder, though the giver can be genuinely helpful as well. For the Irish case, see, for example, Maria Luddy, *Women and Philanthropy in Nineteenth-Century Ireland* (Cambridge: Cambridge University Press, 1995); Margaret Preston, *Charitable Words: Women, Philanthropy, and the Language of Charity in Nineteenth-Century Dublin* (Westport, CT.: Praeger, 2004); Caitriona Clear, " 'The Women Cannot be Blamed:' The Commission on Vocational Organisation, Feminism, and 'Home-makers' in Independent Ireland in the 1930s and '40s" in Mary O'Dowd and Sabine Wichert, eds, *Chattel, Servant, or Citizen?: Women's Status in Church, State, and Society* (Belfast: Institute of Irish Studies, 1995), 184; Rosemary Raughter, "A Natural Tenderness: the Ideal and Reality of Eighteenth-Century Female Philanthropy," in Maryann Gialanella Valiulis and Mary O'Dowd, eds, *Women & Irish History: Essays in Honour of*

Margaret MacCurtain (Dublin: Wolfhound Press, 1997), 88.

41. For a useful summary of maternalism, see Seth Koven and Sonya Michel, "Introduction: 'Mother Worlds,' " in Koven and Michel, eds, *Mothers of a New World: Maternalist Politics and the Origins of Welfare States* (New York: Routledge, 1993), 1–31. See also Martin Pugh, *Women and the Women's Movement in Britain, 1914–1959* (New York: Paragon House, 1993), and, for Ireland, Caitriona Clear, "No Feminist Mystique: Popular Advice to Women of the House in Ireland, 1922–1954," in Maryann Gialanella Valiulis and Mary O'Dowd, eds, *Women & Irish History: Essays in Honour of Margaret MacCurtain* (Dublin: Wolfhound Press, 1997), 200–1.
42. Koven and Michel, "Introduction: 'Mother Worlds,' "6.
43. Sile Ni Chinneide, Lecturer in History at University College Galway, unsuccessfully ran in 1954.
44. See, for instance, Dail Debates, vol. 53, col. 1499; vol. 61, col. 1676.
45. Once, to Concannon's chagrin, domestic responsibilities forced her to stay home and miss a meeting in Dublin, as her housekeeper was in the hospital. Helena Concannon to Eamon de Valera, Department of the Taoiseach Papers, National Archves of Ireland.
46. Clear, "The Women Can Not be Blamed,"179–86. Concannon was at least as unrepresentative of the majority of Irish women as middle-class feminists were. Not only was she an educated, childless married woman with a career, she also represented an elite minority group, Irish university graduates, in the Dail and the Senate.
47. Dail Debates, vol. 61, April 2, 1936, col. 902.
48. Caitriona Clear, "No Feminine Mystique: Popular Advice to Women of the House in Ireland 1922–1954," in Valiulis and O'Dowd, eds, *Women & Irish History*, 190–1.
49. Clear, "No Feminine Mystique," 201.
50. The Constitution angered Northern Irish Unionists by stating, in Articles 2 and 3, that Irish "national territory consists of the whole island of Ireland ... pending reintegration of the national territory." Article 44 announced that "the State recognizes the special position of the [Catholic] Church," as the church of the majority, though other religions were also recognized.
51. Bunreacht na hEireann (Constitution of Ireland), 1937.
52. Maryann Gialanella Valiulis, "Engendering Citizenship: Women's Relationship to the State in Ireland and the United States in the Post-Suffrage Period," in Valiulis and O'Dowd, eds, *Women & Irish History*, 162.
53. Caitriona Beaumont, "Women and the Politics of Equality: The Irish Women's Movement, 1930–1943," in Valiulis and O'Dowd, eds, *Women & Irish History*, 181–4.
54. See Seanad Debates, vol. 23, July 6, 1939, col. 46; vol. 28, January 13, 1944 and January 26–27, 1944.
55. Dail Debates, vol. 67, May 12, 1937, cols. 241–2.

56. Beaumont, "Women and the Politics of Equality ,"181–4.
57. Seanad Debates, vol. 30, November 28, 1945, cols 1057–8.
58. Seanad Debates, vol. 30, November 14,1945, cols 989–91.
59. Censorship legislation was certainly operative in other Western countries besides Ireland at this time. For a recent discussion and assessment of the Irish censorship policy, see Brian Fallon, *An Age of Innocence: Irish Culture 1930–1960* (Dublin: Gill & Macmillan, 1998), 201–11.
60. Seanad Debates, vol. 35, August 11, 1948, col. 892.
61. Seanad Debates, vol. 36, December 10, 1948, cols 117–20.
62. Ibid., col. 120.
63. "Macardle, Sir Thomas Callan, K.B.E.," *Who Was Who*, vol. 2, 1916–28, 657; Birth Certificate of Dorothy Macardle, General Register Office, Dublin; Census of Ireland, 1901,Louth, 41 D.E.D. Dundalk Urban no. 4, 35.
64. Peter Tremayne [Peter Berresford Ellis], "A Reflection of Ghosts," in Stephen Jones and Jo Fletcher, eds, *Gaslight and Ghosts* (London: Robinson, 1988), 87–8; Obituary, *Irish Press*, December 24, 1958.
65. Anne O'Connor and Susan M. Parkes, *Gladly Learn and Gladly Teach: Alexandra College and School, 1866–1966* (Dublin: Blackwater Press, 1984), 109.
66. These included Sinn Fein president Edward Martyn and Constance Markiewicz as well as Maud Gonne MacBride.
67. Tremayne, "A Reflection of Ghosts," 89.
68. Dorothy Macardle, *The Irish Republic: a Documented Chronicle of the Anglo-Irish and the Partitioning of Ireland, With a Detailed Account of the Period 1916–1923. With a Preface by Eamon de Valera* (London: Victor Gollancz, 1937; 4th ed., Dublin: Irish Press, 1951), 318. All references are to the 1951 edition.
69. *Report of the Irish White Cross to 31st August, 1922* (Dublin: Martin Lester, 1922); Margaret Mulvihill, *Charlotte Despard* (London: Pandora Press, 1989).
70. Tremayne, "A Reflection of Ghosts," 90.
71. Lily O'Brennan Diary, Lily O'Brennan Papers, UCDA P13/44, March 14, 1923.
72. Dorothy Macardle to Hanna Sheehy Skeffington, September 13, 1926, Sheehy Skeffington Papers, NLI MS 33,606(13).
73. Dorothy Macardle, "The Nation's Dream of Peace," *Irish Press*, September 13, 1935, 6; "[Mr. De Valera's Speech at Geneva], Deep Effect on Listeners," *Irish Press*, September 17, 1935, 2.
74. Dorothy Macardle, "The Crisis and the Covenant," *Irish Press*, September 25, 1935.
75. Dorothy Macardle, "Women's Meeting at Geneva," *Irish Press*, September 18, 1935, 8; "The Legal Status of Women," *Irish Press*, September 19, 1935, 1; "Women's Cause at Geneva," *Irish Press*, September 30, 1935, 6. Historian Carol Miller has written extensively about women in the League of Nations. See, for instance, Carol Miller, " 'Geneva – the Key to Equality': Inter-war Feminists and the League of Nations," *Women's History Review*, 3, 2, (1994), 219–45.

76. See also Patrick Murray, "Obsessive Historian: Eamon de Valera and the Policing of His Reputation," *Proceedings of the Royal Irish Academy*, 101C, (2001), 57–8.
77. Eunan O'Halpin, "Historical Revisit: Dorothy Macardle, *The Irish Republic* (1937)," *Irish Historical Studies*, 31, 123 (May 1999), 390. See also Murray, "Obsessive Historian," 59–60.
78. O'Halpin, "Historical Revisit," 390.
79. Macardle, *The Irish Republic*, 23.
80. Rosamond Jacob Diary, NLI MS 32,582(48), June 21, 1925, June 26, 1925.
81. Macardle, 36–50.
82. RJD, NLI MS 32,582 (48), 23 June 1925, 31 July 1925; RJD, NLI MS 32,582 (66), March 22, 1931.
83. Macardle, 121–2.
84. Ibid., 184–9.
85. Ibid., 265–7, 453–5.
86. Ibid., 297–8.
87. Ibid., 544–8.
88. Ibid., 809.
89. Ibid., 51, 183–4, 342, 390, 750, 838–9.
90. Ibid., 30, 63.
91. Ibid., 434, 455, 631, 680–3, 729–30.
92. Ibid., 705.
93. Ibid., 624, 701.
94. Ibid., 822, 839–40.
95. Ibid., 748–50, 776.
96. Ibid., 897.
97. Macardle was asked to give a speech on *The Irish Republic* to the Left Book Club, founded by Gollancz, in 1937. Dorothy Macardle to Owen Sheehy Skeffington, Sheehy Skeffington Papers, NLI MS 40,505(5), December 8, 1937. For more on the Left Book Club and its impact, see Stuart Samuels, "The Left Book Club," *Journal of Contemporary History*, 1, no. 2 (April 1966), 65–87.
98. "E.A.," review of *The Irish Republic* by Dorothy Macardle, *Irish Press*, March 17, 1937, 8.
99. "E.A.," review of *The Irish Republic* by Dorothy Macardle, *Irish Press*, March 24, 1937,8.
100. Ibid., 11. When writing about the IRA avenging the execution of republicans during the Civil War by burning Free State politicians' homes, she simply mentioned that when they set McGarry's house on fire, "a child was accidentally injured and afterwards died." Macardle, 824.
101. Review of *The Irish Republic* by Dorothy Macardle, *Irish Independent*, March 15, 1937. Other reviews appeared in *Ireland To-day*, a progressive journal that lasted only two years, and the conservative *Catholic Bulletin*. There was no review in the leading American newspaper, the *New York Times*, until the publication of an American edtion of *The Irish Republic* in 1965. Turning to the British press, a positive review of *The Irish Republic*, written by W.R. LeFanu, appeared in the *Times Literary*

Supplement. Thus, British readers interested in contemporary events were aware of Macardle's book, as the *TLS* review dovetailed with the publicity given *The Irish Republic* by the Left Book Club. W.R. LeFanu, review of *The Irish Republic* by Dorothy Macardle, *Times Literary Supplement*, April 24, 1937, 306.

102. W.A. Phillips, *The Revolution in Ireland* (Dublin, 1923).
103. Bonnie Smith, *The Gender of History*, 147.
104. I owe this point to Ilaria Porciani.
105. For the strictures on contemporary history, see Ronan Fanning, " 'The Great Enchantment': Uses and Abuses of Modern Irish History," in Ciaran Brady, ed., *Interpreting Irish History: the Debate on Historical Revisionism* (Dublin: Irish Academic Press, 1994), 150–1.
106. R.D. Edwards Papers, UCDA [University College Dublin Archives], LA22/1135 (7).
107. Dorothy Macardle, *Children of Europe* (London: Gollancz, 1949); Blom, "Women in Norwegian and Danish Historiography," 144.
108. J.J. Lee, *Ireland, 1912–1985: Politics and Society* (Cambridge: Cambridge University Press, 1989), 270.
109. O'Halpin, "Historical Revisit," 390.
110. O'Halpin, "Historical Revisit," 389–90.
111. Rosamond Jacob Diary [RJD], NLI MS 32,582(1), April 1903.
112. W.J. Jacob, "The Dublin Family of Jacob," *Dublin Historical Record*, 3 (1939–40), 134–7.
113. Damian Doyle, *A Bio-Critical Study of Rosamond Jacob and Her Contemporaries* (University of Colorado, PhD Dissertation, 2000), 17–20.
114. Jacob, "The Dublin Family of Jacob," 136–7.
115. Doyle, *A Bio-Critical Study of Rosamond Jacob*, 19–20.
116. On eighteenth-century Irish Quakers and republicanism, see Kevin O'Neill, "Mary Shackleton Leadbeater: Peaceful Rebel," in Keogh and Furlong, eds, *The Women of 1798*, 137–62. A prominent Quaker republican of Rosamond Jacob's time was Bulmer Hobson, head of the IRB (Irish Republican Brotherhood).
117. Rosamond Jacob Papers, NLI MS 33,127 (1).
118. Doyle, *A Bio-Critical Study of Rosamond Jacob*, 21.
119. Rosamond Jacob Diary [RJD], NLI MS 32,582(2), 10 April 1900; NLI MS 32,582 (3), December 31, 1901.
120. Rosemary Cullen Owens, *Smashing Times: A History of the Irish Women's Suffrage Movement, 1889–1922* (Dublin: Attic Press, 1984), 42. In 1876, Jacob's fellow Quaker Anna Haslam formed the first Irish feminist group, the Dublin Women's Suffrage Association, later called the IWSLGA (Irish Women's Suffrage and Local Government Association). Cullen Owens, *Smashing Times*, 23–5.
121. Doyle, *A Bio-Critical Study of Rosamond Jacob*, 29.
122. Ibid., 32.
123. Ibid., 158–61.
124. Margaret Ward, *Unmanageable Revolutionaries: Women and Irish Nationalism* (London: Pluto Press, 1989, reprinted 1995), 183–4.

125. Rosamond Jacob Diary, March 9–11, 1926, April 8, 1926, NLI MS 32,582 (47).
126. Brian Hanley, *The IRA 1926–1936* (Dublin: Four Courts Press, 2002), 104–5.
127. Pugh, *Women and the Women's Movement in Britain*, 104–6. See also Carol Miller, " 'Geneva – the Key to Equality': Inter-War Feminists and the League of Nations," *Women's History Review*, 3, 2 (1994), 219–45.
128. Rosemary Cullen Owens, "Women and Pacifism in Ireland, 1915–1932," in Valiulis and O'Dowd, eds, *Women & Irish History*, 231–5.
129. For Agerholt and Lunden, see Blom, "Women in Danish and Norwegian Historiography," 140–3.
130. Doyle, *A Bio-Critical Study of Rosamond Jacob*, 54.
131. USSR Diary, Rosamond Jacob Papers, May 1, 1931, NLI MS 33,129(1).
132. On Communism in Ireland, see Mike Milotte, *Communism in Modern Ireland: the Pursuit of the Workers' Republic Since 1916* (Dublin: Gill and Macmillan, 1984).
133. Doyle, *A Bio-Critical Study of Rosamond Jacob*, 54, 56–7.
134. In response to the Constitution, feminists formed the Women's Social and Political (later Progressive) League in 1937. Members included historians Mary Hayden, Dorothy Macardle, and Rosamond Jacob. The WSPL's intent was to be a women's political party that would nominate feminists for election to the Dail, where they would advocate equal rights and New Feminist legislation. When the independent female candidates lost in the 1943 election, the WSPL focused more on a program of citizenship education for women. Beaumont, "Women and the Politics of Equality," 185.
135. Doyle, *A Bio-Critical Study of Rosamond Jacob*, 63–4, 67, 69–70.
136. Kevin Whelan, "'98 After '98," in Whelan, *The Tree of Liberty: Radicalism, Catholicism, and the Construction of an Irish Identity 1760–1830* (Cork: Cork University Press), 170–1. Whelan discusses other interpretations of the 1798 Rebellion and their nineteenth-century origins. See also Ian McBride, "Reclaiming the Rebellion: 1798 in 1998," *Irish Historical Studies*, xxxi, 123 (May 1999), 396–410, for discussions of other interpretive traditions, such as the Ulster liberal interpretation.
137. Leo McCabe, *Wolfe Tone and the United Irishmen: For and Against Christ* (London: Health Cranton, 1937). Cited in James Quinn, "Theobald Wolfe Tone and the Historians," *Irish Historical Studies*, xxxii, no. 125 (May 2000), 115.
138. Doyle, *A Bio-Critical Study of Rosamond Jacob*, 59.
139. Rosamond Jacob, *The Rise of the United Irishmen, 1791–4* (London: George G. Harrap, 1937), 251–3.
140. McBride, "Reclaiming the Rebellion," 401.
141. Jacob, *The Rise of the United Irishmen*, 15–17.
142. Ibid., 67.
143. Rosamond Jacob Diary, NLI MS 32,582 (81), March 5, 1937. She was referring to Maxwell's *Country and Town Under the Georges* (London, 1940).
144. Des Jardins, *Women and the Historical Enterprise in America*, 68.
145. R.H., review of *The Rise of the United Irishmen*, by Rosamond Jacob, *The Irish Book-Lover* (July-December 1937), 118.

146. R. Dudley Edwards, review of *The Rise of the United Irishmen*, by Rosamond Jacob, *Dublin Magazine*, 13, 3 (1937), 70.
147. Ibid., 72. Other reviews appeared in *Irish Historical Studies, History*, and the *English Historical Review*, demonstrating that *The Rise of the United Irishmen* reached an academic audience, despite having been written by a non-professional historian. See *Irish Historical Studies*, 1 (1938), 89–90; *History*, 23 (December 1938), 271–2; *English Historical Review* (April 1938), 371. Reviewers commented on how her politics shaped her work and on her reliance on printed sources, but generally thought Jacob's book provided an insightful and readable narrative of the political and social world of the United Irishmen.
148. Rosamond Jacob, *The Rebel's Wife* (Tralee, 1957); Doyle, *A Bio-Critical Study of Rosamond Jacob*, 657.
149. See, for example, Keogh and Furlong, eds, *The Women of 1798*.
150. Bonnie Smith, *The Gender of History*, 3, 7–8, 147.
151. See Thomas C. Kennedy, "History and the Quaker Renaissance: The Vision of John Wilhelm Rowntree," *Journal of the Friends' Historical Society*, 55 (1983–84), 35–6.
152. Isabel Grubb, *J. Ernest Grubb of Carrick-on-Suir* (Dublin: Talbot Press, 1928), 12–25, 52–4.
153. Berg, "The First Women Economic Historians," 308–20; Smith, *The Gender of History*, 198–201.
154. William M. Glynn, "Isabel Grubb 1881–1972," *Friends Journal*, April 15, 1972, 253–4; *History*, 4 (October 1919), 178.
155. Herbert M. Hadley, *Quakers World Wide: A History of Friends World Committee for Consultation* (London: Friend's World Committee for Consultation, 1991), 10–18.
156. Glynn, "Isabel Grubb 1881–1972," 254.
157. Isabel Grubb, *Quakers in Ireland, 1654–1900* (London: Swarthmore Press, 1927).
158. Grubb, *J. Ernest Grubb of Carrick-on-Suir*
159. Grubb *J. Ernest Grubb of Carrick-on-Suir*, 86–7.
160. Isabel Grubb, *Quakerism and Industry Before 1800* (London: Williams and Norgate, 1930).
161. R.H. Tawney, *Religion and the Rise of Capitalism: a Historical Study* (1922: London, 1926). See also Maxine Berg, *A Woman in History*, 148–52, for Tawney's work and its influence.
162. "J.F.R.," review of Isabel Grubb, *Quakerism and Industry Before 1800, English Historical Review*, 47 (January 1932), 170.
163. Kevin O'Neill, " 'Almost a Gentlewoman:' Gender and Adolescence in the Diary of Mary Shackleton," in Mary O'Dowd and Sabine Wichert, eds, *Chattel, Servant, or Citizen: Women's Status in Church, State, and Society* (Belfast: Institute of Irish Studies, 1995), 91. The diaries of Rosamond Jacob, another Quaker woman, also detail "one of the most complete records of the private life of any individual who has lived in Ireland."
164. Francesca de Haan, "A 'Truly International' Archive for the Women's Movement (IAV, now IIAV): From Its Foundations in Amsterdam in 1935

to the Return of its Looted Archives in 2003," *Journal of Women's History*, 16, 4 (2004), 148–62; Des Jardins, *Women and the Historical Enterprise in America*, 225–40.

165. Obituary of Philip George Lee, *Journal of the Cork Historical and Archaeological Society*, 38 (1933).
166. I am grateful to Aisling Lockhart for checking the student admissions register and providing the dates of Lee's undergraduate career at Trinity. See also Parkes, *A Danger to the Men?*, 99.
167. Later works on Huguenots in Ireland included short histories such as Alicia St. Leger's *Silver, Sails, and Silk: Huguenots in Cork, 1685–1850* (Cork: Cork Civic Trust, 1991), and a collection of essays edited by C.E.J. Caldicott and Hugh Gough, entitled *The Huguenots in Ireland: Anatomy of an Emigration* (Dun Laoghaire: Glendale Press, 1987). The latter was the outcome of a 1985 conference marking the 300th anniversary of the Revocation of the Edict of Nantes.
168. Grace Lawless Lee, *The Huguenot Settlements in Ireland* (London: Longmans Green, 1936), 264. *The Huguenot Settlements in Ireland* went through several editions. It was reprinted in 2001 by Heritage Books, a Maryland publishing company specializing in genealogical works. The book was marketed towards Americans researching their Huguenot ancestry, who were advised to look to Ireland for possible leads.
169. Constantia Maxwell, review of *The Huguenot Settlements in Ireland* by Grace Lawless Lee, *History*, 21 (September 1936), 163–5.
170. Marriage announcement in the *Times*, October 8, 1933, 17; "Obituary: Grace Lawless Gwynn," *Proceedings of the Huguenot Society of London*, 20 (1958/64), 664–5.
171. Mairead Dunlevy, "Ada K. Longfield (Mrs. H.G. Leask) 1899–1987," *Journal of the Royal Society of Antiquaries of Ireland*, 18 (1988), 169–70; University Research, Session 1926–27," *History*, 12 (1927–28), 375.
172. Berg, *A Woman in History*, 151–2.
173. Natalie Zemon Davis, "Women and the World of the *Annales*," *History Workshop Journal*, 33 (1992), 122. For the historians associated with the *Annales* school and their interests in social and economic history, see Peter Burke, *The French Historical Revolution: the Annales School, 1929–1989* (Stanford, CA: Stanford University Press, 1990); for their interactions with LSE historians in the interwar era, see Maxine Berg, *A Woman in History*, 210–15. See also Mary Spongberg, *Writing Women's History Since the Renaissance* (Basingstoke: Palgrave Macmillan, 2002), 164–5.
174. Ada K. Longfield, *Anglo-Irish Trade in the Sixteenth Century* (London: Routledge, 1929), 202.
175. Ibid., 20–1.
176. Philip Wilson, review of *Anglo-Irish Trade in the Sixteenth Century* by A.K. Longfield, *History*, 16 (1931), 69–70.
177. "A.R.," review of *Anglo-Irish Trade in the Sixteenth Century* by A.K. Longfield, *English Historical Review*, 46 (April 1931), 325.

178. "Glensman," "Unchanging British Exploitation: Trade in Tudor Days" [a review of A.K. Longfield's *Anglo-Irish Trade in the Sixteenth Century*], the *Nation*, July 26, 1930, 6.
179. Ibid., 6.
180. Dunlevy, "Ada K. Longfield", 169; O'Dowd, "From Morgan to MacCurtain," 299.
181. Dunlevy, "Ada K. Longfield," 169–70.
182. Blom, "Women in Norwegian and Danish Historiography," 130–51; Mervi Kaarninen and Tiina Kinnunen, " 'Hardly Any Women At All': Finnish Historiography Revisited," *Storia della Storiografia*, 46 (2004), 152–70; Davis, "Women and the World of the *Annales*," 121–30; Spongberg, *Writing Women's History*, 164–5.

6 Conclusion

1. Maeve Binchy, *Echoes* (New York: Dell, 1985), 262–3.
2. Mary O'Dowd, "From Morgan to MacCurtain: Women Historians in Ireland From the 1790s to the 1990s," in Maryann Gialanella Valiulis and Mary O'Dowd, eds, *Women & Irish History: Essays in Honour of Margaret MacCurtain* (Dublin: Wolfhound Press, 1997)," 54.
3. Eda Sagarra, "Jobs For the Girls," in Anne Macdona, ed., *From Newman to New Woman: UCD Women Remember* (Dublin: New Island, 2001), 89.
4. See Gerard O'Brien, "Introduction," and Tom Dunne, "Maureen Wall (nee McGeehin), 1918–1972): a Memoir," in Gerard O'Brien, ed., *Catholic Ireland in the Eighteenth Century: Collected Essays of Maureen Wall* (Dublin: Geography Publications, 1989).
5. O'Dowd, "From Morgan to MacCurtain," 57; Ilaria Porciani and Mary O'Dowd, "History Women," *Storia della Storiografia*, 46 (2004).
6. Anthony Brundage, *The People's Historian: John Richard Green and the Writing of History in Victorian England* (Westwood, CT.: Greenwood Press, 1994), 165.

Index